RUTH AND ESTHER

BERIT OLAM
Studies in Hebrew Narrative & Poetry

Ruth

Tod Linafelt

and

Esther

Timothy K. Beal

David W. Cotter, O.S.B.
Editor

Jerome T. Walsh
Chris Franke
Associate Editors

A Michael Glazier Book
THE LITURGICAL PRESS
Collegeville, Minnesota

A Michael Glazier Book published by The Liturgical Press.

Cover design by Ann Blattner.

1   2   3   4   5   6   7   8   9

Library of Congress Cataloging-in-Publication Data

Linafelt, Tod, 1965–
    [Ruth]
    Ruth / Tod Linafelt. And, Esther / Timothy K. Beal ; David W. Cotter, editor ; Jerome T. Walsh, Chris Franke, associate editors.
        p.   cm. — (Berit olam)
    Includes bibliographical references and index.
    ISBN 0-8146-5045-7 (alk. paper)
    1. Bible. O.T. Ruth—Commentaries. 2. Bible. O.T. Esther--Commentaries. I. Cotter, David W. II. Walsh, Jerome T., 1942–. III. Franke, Chris. IV. Beal, Timothy K. (Timothy Kandler), 1963–   Esther. V. Title. VI. Title: Esther. VII. Series.
BS1315.3.L45   1999
222'3507—dc21   99-11352
                                                                         CIP

Ruth

Tod Linafelt

for
Rebecca
and
Eleanor

CONTENTS

ACKNOWLEDGMENTS

Much of the initial writing of this book was facilitated by a summer research grant from the Theology Department at Georgetown University, for which I am very grateful. My student Adam Heyman, a fine biblical scholar in his own right, deserves many thanks for the invaluable research he did on the history of Jewish interpretation of the book of Ruth and for his suggestions on how I might improve an early draft of the manuscript. As always, Tim Beal has served as an indispensable conversation partner; I am thankful to have such a colleague as Tim. My thanks also to David Cotter, O.S.B., for allowing me to take on the task of commenting on Ruth and for taking missed deadlines in stride.

The primary reason for such missed deadlines was my first child, Eleanor Elizabeth. She was born as I was in the midst of writing this commentary, and I will always associate it with her wonderful, demanding presence in the world. I am happy to dedicate the final product of my work to Eleanor and, especially, to my wife Rebecca. It is common for male commentators on the book of Ruth to dedicate their books to their spouses, with a statement such as "she is my very own Ruth." I will avoid this practice, and I will endeavor instead to be her Ruth.

INTRODUCTION

The book of Ruth, if one were to follow the consensus of modern interpreters, tells a story of such utter simplicity and naivete as to verge on the banal. To be sure, one would be hard-pressed to find a commentator who would actually describe the story as banal, yet the adjectives one does find applied to the book—pretty, sentimental, idyllic, charming, beautiful, and delightful, to name the most common—betray a view of the narrative as fundamentally facile. Yet the more time I have spent with the book the more convinced I have become that it is exceedingly complex and ambiguous. In this commentary, then, I intend to highlight that which is most unresolved and even perplexing about the narrative.

This makes for a rather unsettling interpretation of the book in certain respects. It is "unsettling" in the sense that I will often refuse to "settle" on a single, unequivocal meaning of a particular word, phrase, or theme, preferring to underscore the dual or even multiple meanings that the narrative so often hosts. This is not, of course, the typical way of approaching the task of the commentator, most often seen precisely as one who weighs evidence and settles the meaning for the reader out of his or her expertise. I am convinced, however, that such an approach is wrong for the book of Ruth (and perhaps for all Biblical texts) and that, instead, the task of the commentator is to enable the reader to apprehend and negotiate the uncertainties of the text and, when possible, to demonstrate how these uncertainties are not pesky problems to be solved but rather are integral to the narrative art of the book.

Characterization, Human and Divine, in the Book of Ruth

My interpretation of the book of Ruth may seem unsettling in another way as well. Even those recent commentators who have recognized

the artfulness of the story—reflected especially in its clear formal design and numerous wordplays—refuse to entertain the possibility that
there might be any complexity or ambiguity with regard to the various
characters' motivations, the presentation of God, or the book's purpose.[1] Thus one recent commentator, who provides an exhaustive and
insightful analysis of the rhetorical art of the narrative, nevertheless
reduces the "theme of the book" to a series of timeworn character
traits: "the loving loyalty, faithfulness, and obedience of Ruth . . . the
kindness, graciousness, and sagacity of Boaz . . . the loving concern of
Naomi . . . [and] Yahweh's gracious provision of fruitfulness for field
and womb."[2] On this reading the characters become character *types*,
even stereotypes. Not only do they reflect traditionally defined gender
roles, but they lack precisely that which makes characters compelling
in a story: complexity, indecisiveness, and mixed motives, in short, an
inner life. By making them into models of piety and altruism, such an
interpretation flattens the characters and threatens to turn them into
cliches. When it comes to the character of God, interpreters are especially reticent to admit any ambiguity. The story is said to evince "the
absolute sway that God exercises over the affairs and actions of his
world,"[3] God's "never-failing presence,"[4] and "God's continuous all-
causality."[5] In contrast to the surety of these interpreters, my own
experience with the book of Ruth is that the more one explores the ambiguities of meaning built into the grammar, syntax, and vocabulary of
the story, the more one begins to see that these ambiguities carry over
to the larger interpretive issues of characterization, theology, and purpose.

With regard to the human characters and their motivations, for example, I find that far from exemplifying a simple godliness and un-

[1] One very notable exception to this tendency is the treatment offered by Danna
Fewell and David Gunn in their provocative book, *Compromising Redemption,* Literary Currents in Biblical Interpretation (Louisville: Westminster John Knox Press,
1990). I had read the book years ago and deliberately avoided going back to it until
completing most of my exegesis for the present commentary. After re-reading it,
however, I realize that my debt is quite substantial, and I have endeavored to cite
them where their influence on my reading is most pronounced.

[2] Frederic Bush, *Ruth, Esther,* Word Biblical Commentary (Dallas: Word Books,
1996) 52.

[3] Ibid, 46 (repeated nearly verbatim on pp. 52 and 56).

[4] Kirsten Nielsen, *Ruth,* The Old Testament Library (Louisville: Westminster
John Knox Press, 1997) 30.

[5] Robert L. Hubbard, *The Book of Ruth,* The New International Commentary on
the Old Testament (Grand Rapids: William B. Eerdmans Publishing Company,
1988) 69.

questioned morality, they are a mass of conflicting desires and vested interests, each of them existing within the bounds of a societal structure that limits a person in severe ways depending on one's gender, social class, and nationality, yet each struggling in some way to transcend or subvert those bounds. On my reading, Ruth the obedient and submissive recedes before a Ruth who demonstrates a fierce solidarity with Naomi, but who is far from obedient and never entirely forthcoming. She clearly demonstrates a strong agency in the narrative, pushing Boaz to drop his veneer of social acceptability by her verbal sparring in which she employs subtle yet recognizable double entendres. Yet the narrator never tells the reader whether these double entendres, as well as her approaching Boaz in the middle of the night at the threshing floor, are meant to signal a genuine romantic interest in Boaz on the part of Ruth, a desire to provide Naomi with a secure household and/or an heir, her own desire for an heir, or some combination of these possibilities. Nor are we ever told why Ruth's reports to Naomi after her encounters with Boaz in chapters 1 and 2 are not completely truthful. Likewise, Boaz the kindly and pious pillar of the community slips easily into a blustering paternalistic figure who is caught off guard by the surprisingly quick-thinking and mock-deferential Ruth. When Ruth appears next to Boaz in the middle of the night in chapter 3, he is clearly flustered, more than a little frightened, and acquiesces to her suggestions quite easily. Boaz has already demonstrated an interest in Ruth before the nighttime encounter, yet he demonstrates virtually no interest in familial responsibilities to Naomi. If he is as altruistic as interpreters take him to be, why has he not volunteered his help earlier in the narrative, and why does he only mention the redemption of Naomi's land after Ruth has tied land redemption to marriage in chapter 3? And finally, if Naomi is a model of loving concern toward Ruth, why does she virtually render Ruth invisible when she declares herself "empty" upon her return to Bethlehem at the end of chapter 1? Why does she allow Ruth to go off into the fields to glean at the beginning of chapter 2 without so much as a warning, but then exhibit an exaggerated motherly care at the end of the chapter after seeing the interest that Boaz has shown in Ruth? Is it possible that her strenuous attempt to dissuade Ruth and Orpah from returning with her from Moab resulted from a desire not to be burdened with two Moabite women in Judah? And why does Naomi have to be reminded by the neighbor women in chapter 4 of the importance of Ruth in her life? The story, in a style typical of Hebrew narrative, simply does not give the reader enough information to answer these questions with any hard-and-fast certainty, which is not to say that the questions are unimportant or that the author has no interest in them. On the contrary, these questions are central to the plot; but by not providing the answers, the narrative forces the reader to formulate his or her own suppositions while never knowing for sure if they are correct.

The questions I raise about mixed motivations are not meant to impugn the characters in the book, but rather to show that they are presented as complex manifestations of humanity. Bush argues that the book "places a significant stress on the *imitable*, 'go thou and do likewise.'"[6] But it is not so much that the story offers up the characters as unambiguous moral examples to be followed by the reader, but that it compels the reader to constantly re-negotiate the complexities of moral decision-making in a world where everyone is in some way compromised or limited by the rules of the game. The Bible does not have to be read everywhere and always as moral literature in which every character is a potential model for the reader's behavior. Moreover, even when we do choose to read it as moral literature, it does not have to be simplistic or transparent. Hebrew narrative thrives on ambiguity and even ambivalence, and we do well to allow these qualities into our ethical and theological reflections on the literature.

With regard to the theological implications of the narrative, one can only be amazed at the consistency with which interpreters have inserted God into a book that only attributes one direct action to God, that is, allowing Ruth to conceive (4:13). Other than this action, which arguably could take place without God's intervention, one finds only the statement that Naomi had *heard* that "the LORD had considered his people and given them food" (1:6), and the references to God in the speeches of the characters, which primarily take the form of complaints and blessings rather than assertions of divine activity. To bolster the claims for God's "all-causality" or "never-failing presence" commentators must engage in some unabashedly circular argumentation. R. M. Hals, in an oft-cited monograph, argues that the virtual absence of God in the story represents "a kind of underplaying for effect."[7] Hubbard has pursued this line of thought most rigorously, arguing that the narrative speaks of God's activity with "startling indirectness" but that "extreme understatement served as effective overstatement to stress forcefully that Yahweh is indeed very much at work"[8] Nielsen falls back on the repeated statement that one "senses" the hand of God at work in the story.[9] But one reader's sense of hidden

---

[6] Bush, *Ruth, Esther*, 52.

[7] R. M. Hals, *The Theology of the Book of Ruth* (Philadelphia: Fortress Press, 1969) 12.

[8] Hubbard, *The Book of Ruth*, 70.

[9] Nielsen, *Ruth*, 30–31.

providential workings is another reader's sense of God's absence, and the circular argumentation that assumes God's presence and then works diligently to find it remains unconvincing. Thus to argue that God is "the primary actor in the drama"[10] is a serious, if common, misreading of the text. The human characters are quite obviously the primary actors, with God's presence neither veiled nor hidden but, up until 4:13, simply missing. The character of Ruth especially is the drive behind the narrative and her actions are what propels the plot forward; her subtle displacement of Boaz's pious-sounding references to God in their first encounter in chapter 2 of the book reinforces this role. To be sure, God steps in at the point of Ruth and Boaz's consummation of their marriage and allows conception, but this is only possible because Ruth (with Naomi and Boaz doing their parts) has gotten the story this far.

One must be careful, then, not to attempt to build a theological reading of the book based on preconceived notions of God's omnipotence and omnipresence. While such categories sit well in systematic theology, they are rather foreign to biblical narrative in general and to the book of Ruth in particular. Any theological reflection on the book must start with the recognition that human action is of primary importance, and that human actors have the ability, indeed perhaps the responsibility, to resist and challenge social systems that tightly circumscribe such action but which are never entirely free from ideological gaps. The hope is that God will in turn respond to such initiative and bring to fruition what human actors have worked toward. To the extent that the book of Ruth has a "theology," it is one that is less traditional but also less simplistic than has generally been recognized. It is a theology that refuses to see the human characters in the drama as puppets of God's providence and that, because of this refusal, may ultimately prove more relevant to the modern world than we might suppose.

Rethinking the Purpose of the Book of Ruth

If the book's narrative art, characterization, and theology are more complex and ambiguous than has generally been recognized, we might expect that its purpose is similarly complex and ambiguous. It is of course simplistic to speak of any piece of literature as having a

---

[10] Edward F. Campbell, *Ruth: A New Translation with Introduction and Commentary,* The Anchor Bible (Garden City: Doubleday & Company, 1975) 29.

single, defining purpose; literature resists such reduction and tends to
function in a variety of ways, not all of which may be intended by the
author. Nevertheless, I want to pursue one particular purpose or function of the book of Ruth that has yet to be recognized by commentators
and that manifests the same sort of ambiguity that is elsewhere so important to the narrative.

It has occasionally been noted—though not as often as one might
imagine—that the book of Ruth begins with the phrase "in the days of
the judges" and ends with the name "David," thus serving as an especially appropriate link between the book of Judges (which recounts
precisely the time in which the main action of the book of Ruth is set)
and the books of Samuel (which recounts the rise and reign of David).
Many readers are, of course, quite used to finding Ruth placed between these two other books, since that is where the Septuagint and
consequently most modern English translations (such as the NRSV)
have it. But Jewish canonical lists and modern Jewish translations
(such as the JPSV) place the book among the Writings, the third section
of the Hebrew Bible. The traditional scholarly view of the process of
canon formation held that the Septuagint ordering of the books was a
later development among Hellenized Jews who rearranged a previously
existing Palestinian canon. Such a view would make Ruth's placement
between Judges and 1 Samuel secondary and derivative. More recent
scholarship, however, has demonstrated that the process of canonization is much more complex and uncertain than this scenario allows,
particularly in the relationship between Jews of Palestine and Hellenistic Jews; it is simply no longer tenable to assume the Septuagint order
to be late and derivative. This has opened up the possibility that Ruth
was not moved to its position between Judges and 1 Samuel because it
seemed to fit there, but that it has a more intrinsic connection with
those books. In fact, it becomes possible to speculate that the book of
Ruth was written as and intended to be a connector between these two
books.

The more I have worked on the book of Ruth, the more I have become convinced that this claim—that the book is intended to be read
as an interlude between Judges and Samuel—is not only plausible, but
that it also opens up an important new line of interpretation with regard to the larger function of the book. First, I will present the case for
the plausibility of this claim. I begin by noting Pfeiffer's claim that the
opening phrase of the book of Ruth indicates that the author knew of
the Deuteronomistic edition of the book of Judges.[11] While Pfeiffer gives

[11] R. H. Pfeiffer, *Introduction to the Old Testament* (New York: Harper and Brothers, 1948) 716.

no evidence for this claim, it is supported by the fact that nowhere in the book of Judges are the various leaders who are said to have "judged" (*šapat*) Israel referred to by the noun form of "judges" (*šōpᵉtîm*). The title appears to be a later development and indicates that perhaps the author of the book of Ruth knew it from the title of a completed, or nearly completed, book of Judges. Following Boling, Campbell argues that the book of Ruth was constructed by a Deuteronomistic editor of the exilic period as a sort of coda to the book of Judges.[12] In support of this argument, Campbell notes the many verbal correspondences between Ruth and the ending of Judges (especially chapters 19–21): of only six occurrences of the Hebrew particle *ʾal* as an independent negative, two are in Judg 19:23 and Ruth 1:13; the book of Ruth repeatedly uses an unusual and probably archaic feminine dual suffix that is also found three times in Judg 19:24; Judg 20:40 employs the Hebrew *hinnēh* as an indicator of a shift in point of view in a manner similar to its use in Ruth 2:4 and 4:1;[13] both Judg 19:22 and Ruth 3:7 portray someone drinking until their hearts become "good" (or "merry"), with the clear implication that in both cases they are placing themselves in a vulnerable position; the levite's concubine in Judges 19 is said to come from Bethlehem, which is of course the geographical focus of the story in Ruth; and finally, in both Judg 21:23 and in Ruth 1:4 one finds the unusual use of the Hebrew verb *nś'* (rather than *lqḥ*) to express the idiom "to take a wife." To this list of correspondences we may add the theme of "house" and its ambiguous status a place of both safety and threat. Thus in Judges 19 the concubine returns to her father's house (v. 2), from which she is taken by the Levite to another man's house, from which in turn she is taken to be raped and murdered (vv. 22-6); likewise, in the opening verses of Ruth, the house of a husband is shown to be no guarantee of security, perhaps motivating Naomi to adjure Ruth and Orpah each to return to their "mother's house" (1:8).

It would seem to be the case, then, that the book of Ruth shows convincing evidence of a connection to the ending of the book of Judges. What has not been noticed—and what opens up a new line of interpretation that I want to pursue—is that the book of Ruth also shows convincing evidence of a connection to the books of Samuel. If this is

---

[12] Campbell, *Ruth*, 35–36; see also Robert G. Boling, *Judges: Introduction, Translation, and Commentary,* The Anchor Bible (Garden City: Doubleday & Company, 1975).

[13] Actually, Campbell argues that *hinnēh* is used in these instances as an expression of surprise, but Adele Berlin, *Poetics and Interpretation of Biblical Narrative* (Sheffield: Almond Press, 1983), 91–95, has convincingly demonstrated its function as a marker of a shift to a particular character's point of view.

in fact the case, then rather than thinking of the book of Ruth as a coda to the book of Judges, it is more appropriate to see it as a connector between Judges and Samuel. Before exploring the evidence for this claim, a few words about the dating of the book are in order. For Ruth to serve as an intentional link between the books of Judges and 1 and 2 Samuel, it must be at least potentially datable to a period in which the books it connects existed in written form, but before the canonical section of the prophets was sufficiently "closed" to the point that nothing more could be added to it. Thus if the book can be shown to be too late or too early, the theory would break down. To my mind, the most convincing attempt to date the book of Ruth is Bush's detailed comparison of the Hebrew of Ruth to what has been called the Standard Biblical Hebrew of the pre-exilic era and the Late Biblical Hebrew of the post-exilic era.[14] Bush finds ten convincing examples of Standard Biblical Hebrew in the book and eight convincing examples of Late Biblical Hebrew, indicating that the writer of Ruth lived in the transitional period between the two phases of the language's development, or the late pre-exilic to early post-exilic period. This dating, while not conclusive, would place the book late enough that the author could know the written versions (or some written versions) of the books of Judges and Samuel, but early enough that Ruth's canonical placement between these books would not have to be considered secondary.

In support of the connection to the books of Samuel, we may note, once again, that the book of Ruth ends with the name David, who is, of course, from Bethlehem. Moreover, nowhere else in the Bible is a genealogical list used at the end of a narrative; they are always used to introduce a story that follows. Unless one takes Ruth as the only exception to this otherwise quite consistent feature of genealogies, one must assume that the ending of Ruth actually functions to open out to another story. And the most natural story to follow a genealogical list that leads to the name of David would be the story of David's succession to the throne of Israel, told in the books of Samuel. These few clues about the connection between the book of Ruth and the books of Samuel do not in and of themselves add up to an argument. However, there is one other piece of evidence that leads me to believe that the author of Ruth not only knew and echoed the book of Judges, but that he or she also knew and anticipated the books of Samuel: namely, the structural parallels between the book of Ruth and a key section of Samuel.

---

[14] Bush, *Ruth, Esther,* 18–30.

First, let us look at the overall structure of the book of Ruth, which as Bertman has shown is a balanced chiasm or envelope design.[15] Modifying Bertman's proposal, the book may be outlined as follows:

A) 1:1-5   Informal family history (oriented around the tribe and
        the clan)

  B) 1:6-18   Informal kinship ties among women
    1:19-22   Naomi and the women of Jerusalem

    C) 2:1-23   Ruth and Boaz in the field
            a—Exchange between Ruth and Naomi
            b—Ruth goes to the field
            c—Boaz seeks identity of Ruth
            d—Boaz deems Ruth worthy, gives her food and
               protection
            e—Ruth returns and reports to Naomi

    C[1]) 3:1-18   Ruth and Boaz at the threshing floor
            a—Exchange between Ruth and Naomi
            b—Ruth goes to threshing floor
            c—Boaz seeks identity of Ruth
            d—Boaz deems Ruth worthy, gives her food and
               protection
            e—Ruth returns and reports to Naomi

  B[1]) 4:1-13   Formal kinship ties among men
    4:14-17   Naomi and the women of Bethlehem

A[1]) Formal family history (oriented around the monarchy)

While the main sections in this chiastic outline are obviously parallel to each other and exist in a balanced relationship, the structure of the book is not by any means static. That is, there is a clear movement from the beginning of the book to the end, a contrast between the first half and the second half of the structure, which can best be described as a movement from the informal and decentralized to the formal and centralized.

This movement or contrast is indicated in the first instance by the explicit bracketing of the story between the "days of the judges" and "David," or between the tribal confederacy and the monarchy, but it characterizes the structure as a whole. Thus the two "family histories" (labeled A and A[1] above) not only match each other but differ in strik-

---

[15] S. Bertman, "Symmetrical Design in the Book of Ruth," *Journal of Biblical Literature* 84 (1965) 165-8.

ing ways as well. The first (1:1-5) is focused on a single family that is
designated by tribal affiliation (e.g., Judah) and by clan (e.g., Ephrathah). This informal family history—by which I mean that it is not in
the form of a strict genealogy—is decentralized further by the death of
the man Elimelech around whom it is initially organized. The second
family history (4:19-22) is comprised of a much more formal genealogical list. As many commentators note, this sort of genealogical list
tends to function to legitimate the political claims of whomever occupies the final spot in the list. Here of course that spot is occupied by
David, marking the genealogy that closes the book as not only formal
but also concerned with the centralization of power in the Israelite
monarchy. Similarly, with the second level of the chiastic structure of
the book (labeled B and B¹ above) one sees a movement from an informal, private negotiation of kinship ties among women (1:6-18) to a formal, public negotiation of kinship ties among men (4:1-13). In the
former, Naomi, Ruth and Orpah debate matters of loyalty and survival
at the family level, while in the latter, Boaz and Mr. So-and-so debate
matters of property rights and inheritance laws. Even the exchanges
between Naomi and the women of Bethlehem, which form the second
element in each of these sections, reflect this movement: in the first exchange (1:19-21) the focus is on Naomi herself, while in the second exchange it is on the newborn child who is given the legal designation of
"redeemer" (gōʾel) and is identified as the ancestor of David. The decisive shift in the book comes between the central sections represented
by chapters 2 and 3 (identified as C and C¹ above). As with the other
sections in the outline of the book, these match each other extraordinarily closely, down to the five major elements of each episode. But in
chapter 2 the issue is still primarily the welfare of the two women as
Ruth works to provide food for them both, while in chapter 3 the issue
becomes the relationship between Ruth and Boaz and the legal question of who is the nearer redeemer. Admittedly, the two chapters overlap in significant ways, with Ruth interacting with both Naomi and
Boaz in each chapter, but the focus and vocabulary have shifted
slightly but perceptibly. For example, while Boaz's statement of Ruth's
worthiness in chapter 2 centers on her commitment to Naomi and is
couched in terms of family (v. 11), his statement of her worthiness in
chapter 3 centers on the public perception of her and is couched in the
quasi-legal terminology of "all the assembly of my people" (v. 11).

We may compare this dialectic found in the book of Ruth, between
a structure of strict parallelism and a movement from one contrasting
state to another, with a similar rhetorical pattern in 2 Sam 5:13–8:18.
These chapters represent a literary keystone of sorts for the story of
David, connecting as they do the large sections of narrative that re-

count the rise of David (1 Samuel 16–2 Samuel 5:12) and the succession to the throne of David (2 Samuel 9–2 Kings). These sections of the books of Samuel have been characterized, respectively, as the story of David under "blessing" and David under "curse," since in the first he is successful in every venture and appears to be able to do no wrong whereas in the second section David's hold on power begins to slip and his "house" (both in terms of his family and his dynasty) is thrown into a great deal of turmoil. As James Flanagan has shown and Walter Brueggemann has elaborated upon, the seemingly diverse narrative elements that comprise 2 Sam 5:13–8:18 are actually a carefully constructed link between these larger sections and between the ambivalent views of David that they represent.[16] Following Flanagan and Brueggemann, we may outline this central section as follows:

A) 5:13-16   Family list (children born to David)

  B) 5:17-25   Accounts of Philistine wars

    C) 6:1-23   The transfer of the ark to Jerusalem

    C^1) 7:1-29   David's plan to build the temple and a dynastic oracle

  B^1) 8:1-14   Accounts of wars of empire-building

A^1) 8:15-18   Bureaucratic list (David's court officers)

As with the book of Ruth, one immediately notices that this section is constructed by three sets of parallels that have been arranged in a chiastic or envelope design: the list of David's sons is balanced by a list of his court officers, accounts of battles with the Philistines are balanced by battles with other neighboring peoples, and the story of the ark is balanced by the story of David's desire to build a temple for God in Jerusalem. Within these balanced sections, however, there is a movement from one contrasting state to another, in a similar manner to that we identified in Ruth. That is, we find the same move from a decentralized, tribal mode of social life to a centralized, monarchical system. Thus the outside elements in the design (labeled A and A^1 above) are similar in form but contrastive in function; the first focuses on David's immediate family, the second on his creation of an elite political class,

---

[16] James W. Flanagan, "Social Transformation and Ritual in 2 Samuel 6," in *The Word of the Lord Shall Go Forth: Essays in Honor of David Noel Freedman in Celebration of His Sixtieth Birthday,* ed. C. L. Meyers and M. O'Connor (Winona Lake, IN: Eisenbrauns, 1983) 361–72; Walter Brueggemann, *First and Second Samuel,* Interpretation (Louisville: Westminster John Knox Press, 1990) 243–5.

which appears not to have existed under Saul. And while the wars
against the Philistines are defensive wars reminiscent of the days of
the judges when God would raise up a charismatic leader to accompany Israel into battle—and we may recall that in 1 Samuel 7 the
people demand a king precisely for this reason, to lead them in battle
against the Philistines—the wars against the neighboring peoples recounted in B¹ serve to extend the borders of David's empire and to
amass wealth. The two central elements in the outline (labeled C and
C¹) both represent modes of God's presence in Israel, but the ark is tied
to the tribal confederation and represents God as a mobile, untamable
force (see 2 Sam 6:6-11), whereas David's desire to build a temple and
the subsequent dynastic oracle from Nathan represent a clear move toward not only the centralization of political power in Jerusalem but
also toward an appropriation of God's presence in the service of the
monarchy. The similarity in design and in theme between these chapters in 2 Samuel and book of Ruth lead me to wonder if the author of
Ruth imitated this section in the construction of his or her story, or
even if they are from the same hand.

As is typical with Hebrew narrative, the narrator never comes out
and tells the reader how to interpret these parallel yet contrasting elements in this central section of the David story. Clearly the older tribal
socio-political structures and theological assumptions are portrayed as
giving way to the institution of monarchy and to its attendant theological assumptions, but one must ask what the implications of this
shift are for the narrative. We may begin to answer this question by
noting that while the narrator of the book of Judges condemned the
lawlessness and inter-tribal warfare of the time with the repeated refrain, "In those days there was no king in Israel; all the people did
what was right in their own eyes" (21:25; cf. 17:6; 18:1; 19:1), thereby
encouraging the reader to look forward to the monarchy as a positive
force for order, the books of Samuel manifest a more pronounced ambivalence about kingship in Israel. This ambivalence is signaled in 1
Samuel 8 when Samuel, who represents the last of the judges, tries to
dissuade the people from their demand for a king even as the Lord approves their request, but it is most keenly embodied by David, who is
both the ideal king (see especially 2 Sam 16:6-18) and at the same time
one who abuses his power in precisely the terms Samuel predicted (see
especially 2 Samuel 11–12). David represents both the possibility and
the failure of the institution of monarchy in Israel. By the time the
reader of the Deuteronomistic history gets through the books of Kings,
the failures of the monarchy have rather decisively eclipsed its possibilities. It seems to me, then, that we are to interpret 2 Sam 5:13–8:18 as
a subtle negative evaluation of the move from a decentralized, tribal

organization to a centralized monarchical bureaucracy, or at least a manifestation of the narrative's ambivalence about that move. From the perspective of a writer or editor living late in the monarchy, the days of the judges become, rather than a time of social and political chaos, an idealized period of social and political autonomy for the tribes in which God had not yet been co-opted in service of the centralization of power in Jerusalem. This period had its own dangers and excesses, as the book of Judges shows, but they were different dangers and excesses than those evinced by the monarchy.

Returning to the book of Ruth, I admit that I have not presented by any means an airtight case for an intrinsic connection between it and the books of Judges and 1 and 2 Samuel, but the echoes and parallels between the end of Judges and the story of David in the books of Samuel are striking enough to allow me to ask the reader to continue this thought experiment long enough to rethink the purpose, or *a* purpose, of the book of Ruth: namely, that it was intended to function as a narrative link between the stories of the judges and the story of David and the monarchy. And if this is the case, then we have a warrant for seeing in the book of Ruth a more complex attitude toward the David and, consequently, for reading the end of Ruth in a more ambiguous light than interpreters have been wont to do. I will explore the implications of this more fully in my comment below on the end of chapter four, but for the time being it is enough to note that the story may not have the unequivocally happy ending that commentators so often claim for it. Rather than contrasting the positive connotations of the name David at the end of the narrative with the negative connotations of the setting in the days of the judges at the beginning, we might do well to recognize the massive ambiguity in both, and then to read the story of Ruth and Naomi in light of this ambiguity. I will do just this in the commentary that follows.

Chapter 1
THE BOND BETWEEN RUTH AND NAOMI

Chapter one of the book of Ruth is the story of a family. It is a family transformed from a conventional configuration centered on a man and his sons to a less conventional configuration centered on a woman and her daughter-in-law. The fact that the chapter is focused on the motif of a family is reinforced by the repeated use of familial and relational terms, such as wife, husband, daughter, son, mother-in-law, daughter-in-law, and sister-in-law. The fact that the chapter is equally concerned with the *transformation* of that family is indicated by the repeated use of verbs of movement, foremost among them the two key words "to go" *(hālak)* and "to return" *(šûb)*. As this family moves from Judah to Moab and back to Judah, it also moves symbolically from fullness to emptiness, an emptiness that is countermanded only by the bond between the two women—Naomi and Ruth—who remain after the men of the family have dropped from the plot. This bond, or solidarity, that exists between the two women is expressed most eloquently in Ruth's speech in verses 16-17, and it is what ultimately staves off the pervasive sense of death and despair that otherwise overshadows the chapter.

The chapter divides into three main parts. In verses 1-5 the narrator recounts the family history that starts the plot in motion. In verses 6-18, narration gives way to dialogue, as the story negotiates the meaning of kinship ties. In verses 19-21, the transformed family—transformed both for better and for worse—returns to its roots in Bethlehem, where Naomi encounters and speaks with a group of women. As noted in the Introduction above, each of these three parts corresponds in theme to the three parts of chapter four of the book.

1:1-5

[vv. 1-2]

The opening sentences of the book of Ruth recall the book of Judges explicitly as well as in more subtle ways. Judges ends with the refrain, "In those days there was no king, and everyone did what was good in their eyes" (21:25; cf. 18:1; 19:1), and the book of Ruth begins by referring precisely to "those days" by way of the narrator's setting of the context "in the days when the judges ruled" (1:1). The same Hebrew word *(špt)* lies behind both the noun "judges" and the verb "ruled." It is worth noting that the word appears elsewhere in the Hebrew Bible in parallel to the word for "king" (1 Sam 8:5, 6, 20; 1 Kgs 3:9). Particularly relevant are the occurrences in 1 Sam 8:5-6, where the people demand that Samuel give them a king to "judge,"or rule over, them. The repetition of the demand, voiced first by the people in verse 5 and then again by Samuel in verse 6, indicates the importance that it holds in the narrative. Chapter 8 is a turning point in the books of Samuel, away from the days of the judges—quite explicitly represented by Samuel (7:15) and his sons (8:1)—and toward the establishment of the monarchy, which is taken up immediately following with the introduction of Saul in chapter 9 and which leads inexorably to David. This transition is obviously crucial to Israel's self-understanding, even as it is also quite obviously freighted with ambiguity. (See the Introduction above.) The book of Ruth, of course, moves the reader from the days of the judges, wherein it opens, to the days of the monarchy, which are symbolically condensed into the final word of the book (in 4:22), the name of the one person who most clearly embodies Israel's image of kingship: David. Thus the book takes the paired concepts of "judging/ruling" *(špt)* and "king" *(melek)*, separates them, and uses them as a frame for the story.

In this regard, the name Elimelech takes on a tacit symbolic value. It is often noted that the names of the characters in the book, even if not directly translatable into symbolic meanings, seem to be at least wordplays on concepts that the reader is to associate in some way with the characters. Thus Naomi, as the character herself notes with irony in 1:20, is associated with the Hebrew word meaning "pleasant"; Mahlon and Chilion, the children of Naomi and Elimelech who die off abruptly in 1:5, call to mind the words for "sickness" and "consumption"; Ruth sounds a good deal like the word for companion, which of course she is *par excellence* to Naomi; and the name Orpah seems to hint at the word indicating the back of the neck, perhaps reflecting her decision to return home to Moab rather than continue on with Naomi to Judah. Scholarly attention to the names of the characters has tended to focus on whether or not one can *prove* an etymological relationship between the names and these symbolic concepts, thus overlooking the fact that wordplays do not depend necessarily on genuine etymologies, but rather work through hints and allusions. The name Elimelech, then, which may be translated literally as "my god is king," is a symbolic parallel to the opening phrase of the book, "in the days of the judges." That is, as both Judges 21 and 1 Samuel 8 indicate, the time of the judges was a time when there was no human king and Israel was ruled over by the LORD. Elimelech, by his very name declaring the rule of God rather than a human king, represents this era. It is, as noted above, an era that by the end of the book will have vanished, and therefore the death of Elimelech in the opening verses may be subtly symbolic of the passing of that era.

The book of Ruth is a very complex and tightly designed tale (see Introduction above), with a number of structuring patterns, both large and small, that tend to overlap one another. The opening verse not only represents one side of the book-length frame that leads the reader from the days of the judges to David, but also represents the initial element of an inclusio that frames the first chapter. In verse 1 we read of Elimelech and "his wife and his two sons" leaving Bethlehem to travel to Moab, while in verse 22 we read of Naomi and "her daughter-in-law" returning from Moab to Bethlehem. The chapter's opening with the movement of a family away from Bethlehem and its closing with the movement of that family back to Bethlehem creates a thematic parallel that frames the chapter; but, as is often the case with the use of such an inclusio in Hebrew narrative, what is perhaps most interesting are the differences that exist within the parallel. That is, although the chapter begins and ends with the same family in the same city, both the family and the city have undergone drastic changes by the time the reader reaches the enclosing final verse. When the family set out in the opening verses the members were identified in relation to the man Elimelech (e.g., "*his* wife" and "*his* two sons"); when it returns the one remaining member is identified in relation to the woman Naomi ("*her* daughter-in-law"). When the reader first encounters Bethlehem in the opening verses it is a city suffering under a famine; when the reader encounters Bethlehem at the end of the chapter it is a city at the start of a barley harvest.

The name Bethlehem, then, becomes the object of an ironic wordplay. The construct phrase, *bêt-leḥem* means literally "house of bread," but the narrative gets underway by noting that in this house of bread there is no food. This irony is compounded by the identification of Moab as the place to which the family emigrated in order to find food. The land of Moab and the Moabites are freighted with animosity in

Israel's memory (cf. Num 21:29-30; 22; Amos 2:1-3; Jer 48:1-9), and when the book of Deuteronomy sees fit to articulate a rule excluding the Moabites from the congregation of Israel, one of the reasons it gives is that "they did not meet you with food and water on your journey out of Egypt" (Deut 23:3). So not only is Bethlehem (the "house of bread") the site of a famine, but Moab, the place associated in Israel's memory with the withholding of food (in the Hebrew, *lehem*, or "bread"), becomes the destination of an Israelite family seeking to escape the famine. This paradoxical reversal of expectations in the first verse of the book sounds a leitmotif that will recur throughout the story: the dialectic between emptiness and fullness. This leitmotif is often presented by commentators as a movement from emptiness to fullness, and as we will see below there is a good deal of truth to this characterization. It is, however, a bit more complicated than this, since what appears to be emptiness is not always the case and what appears to be fullness can be misleading. We see this not only with the unexpected reversal of Bethlehem and Moab with regard to famine, but also in the family situation at the end of chapter 1. As Naomi herself notes in verse 21, the family that left so full at the beginning of the chapter—with a wife, a husband, and two children—has returned in what seems a dissipated state. The attentive reader, however, will know that this dissipation is not complete: as tragic as the deaths of her husband and two sons may be, Naomi does not in fact return empty, but with Ruth, who represents an almost hyperbolic abundance of commitment and loyalty (see the comment on 1:16-17 below). As the women of Bethlehem inform Naomi near the end of the story, Ruth is "more to you than seven sons" (4:15).

[vv. 3-5]

Still, at this point in the narrative it is family history under curse, and in the larger chiastic structure of the book it matches up with, and is in a sense abrogated by, the family history represented by the genealogy of 4:18-22. Genealogies can serve many functions in biblical narrative, but one thing that they communicate most effectively is sheer fecundity: the regular, rhythmic movement of a genealogical list conveys a nearly unassailable sense of confidence in the future of a family or a people. But in these opening verses there is no such confidence. In many ways a bleaker family history than what the reader encounters in 1:1-5 can hardly be imagined. Once in the land of Moab, Elimelech dies and, after ten years of childless marriage (probably coinciding with the ten generations of the genealogy of 4:18-22), both sons Mahlon and Chilion die as well. On the other hand—and in harmony with the book's complex, often ambivalent, outlook—the dying off of the three men of the family opens up room for the development of the women into more fully imagined characters. That is, the death of the men is in a sense not presented as a great tragedy, but rather as something that must happen in order for the narrator to move on to the more compelling tale of the women. Thus, the death of the men is presented in a quite matter-of-fact manner with little elaboration. In a book that places a peculiar emphasis on dialogue between the characters (fully fifty-six of its eighty-five verses are taken up by dialogue), none of the three men are given a single line to speak. The relative unimportance of Mahlon and Chilion to the narrator's larger story is communicated not only by the wordplays evoked by their names ("sickness" and "consumption"), but also by the fact that neither exists as a genuine character in his own right, but only as one in a pair of un-differentiated brothers. For example, the reader is never told which brother is married to which woman (until it is revealed as part of the legal transaction in 4:9), and the rhyming, sing-song quality of their names foreshadows the nonsense name, *pelōnî 'almōnî*, or "Mr. So-and-so," that is assigned to Boaz's rival in chapter 4. (On the mocking tone of *pelōnî 'almōnî*, which the NRSV elides with its rendering "friend," see the comment on 4:1 below.) Mahlon and Chilion exist almost as a hendiadys, two words that together communicate one concept, i.e., "the sons."

With the deaths of the father and the sons, what has promised to be a story of men quickly and decisively becomes a story of women. Notice how the wording of verse 1, "a certain man . . . *his* wife and *his* two sons," has been replaced by the end of this introductory section to "the woman was left without *her* two sons and *her* husband" (v. 5). The introductory section is rounded off nicely in verses 3-5 with one of the author's trademark chiastic structures. Restoring the Hebrew syntax, Bush outlines the verses as follows:[1]

A **Then died Elimelech, the husband of Naomi, and she was left alone with her two sons.**

  B *They took* Moabite wives, the name of one Orpah and the other Ruth,

  B[1] *And they lived* there about ten years.

A[1] **Then died also both Mahlon and Chilion, and the woman was left alone without her two boys and without her husband.**

---

[1] Bush, *Ruth, Esther,* 60.

With verse 5 the narrator essentially closes the book on Elimelech and his two sons, who will figure no more in the story, and opens up space for the story of Naomi and her two daughters-in-law. A midrashic interpretation of verse 3 captures in its own subtle, intertextual way this dynamic:

> The death of a man is felt by none but his wife, as it is said, "And Elimelech, Naomi's husband, died." The death of a woman is felt by none but her husband, as it is said, "And as for me, when I came from Paddan, Rachel died unto me" (Gen 48: 7). R. Johanan said: [The meaning is] the death of Rachel is [heavy] upon me. Our Patriarch Jacob said, "The death of Rachel is more grievous to me than all the calamities which have befallen me."[2]

By comparing Naomi with the great patriarch Jacob, and likening the death of Elimelech with the death of Rachel, the midrash tacitly acknowledges the shifting focus of the story from the expected story of men to the unexpected story of women.

1:6-18

This section, dealing with the negotiation and definition of kinship ties, matches up in the structure of the book as a whole with 4:1-13, which also deals with the negotiation and definition of kinship ties. As discussed in the introduction above, while these two sections are thematically parallel and occupy parallel places in the chiastic design of the book, the differences between the two bear scrutiny. While the negotiation of kinship ties in chapter 4 is a formal, public matter adjudicated by men (4:1-2), in the presence of a quorum of male elders (4:2), and ostensibly serving the interest of a man's posterity (4:10), the negotiation of kinship ties in 1:6-18 is an informal, private matter between women and concerning the interests and security of women.

[vv. 6-7]

Verses 6-7 properly begin the next scene in chapter 1, which extends through v. 18. As Berlin has noted, the opening verb of verse 6, *qûm* ("She arose . . ."), is used also in Gen 23:3, Exod 1:8, and 1 Sam 1:9 to

---

[2] All references to the midrash *Ruth Rabbah* are from the Soncino Press edition of the *Midrash Rabbah*, ed. H. Freedman and M. Simon (New York: Soncino Press, 1983), cited *ad loc*.

introduce the main action of the narratives.[3] While verses 6-7 certainly begin the story in earnest, they also serve as a transition between the setting of the scene in verses 1-5 and the beginning of the main action of the story. It is a transition that takes place on numerous levels: as noted above it is the transition from a story of men to a story of women, from the land of Moab to the land of Judah, and from narration to dialogue.[4] Formally, since they are spoken in the voice of the narrator rather than in dialogue, there is a sense in which the verses belong with the introductory section. Of course the nature of any narrative transition is to pick up on what comes before in order to move the reader to what comes next, and these two verses perform this task extraordinarily well.

We may note that once again the author has used a chiasm to structure this brief section, overlapping the chiasm with a more strictly parallel relationship between lines. First, by restoring the Hebrew word order as much as possible, we may note the parallel design of the verses:

A Then she started to return, *with her daughters-in-law*, from the country of Moab, for she had heard in the country of Moab, (v. 6a)

 B that the Lord had visited his people in order to give them food. (v. 6b)

A[1] She departed from the place, there where she had been living, *along with her two daughters-in-law*, (v. 7a)

 B[1] and they set out on the road to return to Judah. (v. 7b)

Three parallel elements comprise lines A and A[1], or verses 6a and 7a: (1) each begins with a verb of movement (*wattāqām* and *wattēṣēʾ*, respectively); (2) each makes reference to her daughters-in-law accompanying Naomi; and (3) each mentions twice the geographical location from which Naomi is setting out. Lines B and B[1] are likewise parallel in that each indicates the geographic location to which Naomi is returning.

The differences that exist within these parallels are, however, equally instructive. The dual reference to the proper name Moab in line A is replaced in line A[1] by a dual generic reference: "the place" (*hammāqôm*), and "there" (*šāmmâ*). In a similar way, the statement that Naomi had

---

[3] Berlin, *Poetics and Interpretation of Biblical Narrative*, 104.

[4] Phyllis Trible, *God and the Rhetoric of Sexuality* (Philadelphia: Fortress Press, 1978), 166-68.

heard that the Lord had given his people food in line B is made more specific by the use of the proper name Judah in B¹ to indicate where the Lord had done so. Thus, overlaying the parallel design of the lines is a chiastic design as well, which may be outlined as follows:

A   Place name: Moab. (v. 6a)

   B   No place name: Moab implied. (v. 6b)

   B¹ No place name: Judah implied. (v. 7a)

A¹ Place name: Judah. (v. 7b)

The author of the book of Ruth obviously has a certain literary flair and likes to employ rhetorically complex structures and figures, no doubt often for their own sake. For example, we may also note that in these lines the author makes fine use of alliteration and assonance. The end of verse 6 incorporates both in the wonderful Hebrew phrase, *lātēt lāhem lāhem* ("to give to them bread"). Likewise, verse 7a makes use of a string of rhyming final syllables in the Hebrew, *hāytâ šāmmâ uš*ᵉ*tê kāloteyhâ ᶜimmâh* ("there where she had been living along with her two daughters-in-law"). But in this case there seems to be more than simply literary artfulness involved. That is, the chiastic overlay introduces an element of meaning that the parallel lines did not have: the erasing of the name Moab and the inscribing of the name Judah. It is by no means accidental that this transitional section begins with explicit reference to Moab and ends with explicit reference to Judah, for this is exactly the movement that the chapter as a whole makes.

This movement from Moab to Judah is also indicated in this section by the introduction of two *leitworten,* or leading words, for the chapter: "to return" (*šûb;* v. 6) and "to go" (*hālak;* v. 7). Forms of the Hebrew word for "return" occur twelve times in chapter 1 (vv. 6, 7, 8, 10, 11, 12, 15 [twice], 16, 21, 22 [twice]), while forms of the word for "to go" or "walk" occur ten times (vv. 1, 7, 8, 11, 12, 16 [twice], 18 [twice], 19, 21). These verbs of movement interlock throughout the chapter to construct a pervasive journey motif. Taken most literally, the journey is of course from Moab back to Judah, since the first occurrence of *hālak* was in 1:1 when the family "went" to live in Moab. But symbolically it is a movement from emptiness to fullness, and from ubiquitous death to abundant life. There is a provisional inclusio with the introduction of the *leitwort* "return" in 1:6 and its resumption in 1:22 when we read that Naomi "returned" to Bethlehem, along with Ruth the Moabite who "returned" with her. I call this inclusio "provisional" because it completes the journey motif only in the most literal, geographic sense, with the symbolic meanings of the journey still to be worked out in the remaining chapters of the book.

[vv. 8-10]

With verse 8, the reader encounters the first spoken dialogue of the book, placed in the mouth of Naomi. Campbell has noted that much of the archaizing language in the book of Ruth occurs in the speeches of Naomi and Boaz as a means of communicating their elderly status over against the other characters.[5] Whether this is meant to communicate to the reader their wisdom or rather the idea that they are out of touch with what is going on around them is up to individual readers to decide. In any case, Naomi's speeches in chapter 1 do have a decidedly formal air about them.

In her lengthy initial address to Ruth and Orpah, and in their brief response to her, the author ties together in a highly stylized way the central themes of the plot. Though not designed in a strict chiasm, the verses do seem to reflect a basic envelope structure: contained within the frame created by the repetition of the key word "return" *(šûb)*, one finds two parallel oaths of Naomi, followed by two narrated gestures:

A   But *Naomi said to her two daughters in law,* "<u>Go back</u> *(šûb)* each of you to <u>your mother's house</u>. (v. 8a)

   B   *May the* Lord *deal kindly with you,* as you have dealt with <u>the dead and with me</u>. (v. 8b)

   B¹ *The* Lord *grant that you may find security,* each of you in <u>the house of your husband</u>." (v.9a)

   C   Then she kissed them, (v. 9b)

   C¹ and they wept aloud. (v. 9c)

A¹ *They said to her,* "No, <u>we will return</u> *(šûb)* with you to <u>your people</u>." (v. 10)

Parallelism and movement combine to create a rounded outline while also advancing the plot. In line A, Naomi urges the two to return each to their mother's house; but in line A¹, they respond by using the same syntactical construction with the same verb but replacing "your mother's house" with "you." The parallel oaths that Naomi employs in lines B and B¹ evidence a similar dialectic between symmetry in form and progression of plot. Each line opens with a blessing invoking

---

[5] Campbell, *Ruth,* 110.

the name of the Lord on behalf of the two women, and each blessing is qualified by a further phrase. In line B this qualification looks to the past, as Naomi refers to the women's exemplary dealings "with the dead and with me" (v. 8). In line B^1 this qualification looks to the future, as Naomi refers to her hope that each may find security in the house of a new husband. Likewise, in lines C and C^1 parallel narrated gestures evince very different intents on the parts of the subjects of each line. Naomi, the subject of the first line, clearly intends her kiss to be a farewell gesture (cf. Gen 31:28; 1 Kgs 19:20); while the weeping of the two daughters-in-law, the subjects of the second line, forestalls any such parting. That the proper parallel response of parting would be a kiss in return is shown by Orpah's farewell kiss in 1:14; Ruth, who never parts from Naomi, never offers such a kiss.

There is a good deal of subtle irony in Naomi's speech, some of it perhaps intended by the character Naomi, and some of it perhaps intended by the narrator at Naomi's expense. For example, Naomi clearly identifies herself with "the dead" in line B (v. 8). This identification is in keeping with her speech in verses 11-13, where she makes explicit that her sense of self-worth is solely in relation to her ability to produce sons. "The dead" in this line are, of course, Naomi's two sons, and thus in her estimation she might as well be dead herself. The narrator seems to use this reference to the dead as an occasion for a wry comment on the men of this family. Naomi's stated wish is for Ruth and Orpah each to find "security" or "rest" (*m^{e}nûḥâ*) in the house of a husband. But the reader knows what Naomi refuses to recognize: that the house of a husband is, in this story, a place of neither security nor rest. Against the claim in the midrash *Ruth Rabbah* that "from this we see that a woman has no contentment except in her husband's house," it is precisely the deaths of no less than three husbands in a row that has put these women at risk and occasioned the journey motif of chapter 1. It is worth noting that elsewhere in the Bible, the Hebrew word *m^{e}nûḥâ* tends to be used as a positive alternative to the notion of wandering (e.g., Deut 12:9; Jer 51:59; Ps 95:11); but in this chapter the relationship between the terms is reversed, or at least made much more complicated. That the narrator (if not the character Naomi) intends this ironic counterpoint between the dead husbands of the narrative and the reference to security in the house of a husband is suggested by the parallel placement of the two terms in Naomi's two oaths (lines B and B^1 above).

Naomi's speech in these verses is loaded with key words of the story, beginning with the word pair *lēknâ šobnâ*, "go back." In her attempt to persuade the two women to return to Moab, Naomi employs the imperative forms of the *leitworten* "go" and "return" (*hālak* and *šûb*). The combination of the words elsewhere in the Bible seems to convey a certain urgency, and even a hint of risk—see for example the same word pair in Exod 4:19, where God sends Moses back into Egypt after he has fled, and in 1 Kgs 19:15, where God sends Elijah back to undertake the subversive act of anointing Jehu as king of Israel after Elijah has fled from Ahab and Jezebel. One also finds in Naomi's first speech the first occurrence of the word *ḥesed*, a theologically freighted term that has received much attention in scholarship on the book of Ruth as well as in scholarship on the Hebrew Bible in general. As Sakenfeld has shown, *ḥesed* in the Bible indicates a stance of loyalty or solidarity leading to actions that go above and beyond what would normally be expected.[6] The concept of *ḥesed* is applied to both God and humans, and it is a key word in the book Ruth not by frequency of occurrence but by its occurrence in particularly crucial passages (e.g., 2:20; 3:10). In the present verse, Naomi wishes for Ruth and Orpah that God would show as much *ḥesed* toward them as they have shown toward Naomi and her family. Human actions of *ḥesed* thus become the measure of God's actions, a theme that will resonate with later plot developments.

Of particular interest in Naomi's first speech is her use of the phrase "mother's house" *(bêt ʿēm)*. The term is unusual in the Hebrew Bible, occurring elsewhere only in Gen 24:28 and Cant 3:4 and 8:2. It is more common in biblical literature for a widow to be portrayed as returning to her father's house *(bêt ʾāb;* perhaps a technical term for the household as a social unit), as in Gen 38:11 and Lev 22:13 (cf. Num 30:16; Deut 22:21; Judg 19:2-3). Some scholars have speculated that the use of "mother's house" is an indication that the fathers of the two young women are dead, and often the same is claimed for Rebekah's father in Genesis 24. It seems clear however that Rebekah's father, Bethuel, is not dead (see v. 50), and there is no support in the text for the claim that Ruth's and Orpah's fathers are dead. Other scholars argue that the context for the term in all three books has to do with arranging marriages and that the "mother's house" (perhaps meaning something more like "mother's quarters") may be taken as "the locus for matters pertinent to marriage, especially for discussion and planning for marriage."[7] The main problem with this theory is that, contra Campbell, the references in Canticles simply do not refer to or even hint at marriage. The two young lovers in Canticles are quite clearly unmarried—we may notice, for example, they are portrayed as sneaking out to meet each other at night and in the fields, and they fantasize about being siblings so that they might hold hands and kiss in public.

---

[6] Katherine Doob Sakenfeld, *The Meaning of Hesed in the Hebrew Bible: A New Inquiry,* Harvard Semitic Monographs (Missoula: Scholars Press, 1978).

[7] Campbell, *Ruth,* 64.

Rather than looking for a common custom or sociological unit to which mother's house refers and which would then explain its usage in all three biblical books, it seems better to glean what one can from the other occurrences but to go on to note the ways in which the phrase inheres in each of the narratives. In Genesis 24, the way that Rebekah uses the term mother's house to replace the reference by Abraham's servant to her father's house seems to coincide well with her character's force of personality in the narrative—that is, she is a more fully developed and more active character than Isaac. Likewise, in Canticles the woman's voice is dominant in the poetry, both in terms of the sheer number of lines attributed to the female voice in contrast to the male and also in light of the fact that she does most of the planning and initiating of their trysts. Moreover, the use of the phrase in Canticles is less sociological than poetic, serving as the ultimate symbol of safety over against the threatening outside world. (Note too that in both occurrences in Canticles the mother's house is not far from an archetypal symbol of the safety of a womb.) Returning to our present text, the most obvious thing to note is that, as in Genesis and Canticles, the reference to a mother's house occurs in a context focused on women and voicing women's concerns to an unusual degree for the Hebrew Scriptures. Carol Meyers may well be correct in arguing that mother's house is simply another way, like father's house, of referring to the household unit and that while its use was more widespread in ancient Israel than biblical literature indicates, it tends to be preserved in texts that more prominently feature female characters or voices.[8] In addition to this general observation, we may note that the author of Ruth puts the phrase "mother's house" to a particular rhetorical use in this particular story. In the outline above, I noted that in the frame of this initial exchange between Naomi and her daughters in law, Naomi's urging that they return to their mothers' houses is matched with Ruth's and Orpah's vow that they will return with Naomi to her people, thereby framing the exchange with the two options available to the younger women in the story. As it happens, each of the daughters-in-law opts for a different one.

[vv. 11-14]

This second exchange between Naomi and her daughters-in-law mirrors the first exchange, while also serving to intensify and to focus

[8] Carol Meyers, "Returning Home: Ruth 1.8 and the Gendering of the Book of Ruth," in *A Feminist Companion to Ruth,* ed. A. Brenner (Sheffield: Sheffield Academic Press, 1993).

it. Both exchanges consist in an extended and highly stylized address by Naomi, in which she urges Ruth and Orpah to turn back from following her, and a much briefer description of their response to her urging, in which weeping and a kiss of farewell are mentioned. Intensification occurs with Naomi's speech, with her heightened rhetoric conveying her heightening attempt to persuade the two. A focusing movement occurs in the descriptions of Orpah and Ruth, who up until this point have been, like Mahlon and Chilion, undifferentiated—that is, always referred to together and always acting in concert. But with their respective responses to Naomi's second speech they are effectively separated and become individual characters.

Naomi's address to the two women in verses 11-13 is even more tightly constructed than her speech in verses 8-9. It makes such use of parallels and repetitions that one is almost tempted to scan it as verse; though as we have seen this is typical of Naomi's character in general, adding a sort of elderly formality to her dialogue, and in these verses in particular the tight rhetorical construction seems intended to convey the airtight nature of the argument she offers for why Ruth and Orpah should cease from following her. Beginning with the *leitwort* "turn back" *(šûb)*—combined here again (as in verse 8) with the word "go" *(hālak)*, but in a reverse, chiastic order—her speech proceeds by way of a series of couplets introduced by a repeated Hebrew word.

A) Turn back *(šûb)* my daughters, why will you go with me? Do I still have sons in my womb that they may become your husbands? (v. 11)

A¹) Turn back *(šûb)* my daughters, go your way, (v. 12a)

B) for *(kî)* I am too old to have a husband. (v. 12b)
B¹) For if *(kî)* I thought there was hope for me, (v. 12c)

C) Even if *(gam)* I should have a husband tonight, (v. 12d)
C¹) Even if *(gam)* I should bear sons, (v. 12e)

D) Then *(hᵃlāhēn)* would you wait until they were grown? (v. 13a)
D¹) Then *(hᵃlāhēn)* would you refrain from taking a husband? (v. 13b)

A³) No my daughters, (v. 13c)

E) for *(kî)* my lot is more bitter than yours, (v. 13d)
E¹) for *(kî)* the hand of the LORD has turned against me. (v. 13e)

(NRSV; modified)

By means of a series of couplets, Naomi's speech constructs an increasingly unlikely scenario of why Ruth and Orpah might continue to follow her, culminating in the rhetorical questions of verse 13ab, and sealed by the negative evaluation of her situation in verse 13cde.

One notes almost immediately that there is an unusual concentration of familial and relational words in Naomi's speech: three occurrences of "daughters," four occurrences of "husband," and two occurrences of "sons." The three occurrences of "daughters" here matches the three occurrences, to this point in the narrative, of "daughters-in-law," though the reader cannot be sure whether this more intimate address reflects Naomi's genuine emotional attachment to the younger women—perhaps elicited by their choosing her over their "mother's house"—or is simply part of her attempt to persuade them. The focus of this hypothetical scenario is, however, squarely on the male figures that Naomi evokes. This focus becomes especially apparent in the syntactical parallelism of verse 12, in which each opening particle is followed by a first person perfect verb and a direct object. We may note that the first and third direct objects, "husbands," are in parallel, thus leaving the second and fourth in a similar parallel relation that equates "sons" with "hope." Naomi clearly bases all hope for a future with the women on the possibility of her having more sons, who could then become husbands for them. She simply cannot imagine that the women would stay with her for any other reason. The one word that stands out in these parallel sentences—as neither subject, verb, nor object—is the term "tonight," in Naomi's conditional statement, "If I were to have a husband tonight." The term serves to heighten the improbability of this entire scenario and, with its intimations of sexual relations, was deemed indecent by rabbinic interpreters and deleted in the Targum to Ruth.

The response of Orpah and Ruth to Naomi's urging begins in a way similar to their response to her first speech in verses 8-9: "they wept aloud again." While in their previous response both women refused to kiss Naomi goodbye, however, in this instance Orpah takes Naomi's advice and kisses her goodbye, apparently then returning home to her family (v. 15). As I noted above, Orpah and Ruth have up until this point in the story functioned as a sort of plural stock character, "the daughters-in-law," similar to how Mahlon and Chilion always occurred together as "the sons." But while Mahlon and Chilion exited the story before ever being differentiated from one another, here Orpah and Ruth take decisively different paths. Though both rabbinic and modern interpreters have taken a negative view of Orpah's decision to return to Moab rather than continuing on to Judah with Naomi —the former claiming that she was gang-raped upon taking leave of

Naomi and Ruth—the narrator does not offer any clue that we are to condemn her for the decision. Indeed, Orpah is following Naomi's wishes, and the presentation of Ruth's commitment to Naomi as an extravagant gesture of solidarity seems to depend on our understanding Orpah's leaving as the reasonable course of action; it is Ruth that does the unreasonable.

The extravagance of Ruth's solidarity with Naomi is more fully explicated in the verses that follow, but the reader gets a hint of it already in verse 14 with the use of the word "clung." One of the primary contexts of the word (Hebrew, *dābaq*) is that of love and marriage. It is the same word used in Gen 2:24, where we are told, "Hence a man leaves his father and mother and clings to his wife, so that they become one flesh." (See also the use of *dābaq* in Gen 34:3; Josh 23:12; 2 Kgs 18:16.) It is likely that the author is evoking intentionally the language of marriage in an attempt to express the intensification of the relationship between Ruth and Naomi, especially in light of Ruth's taking leave of her "father and mother" to be with Naomi and in light of the oath of commitment that she makes in the following verses (vv. 16-17). The theme of solidarity and commitment between two women, begun here and developed as the story proceeds, offers a poignant counterpoint to Naomi's inability to measure her self-worth except in relation to men.

[vv. 15-18]

Naomi's third speech in chapter 1 is a final attempt to convince Ruth not to follow her back to Judah, employing the keyword "return" (*šûb*) twice, once as a description of Orpah's turning back to "her people and her gods" and once as an imperative for Ruth to do likewise. For the first time in the narrative Naomi addresses one of her daughters-in-law rather than both together, thus reinforcing rhetorically what the reader has just learned, that the two women—unlike their husbands—have become independent characters in the narrative. The content of Naomi's final urging, however, continues to play on the close identification of Orpah and Ruth in its attempt to persuade Ruth not to split herself off from Orpah but to follow after her rather than Naomi. The focus of this response has also shifted from what is lacking in Naomi, e.g., the ability to produce sons, to what is waiting for them upon return to Moab, their people and their gods. With Ruth's response in verses 16 and 17, she becomes a full-fledged character in her own right. And if Robert Alter is right in his claim that in Hebrew narrative the first spoken dialogue by a character is especially important in constructing the reader's perception of him or her, then this first speech by Ruth may be taken as defining her in terms of solidarity and commitment.

It is useful to compare Ruth's speech here with Naomi's speeches. Unlike the formality of tone and the complex, archaic syntactical constructions employed by Naomi, Ruth's words are spare and direct, though for that no less eloquent. Introduced by an imperative, "Do not urge me to forsake you, to turn back *(šûb)* from following you," and rounded off by an oath of self-imprecation, "May the LORD do thus and so to me, and more as well, if even death parts me from you," the heart of Ruth's speech is the series of succinct statements in between. The statements, like Naomi's earlier arguments, make much use of repetition, but in a stripped-down, staccato-like syntax that conveys the irrefutability striven for but never reached in Naomi's more loquacious exhortations. In the central section of Ruth's speech, each statement of solidarity follows quickly upon the previous, with no explication and no transitions. Each is only two or three words long and consists in the repetition of a verb, first in the 2nd person and then in the 1st person:

where you go	I go,
where you lodge	I lodge,
your people	my people,
your gods	my gods,
where you die	I will die,
there I will be buried.	

The series of verbal repetitions culminates in the final phrase, set off by the lack of repetition, which communicates a solidarity in perpetuity. Recognizing that the phrase, "there I will be buried," does not fit the pattern established in the previous paired statements, some Lucianic Septuagint manuscripts omit it. But the technique of adding a third term to parallel versets for emphasis is well known in Hebrew poetry and, although Ruth's speech is not presented as verse, the final phrase functions in this way—Ruth's commitment to Naomi extends even beyond the borders of death. This is reinforced by the oath that closes Ruth's speech, in which she vows that not even death will separate them. "Till death do us part" is not good enough for Ruth.

The sheer resolve of Ruth's speech of solidarity wins out over Naomi's more logical and eloquent arguments for why they should separate. Naomi saw "how determined" Ruth is to continue on with her, and as a consequence "stopped speaking to her" (v. 18). This report by the narrator ends the episode in an abrupt manner—in a story so dependent on dialogue, when one character refuses to speak the story must move on to the next episode. It is worth lingering over this report of Naomi's response, however, precisely for what it does not say, namely, any hint as to Naomi's thoughts or motivations. Hebrew narrative is famous for the way in which it virtually refuses the reader any insight into the inner life of the characters. The narrator will report actions by characters and dialogue between characters, but will very rarely tell the reader why characters chose this or that course of action or what they were thinking when they said this or that line of dialogue, nor does the narrator engage in evaluating the actions or speeches of the characters. In the case of the book of Ruth, this characteristic of Hebrew narrative becomes especially important because of the ways in which the plot is driven precisely by character motivation; that is, the motivations and inner life of the characters are not unimportant, but rather unstated. The reader thus contributes greatly to the meaning of the story depending on how he or she fills in these gaps in characterization. Does Naomi's refusal to speak to Ruth indicate an acceptance of Ruth's companionship? Or does it rather indicate, as Fewell and Gunn argue, "resentment, irritation, frustration, unease"?[9] Does Naomi see the Moabite women as the source of her troubles, even the cause of the deaths of her two sons? Were her earlier protestations against their accompanying her based on a genuine concern for their well-being, or were they perhaps disingenuous attempts to be rid of these women in the same way that Judah wanted to be rid of Tamar (cf. Genesis 38)? Given the laconic nature of Hebrew narrative there is simply no way to decide these questions in any hard and fast way, though every reader will no doubt do so on the basis of his or her continuing negotiation of character and plot, which may well differ with repeated readings. What does become clear in the verses that follow, however, is that Naomi's "bitterness" (first mentioned in verse 13) is very real, and that she has yet to fully grasp the fact of Ruth's solidarity with her.

1:19-22

These verses comprise the second element in the second section of the larger chiastic structure of the book as a whole, matching up with 4:14-17. Both 1:19-22 and 4:14-17 present exchanges between Naomi and the women of Bethlehem that serve both as reactions to the sections on kinship ties that precede them and as connectors with what follows. In 1:19-22 the reader encounters a group of women astonished

---

[9] Fewell and Gunn, *Compromising Redemption*, 104.

at Naomi's return paired with Naomi's own extended description of her bitter lot of emptiness and death, which she attributes to the Lord. In 4:14-17 the reader encounters what is apparently the same group of women who now proclaim the unexpected fullness of Naomi's life, which they attribute to the Lord.

The final episode of chapter 1 begins, as does every episode in the chapter (cf. 1:1 and 1:6), with movement, indicated as we have come to expect by the keyword *hālak* ("to go"): "So the two of them went on *(hālak)* until they came to Bethlehem" (1:19a). No details whatsoever are given about the trip, nor is any dialogue between the two reported. As much as the chapter plays on the journey motif, it is not the actual journey itself that is of interest to the storyteller but rather the two places connected by the journey—Moab and Judah—and the potential these places offer for exploring the nature of kinship ties and the vicissitudes of a life that moves from fullness to emptiness, from abundant life to pervasive death. So the reader immediately finds the two women arriving in Bethlehem, where according to the narrator the whole city was "stirred" because of them.

[v. 19]

The Hebrew verb translated by the NRSV as "stirred" *(tēhōm)* may connote either excitement (1 Sam 4:5) or agitation (Isa 22:2), and how one settles the meaning of it here depends on how one understands the question of the women, "Is this Naomi?" Adding to the ambiguity is the fact that this astonished question may connote either the delight of recognition or shock over Naomi's diminished circumstances. Virtually every commentator argues for one of these lines of interpretation over the other, with something of a consensus having developed that takes the reaction of the city and the question posed by the women as a positive response to the return of Naomi after her prolonged absence, which Naomi sees fit to correct in her speech immediately following. But there is no need to settle on one of these readings over the other. The author of the book of Ruth—as will become clearer below—makes frequent use of ambiguity and double-meanings, and it is likely that such ambiguity is built into this verse as well. The undecidability between shock and joy, between a negative evaluation of Naomi's circumstance and a positive one, may be taken as a cipher for the reader's response to the narrative thus far, a narrative that is negotiating a delicate balance between the poles of blessing and curse. Forcing a decision between a positive or negative perception of Naomi's return to Bethlehem from Moab is analogous to forcing an answer to the question of whether Naomi is returning under blessing or under curse, full or empty. Both answers are, of course, correct: Naomi has lost a husband and two sons, but she has gained a daughter-in-law of extraordinary loyalty and commitment. (Compare the women's evaluation of Ruth in 4:15, explicitly in comparison to the worth of sons.) Naomi's own assessment of her situation in verses 20-21 is unequivocally negative; but this statement of her emptiness is juxtaposed to Ruth's own statement of solidarity in verses 16-17. Although Naomi, by ignoring Ruth in her speech to the women of Bethlehem, conveys an obliviousness to her presence, the reader cannot help but see the presence of Ruth as a compensating factor in Naomi's life.

[vv. 20-22]

Naomi's address to the women in verses 20-21 is characteristically of an orderly symmetrical construction, despite the emotional tenor and theological invective evinced by its content. The speech is composed of two parallel statements of abjection:

A) Call me no longer Naomi,

    a. Call me Mara, for <u>the Almighty has dealt bitterly with me</u>.

    b. I went away full, but <u>the LORD has brought me back empty</u>.

A^1) Why call me Naomi,

    b^1. when <u>the LORD has dealt harshly with me</u>,

    a^1. and <u>the Almighty has brought calamity upon me</u>?

Each statement is introduced by a comment on the inappropriateness of the name "Naomi," which is etymologically related to the Hebrew word for "pleasantness" or "delight," followed by a double complaint against God for her bitter lot.

The first statement employs the divine names *šadday* and *yhwh* (traditionally translated as the Almighty and the LORD) in parallel position and gives a brief explication of the reason for her complaint. Making use of a wordplay on her name, Naomi sardonically rejects its positive connotations and claims that a more appropriate name for her is Mara, etymologically related to the Hebrew word for "bitterness," for God has "dealt bitterly" with her. She then makes explicit the theme that has been implicit throughout the first chapter, the dialectic between emptiness and fullness, while also making explicit the cause of her emptiness, that is, the LORD. This last point is underscored by the only use in the book of the keyword *šûb* ("to return") in its causative sense: "the Lord *made me return* empty." Moreover, the Hebrew reverses the standard word order by placing the adverbs "full" and "empty" before the verbs, thus emphasizing Naomi's abject state. In her second statement (labeled "B" above), Naomi dispenses with the reasons for her complaint against the LORD, which should by now be clear for all to see, and bluntly states her case, once again using the divine names *šadday* and *yhwh* in parallel position but now in a reverse, chiastic order to their use in the previous statement.

Naomi's complaint against God is harsh, but it is by no means unprecedented. The final verb she employs, which the NRSV renders as "brought calamity," is the causative form of the Hebrew verb *ra'a'*. The verb is a strong one, its most common meaning being to "do evil" or to "act wickedly." Now it may well be that its use here means something like, "to bring evil upon," in which case the NRSV is not toning down the verb overly much. But it seems more likely that Naomi is flat out attributing evil or wicked actions to God—that is, unmotivated or wrongly motivated affliction—in the same way that Moses does in Exod 5:22 and Num 11:11 and that Elijah does in 1 Kgs 17:20 (in each case using the same causative form of the verb). It is significant, however, that both Moses and Elijah are directly addressing God in these passages and trying to reverse the circumstances, while Naomi neither addresses God nor expects any chance for reversal. This may be due to the fact that Naomi—unlike Moses and Elijah, the paradigmatic prophets of the LORD—has never herself been addressed by God nor has she been called by God to some great task. Rather, like Ruth—whose leaving of her homeland and parents' household mirrors Abraham's setting out in Genesis 12, with the important caveat that she is never commanded by the Lord to do so[10]—Naomi must endure hardship and uncertainty without the benefit of an active God underwriting and endorsing her affairs.

What Naomi has instead of God's palpable presence is the companionship of Ruth. This is, as we have seen already and will see more fully as the narrative proceeds, no small thing; and the narrator reminds the reader of Ruth's presence as the chapter comes to a close. Verse 22 nicely ties together the major themes of the chapter while maintaining the dialectical tension between emptiness and fullness. The verse represents an obvious inclusio to the opening verse of the chapter: the family that had set out from Bethlehem to journey to Moab here "returns" (*šûb*) from Moab to Bethlehem. While the reader is informed that Ruth returned along with Naomi, there is, in acknowledgment of Naomi's immediately preceding statement of destitution, a distance maintained between the two women. Ruth is referred to

[10] Trible, *God and the Rhetoric of Sexuality,* 178.

again as "the Moabite," despite the fact that she has pledged her loyalty not only to Naomi but to Naomi's god and people, and she is referred to once again as her "daughter-in-law," though earlier Naomi had emended that simply to "daughter." As the chapter ends, the reader certainly would be right to deem Naomi's negative assessment of her situation as correct; but the reader would be just as right to see hints that this negative evaluation is not the final word on the matter. Thus the chapter closes not with fullness, but with the potential for fullness: Naomi left Bethlehem with a husband and two sons, she returns with Ruth; she left during a famine, she returns at "the beginning of the barley harvest."

Chapter 2

FINDING FAVOR IN BOAZ'S FIELD

Chapter two of the book of Ruth, while framed by interchanges between Naomi and Ruth and thus continuing the emphasis on the bond between the two women, nevertheless is centered on the encounter between Ruth and Boaz in the field. It is appropriate then that key words and themes of the chapter are "gleaning" *(lāpat)* and finding "favor" *(ḥen)*. Both of these motifs highlight the developing relationship between Ruth and Boaz, and as the story progresses both are revealed to have double meanings. In addition to these explicit leitworten and leitmotifs, the chapter also works with a series of more implicit binary oppositions, or paired terms that are normally thought of as representing far-removed poles of human existence. Note for example the interplay in the chapter between male/female, old/young, rich/poor, and Judahite/foreigner. The story subverts the strict opposition between these terms, however, showing rather that they exist in a complex dialectical relationship.

Structurally, the chapter corresponds very closely to chapter 3. Both chapters begin and end with Ruth at home with Naomi, and in the middle both chapters recount by means of extensive dialogue an encounter with Boaz. Both of these encounters, I argue, are freighted with ambiguity. Focusing in on the encounters themselves, they exhibit five strikingly similar elements. In chapter two we may identify these (following Bertman, with some modification) as follows:[1]

a) Exchange between Ruth and Naomi (vv. 1-2).

b) Ruth goes to the field and meets Boaz (v. 3).

[1] Bertman, "Symmetrical Design in the Book of Ruth," 165–8.

  c) Boaz inquires as to Ruth's identity (vv. 4-7).

  d) Boaz asks Ruth to stay, deems her worthy, gives her food and
     protection (vv. 8-17).

  e) Ruth reports back to Naomi and receives counsel (vv. 18-23).

Each of these elements has a closely corresponding counterpart in
chapter 3 (on which see the introduction to the next chapter).

2:1-3

[v. 1]

    Dialogue will prove very important for the unfolding of chapter 2,
as it was for chapter 1, but before allowing the characters to speak the
narrator introduces a new character, a relative of Naomi's. In a certain
respect the opening of chapter 2 mirrors the opening of chapter 1: both
are concerned with a man and his family connections. Elimelech is
once again mentioned, but is explicitly identified as the "husband of
Naomi," his status as an independent character having long been lost.
Indeed the first word of the chapter, in the Hebrew, is Naomi ("Naomi
had a relative . . ."). The last word of the opening verse is the name of
that relative, Boaz. As in Ruth's report to Naomi later in the chapter (v.
19), the narrator here withholds the name of Boaz until the very end of
the sentence.

    The withholding of Boaz's name is potentially significant for at
least two reasons. First, when Ruth withholds his name in her report
to Naomi, it is clear from Naomi's reaction that it is a revelation of no
little importance. Perhaps that is the case here—that is, the narrator
may be withholding from the reader the name of a well-known ancestor of David, so that when his name is revealed the reader is to have a
reaction similar to Naomi's. Unfortunately one cannot be sure whether
or not the reader is expected to recognize Boaz as an ancestor of David
since outside of the book of Ruth he is mentioned in the Bible only in
Chronicles, which perhaps depends in turn on the present story. The
withholding of Boaz's name until the end of the sentence, in light of
the narrator opening with the name of Naomi, may also serve as a rhetorical flourish in another way. As numerous commentators have
noted, although the plot of the book puts the two in a complex and in-
tricate relationship to each other—both as kin and as characters dri-
ving the movement of the book—they never in fact meet face to face.
Thus, by splitting the two names and putting them at the beginning
and ending of the opening sentence of the chapter, the narrator sym-

bolically represents the paradoxical relationship between Naomi and Boaz in the story: bound up with each other, yet always separated.

The name Boaz itself, like the other characters' names, may be an allusion to his symbolic role in the story. There is a long tradition, extending at least as far back as the LXX and continuing through rabbinic interpretations and into modern scholarship, to see the name Boaz *(bōʿaz)* as deriving from the Hebrew phrase "in him is strength" *(bô ʿōz)*. As in the discussions of the other names in the book, scholars have tended to get bogged down in arguments over the exactness of the etymology or whether or not "Boaz" is a genuine Ancient Near Eastern name and thus not invented by the author for symbolic purposes. Such argument once again misses the point that an *allusion* does not require a precise etymology, nor does it in this case rule out the possibility that the name exists in other contexts. That is, the author need not have invented the name Boaz in order to make a pun or wordplay on it. When combined with the fact that one of the pillars at the entrance to the great hall of the Solomonic temple is given the name "Boaz" (1 Kgs 7:21), the likelihood of a symbolic value to the name in our story increases. It is hard to avoid using the English cliche "pillar of the community" as a way of summing up the allusion. The etymological wordplay of the name and the punning allusion to the temple pillar are reinforced by the narrator's description of Boaz as *ʾîš gibbōr ḥayil*, translated by the NRSV as "a prominent rich man." Literally, the phrase means something like "mighty man of strength" or "man of heroic strength," but the NRSV is likely correct that the phrase is used here in a symbolic sense indicating his social standing and importance (see 2 Kgs 24:14, where the phrase is used in contrast to "the poorest people in the land"). It is important to note that this is not an evaluation of Boaz by the narrator, who quite consistently refrains from any such explicit judgment of the characters, but is rather an indication of how Boaz is viewed by others in his social world. Whether or not Boaz will live up to his moniker is still to be decided. At this point in the story the significance of Boaz for the two women remains unclear; though by emphasizing that he is kin to Naomi through Elimelech and part of the same clan or family *(mišpāḥâ)*, the narrator opens the possibility that he will be of some help to them.

[vv. 2-3]

Ruth sets in motion the action of chapter 2 with her statement to Naomi of her intention to find a field in which to glean among the ears of grain, thus providing for the two widows, and Naomi assents with the terse reply, "Go, my daughter." In this opening dialogue of chapter

2 the narrator makes subtle reference back to chapter 1. The mention of a field *(śādeh)* to which Ruth will go in order to glean during a time of hardship recalls the "field *(śādeh)* of Moab" to which Naomi and her family went in order to find food during the famine. Moab is also kept in the reader's mind by the designation of Ruth as "the Moabite," which she was called at the end of chapter 1 (1:22). And by having Ruth go out to glean ears of grain, the narrator picks up on the theme of the barley harvest, also introduced in the final verse of chapter 1.

Although provision is made in Israelite law for the poor to glean in the fields of more well-to-do Israelites (e.g., Deut 24:19 and Lev 19:9-10), Ruth's statement implies that she feels the need to seek the permission of the field's owner before doing so. At least this is how most interpreters take the phrase "behind someone in whose sight I will find favor." The rationale behind this interpretation is that even though adherence to the legislation was expected, in practice it was not always the case that landowners conceded the right of gleaning; thus one finds the exhortations of the prophets that seem to presume a lack of compliance (Amos 5:10-15; 8:4-6; Mic 3:1-3; Isa 1:21-24; 5:8-13). It is also possible that we are to understand that Ruth, as a Moabite, does not know the ins and outs of Israelite law or social practices. In this case, the terse reply by Naomi, who presumably *does* know of the provision for gleaners, is little short of negligent for not informing Ruth that there is no need to ask permission. The notion of "finding favor" in someone's eyes carries more subtle meanings as well. We may note that Ruth uses the same phrase twice more in the chapter, both times in her interactions with Boaz (vv. 10, 13), where they imply something more than a simple permission to glean. Thus the narrator sets up the *leitmotif* of "finding favor" by making it a part of Ruth's initial statement of intent, which may have as much to do with its use here as any actual need to request permission. We may also note that the Hebrew word for "favor" *(ḥen)* elsewhere can indicate a woman's sexual desirability to men (Nah 3:4; Prov 11:16; 31:30), and the precise phrase "to find favor" is used in the book of Esther (2:15, 17) to convey Esther's desirability over the multitude of young women brought to King Ahasuerus after their year-long (!) beauty treatments. Though I do not think that it is the case that the narrator is indicating Ruth's intent to "find a man" by use of the phrase, I do think the reader is given a slight hint already of the freightedness of the relationship between Ruth and Boaz and the role that desire and sexuality will play in that relationship.

The phrase "Ruth the Moabite" is used by the narrator three times (1:22; 2:2; 2:21) and by Boaz twice (4:5, 10). Hubbard points out that besides the reference to Ruth and Orpah as "Moabite women" in 1:4, the only other reference to Ruth's nationality is in the description of her given to Boaz by his foreman in 2:6. Hubbard is correct, I think, to see "authorial design" in the designation of Ruth as "the Moabite" in these particular places in the narrative: "It might aim to imply that, once in Bethlehem, Ruth's race became a factor in the story."[2] The clustering of references to her nationality (a better term than "race," which is misleading here) around her entrance into Bethlehem and her attempts to glean in someone's field certainly indicates the vulnerability of Ruth as a foreigner, that is, as one who has no ties to the community in Bethlehem (other than Naomi) and therefore no social safety net in times of hardship such as the present. Indeed, though it is impossible to know if this is intentional on the author's part, Ruth fits all three categories of needy people given permission to glean in the fields of others: the stranger, the fatherless, and the widow (Deut 24:19; cf. Lev 19:9-10). Widowed by the death of her husband in the opening verses, "fatherless" by virtue of her abandonment of all things Moabite in favor of solidarity with Naomi, Ruth is also in the eyes of her new people a "stranger" and a foreigner. Yet not only at issue is her status as a *foreigner* in Israel, which carries the connotation of vulnerability, but also her status as a *Moabite* in Israel, which connotes something other than vulnerability. This other connotation—namely an illicit sexuality—will become important as the chapter progresses.

Picking up on one of the keywords from chapter 1, *hālak*, the narrator reports in rapid succession that "she went *(tēlek)*, she arrived, and she gleaned" (2:3). Campbell is correct to note that the three verbs represent a summation of the scene that follows, rather than imagining that she has already begun to glean in the first half of verse 3. In fact, her arrival in the field of Boaz is narrated in the second half of verse 3. Ruth's arrival in Boaz's field is narrated with the phrase "as it happened" (NRSV) or "as chance would have it" *(wayyiqer miqrehā)*. Virtually every commentator insists that this is a veiled reference to God's providential guiding of the character Ruth's footsteps. Theological judgments such as the following fill the secondary literature on this verse. "The reader is probably to react smilingly, 'Accident? Of course not!'"[3] "The phrase must be taken as an indirect reference to God himself standing behind the apparently chance encounter."[4] "The author's real meaning in 2:3b is actually the opposite of what he says . . . For Ruth and Boaz it was an accident, but not for God."[5] Such theological

[2] Hubbard, *The Book of Ruth*, 137.
[3] Hubbard, *The Book of Ruth*, 141.
[4] Nielsen, *Ruth*, 55.
[5] Hals, *The Theology of the Book of Ruth*, 12.

readings of the verse tend to fall back on a circular logic which claims
that since we know beforehand that the Hebrew Bible attributes all
that happens to God, whenever we come across a text that seems not
to attribute something to God we must endeavor to read God into the
text. The logic is not only circular, but it begins with a faulty premise—
it is simply the case that the Bible does *not* everywhere and always as-
sert a strict providential view of the world's workings, but is quite
diverse in its theological orientation. One need only to read through
the books of Job, Ecclesiastes, Lamentations, Esther, or the Psalms to
find evidence for a more complex and theologically challenging view
of God's relationship to the world. In fact, the only other place in the
Bible where one finds the same linguistic construction that we have in
Ruth 2:3 (the verb *qrh* in combination with its noun form *miqreh*) is in
Eccl 2:14-15, where clearly the notion of an impersonal "fate" or
"chance" is being referred to. Campbell rightly notes that the "best
comparable passage" to the story of Ruth chancing upon Boaz's field
is 1 Sam 6:1-12, where the Philistines devise a test to determine
whether or not their troubles are due to "chance" (our word *miqreh*) or
to having taken possession of the Ark of the Covenant. But because
the results of the test in this story indicate that the cause of their problems is *not* chance, Campbell extrapolates that "few things if any happen by chance, according to biblical thought," then he uses this text as
a basis for claiming providential guidance in the book of Ruth.[6] In
fact, the story in 1 Samuel 6 is nonsensical if one assumes the biblical
writers had no conception of chance: the test is designed to decide between two options, and without the option of chance available there
would be no test. Moreover, as Campbell notes, in the story from 1
Samuel the reader has already been informed by the narrator that God
is behind the events in question, but he elides the fact that in the book
of Ruth this is not the case. For all the references in the secondary literature to God as omnipresent in the book, albeit "in the shadows,"[7]
"behind" the scenes,[8] or "hidden" from the characters,[9] there is only
one direct theological reference to God—in 4:3, a stock formula where
God is said to allow Ruth to conceive (note that 1:6 reports what
Naomi has "heard" about God rather than being a direct theological
statement of God's activity). This is hardly enough to build a context
within the book for interpreting 2:3 against its plain sense of a chance
happening.

[6] Campbell, *Ruth*, 112.
[7] Ibid.
[8] Nielsen, *Ruth*, 55.
[9] Hubbard, *The Book of Ruth*, 69.

2:4-17

Having established Ruth in the field of Boaz in the opening verses, the bulk of the chapter narrates the events and interactions that take place in the field. After the quick movement and terse dialogue of verses 1-3, this section seems distinctively slow-paced, perhaps to emphasize the importance of the meeting between Ruth and Boaz, or perhaps to convey to the reader the length of a day spent working in the fields.

[vv. 4-7]

Boaz appears on the scene for the first time in the book in verse 4, introduced by the Hebrew particle *hinnēh*, usually translated in English Bibles as "look" or "behold." The word *hinnēh* is primarily used to focus the reader's attention on a particularly important and usually surprising piece of information. As Adele Berlin has shown, *hinnēh* is also quite often used as an indicator of point of view, as a way of conveying a character's perspective on what is happening in the narrative. Either of these uses is possible in verse 4. It may be that the reader is given Ruth's perspective here as she looks up and sees the owner of the field approaching. One problem with this reading is that the reader cannot be sure that Ruth knows yet who Boaz is. It is clear that by the end of the chapter she has learned his name, though apparently she does not know the significance of this until Naomi reveals that he is their kinsman, and it may be that we are to assume that she has learned the name of the field's owner upon her arrival. It seems more likely however that the narrator employs *hinnēh* here as an indicator to the reader of the fortuitousness of Boaz arriving in the field as Ruth is there waiting to glean. Not only has Ruth chanced upon the field of Boaz, but "What do you know?" *(hinnēh)*, Boaz himself comes along. *Hinnēh* is thus not used here as the introduction to a temporal clause—not, that is, to indicate that Boaz immediately arrived on the heels of Ruth as implied by the NRSV's "just then"—but rather to indicate a dramatic development in the plot. As we learn in verse 7, Ruth has been in the field for some time before Boaz arrives on the scene.

Boaz's greeting to his workers—"The LORD be with you"—is a convention (cf. Judg 6:12; Ps 129:8) and should not be taken as an indication of his great piety or moral character (contra Campbell, Nielsen, etc.), nor should one use it to buttress such theological claims that "in a simple undramatic way, it affirmed the presence of Yahweh in this scene."[10] To the extent that the exchange between Boaz and his workers

---

[10] Hubbard, *The Book of Ruth,* 144.

is anything more than convention (comparable to the modern English "goodbye," which has lost entirely its original religious meaning), what it affirms is the wealth and power of a landowner over against what are probably itinerant workers. Thus we may notice that both Boaz's wish that the LORD "be with" his workers while they are harvesting *his* field and the workers response—"the LORD *bless* you"— serve Boaz's interests. Put another way, the LORD being with the workers, and thus ensuring a bountiful harvest, implies a blessing on Boaz. All this is to reiterate that, as we were told in 2:1, Boaz is "a prominent rich man." And prominent rich men expect to be blessed.

Boaz's status as a prominent rich man is evinced again in his immediate inquiry as to whom "this young woman belongs." The form of Boaz's question clearly implies an unequal power relation, as shown by the two other occurrences of the form in Gen 32:18 and 1 Sam 30:13 where similarly powerful men address less powerful people. The immediacy of the question—he does not for example ask about the harvest or the condition of the workers or any other matters at hand— communicates Boaz's keen interest in Ruth. As always, the narrator give us no glimpse into Boaz's thoughts, so the motivation behind his interest is left up to the reader to decide. Most commentators, in their desire to portray Boaz as a moral paragon, tend to read his motives in the light of altruism. Thus Hubbard thinks that perhaps his question regarding to whom she belongs reflects not an interest in "acquiring" (cf. 4:10) her, but rather an unspecified "ancient oriental custom" that was meant to avoid offending her, and Nielsen takes his interest in Ruth as evidence of Boaz's "caring for his servants." Rabbinic interpreters, as well as most moderns, assume that Ruth was beautiful, although the story never addresses the issue. But even those who assume her beauty tend to exonerate Boaz of any licentious thoughts. Only Fewell and Gunn explore in any depth the possibility that Boaz's interest in Ruth may be of a sexual nature from the start, though they rightly emphasize that sexual desirability does not necessarily imply conventional beauty.[11]

While the narrator does not make explicit the source of Boaz's curiosity regarding Ruth, there are hints that sexuality plays a part. As Campbell notes, the narrator introduces in this verse another leading theme of chapter 2, that of youth. The foreman is referred to as *naʿar*, Ruth as *naʿărâ*, the male workers as *nᵉʿārîm*, and the women workers as *nᵉʿārôt*. The terms are all variations of the Hebrew word for a young person, sometimes used to indicate a servant. The connotations of sexuality are present due to the fact that the feminine form of the word

---

[11] Fewell and Gunn, *Compromising Redemption*, 40–4.

most often connotes not just a young woman, but a young woman of marriageable age and situation (e.g., Gen 24:14, 16; Deut 22:15, 16; 1 Kgs 1:3, 4; Esth 2:4, 7; etc.). In Judges 19 it refers to a concubine, and in Amos 2:7 it is even more explicitly connected with sexuality. Moreover, sexual overtones are clearly present in Boaz's instructions to his "young men" not to molest Ruth (2:9, 16) and in Naomi's instructions to Ruth to stay close to the young women rather than the young men while she is in the field working. Though there are at most hints of the sexual nature of Ruth's and Boaz's relationship at this point in the story, these hints will be elaborated on and confirmed as the plot progresses. Also, Boaz's status as an unchallenged, powerful man who instigates the relationship will be complicated.

In response to Boaz's request for information about "this young woman" and her attachments, the foreman responds with a distinct emphasis on her nationality as a Moabite: "She's a young Moabite woman *(na'ărâ)*; she returned with Naomi from the field of Moab." As mentioned above, it may be that the mention of Ruth's nationality is meant to connote her economic and social vulnerability as a foreigner. But it may also be an allusion—perhaps even a rather crude one—to a stereotyped view of Moabite women as sexually available and even aggressive. Moab is associated in Gen 19:30-38 and 25:1-5 with such sexuality, and given the fact that author seems to allude to other stories of Moab from the Torah (see the comment on chapter 1 above for the intertextual relationship between Ruth 1:1 and Deut 23:3) the reader might reasonably be expected to make a similar connection to these stories. This would explain nicely why Boaz feels the need to so sternly warn his young men not to molest her. This is also perhaps why the foreman specifies that she has come from Moab *with Naomi*, not because the foreman necessarily even knows who Naomi is or expects Boaz to know but to emphasize that she came *with a woman*. Not only is this a Moabite woman, but a young Moabite woman who does not belong to another man.

The foreman goes on in verse 7 to report Ruth's request and subsequent actions to Boaz. The verse is undoubtedly the most difficult Hebrew in the whole book. Ruth's request in 7a is readable yet confusing; the report of her subsequent actions in 7b is simply unreadable. Regarding her request to the foreman, it is clear that she is requesting to "glean," sounding a keyword for the chapter, but there is much debate among scholars as to the nature of the gleaning at issue. Specifically, is she requesting to "glean and gather *among* the sheaves" (NRSV; emphasis added), that is collecting grain from among the bundles already harvested by the reapers and therefore going beyond that which is allowed by Israelite law, or is she simply requesting what is already allowed by the law, that is, gleaning the leftovers from where the reapers have already gone through? Bush provides a good, detailed summary of the various interpretations of this verse and the evidence marshaled for them.[12] Mainly at issue is the Hebrew word *bāʿomārîm*, which the NRSV takes to mean "among the sheaves" and reads as the indirect object of both "glean" and "gather," which verbs are understood to convey simultaneous action. Bush's explanation— that "glean" and "gather" are sequential verbs, that the object of both is the unstated but implied "ears of grain," and that *bāʿomārîm* is an adverbial phrase—is more convincing. He translates her request as "May I glean stalks of grain and gather them in bundles behind the reapers?"[13] In this reading, Ruth's request is simple and, strictly speaking, unnecessary.

Apparently the foreman had granted her request before Boaz arrived, though because of the garbled Hebrew in the second half of verse 7 it is impossible to be exactly sure what has transpired since Ruth herself arrived at the field. A literal rendering of this problematic passage would yield something like, "She came and stood from then the morning and until now; this is her sitting the house a few." A host of textual emendations and proposed solutions can be found in the secondary literature, none of which has generated a consensus. We simply have to admit that we cannot pin down with precision what the text is saying here, though the general sense is relatively clear and is conveyed well by the NRSV. I would change it only slightly, by accepting Bush's proposal that the foreman does not emphasize that Ruth has been "on her feet" all day (the Hebrew verb *ʿmd* simply does not convey that), but rather that she has "remained" in this field all day. Thus the modified NRSV would read: "So she came, and she has remained here since early this morning until now, without resting even for a moment." The picture is of a long, hot day in the sun with likely very little to show for it if the reapers are doing their job properly and not leaving much behind.

[vv. 8-13]

Boaz's addresses to Ruth in chapter 2, like Naomi's in chapter 1, are long, syntactically archaic, and constructed with a great deal of complex parallelism. As with Naomi's earlier speeches, Boaz speaks nearly in verse. When the rhetoric of his initial address to Ruth in verses 8-9 is outlined, the formal elements of his speech becomes apparent:

[12] Bush, *Ruth, Esther*, 113–9.
[13] Ibid., 107.

A) Have you not heard, my daughter?

> B) Do not go *(hālak)* to glean in another *(ʾaḥēr)* field,
> Do not even step outside of this one.

> B¹⁾ While here, you should stick close to my young women,
> Keep your eyes on the field being reaped as you follow
> *(hālak)* after *(ʾaḥar)* them.

A¹⁾ Have I not commanded the young men to keep their hands off you?

The speech is framed by two interrogatives which, though I have rendered them as questions in order to bring out the formal parallelism, function as emphatic affirmatives—"Listen, my daughter," and "I am commanding . . ." respectively.

Between the framing questions occur four imperative sentences in overlapping patterns of parallelism. The first pair and the second pair evidence a common poetic parallelism in which the second phrase seems to repeat the first but in fact intensifies it or makes it more concrete.[14] Thus, in the first pair (labeled B above) Boaz is telling Ruth not only to eschew other fields as potential opportunities for gleaning, but that she should not even set foot outside of this field. The intensification is highlighted by the switch from the Hebrew negative *loʾ* ("do not") to *ʿal* ("do not, now or ever"), though this is lost in the English since both are routinely rendered as "not." The relationship between the two phrases is not only one of intensification, but also of concretization, as the general verb of movement *hālak* ("go") is replaced by the more concrete verb *ʿabar* ("to pass over, step outside"), and of geographical focusing, as the perspective narrows from all possible surrounding fields to this particular field. Likewise the second pair (B¹) moves from an imperative that Ruth should stick close or "cling" *(dbq,* the same verb used by Ruth in 1:14) to the young women to the more radical imperative that she should not even lift her eyes from the field as she follows after them. Moreover, the author's use of a "poetic" intensification in a prose context extend also to the relationship between the two pairs (B and B¹). That is, while the first pair of imperatives both deal with the question of whether or not Ruth will stay in this particular field, the second pair both focuses the issue and makes it more concrete by specifying how Ruth is to relate to the people who are in the field. The transition between the two pairs is the Hebrew word *kōh*, meaning "While you are here [this is what you should do]." Adding to

[14] For this phenomenon in Hebrew poetry, see Robert Alter, *The Art of Biblical Poetry* (New York: Basic Books, 1985).

the rhetorical complexity, and thus to the formality, of Boaz's speech is the fact that the first line of B and the second line of B¹ are parallel by means of the vocabulary they use. These two sentences, which contain only four words and five words respectively, nevertheless have three words in common: *hālak* ("go"), *śadeh* ("field"), and *ʾahr* (the same root word used in two different senses of "another" and "behind").

Like Naomi's earlier speeches, Boaz's speeches utilize archaic syntax and vocabulary.[15] Boaz's speech in vv. 8-9 thus identifies him with Naomi both by its formal, almost poetic quality as well as its archaic tone. It also echoes much of the vocabulary used by Naomi, including his referring to her as "my daughter" (cf. 1:11, 13; 2:2), his use of *hālak* ("to go"; cf. 1:8, 11), and in the exchange with his workers the use of the divine name YHWH ("the LORD") which, though used repeatedly by Naomi, is used only once by Ruth (1:17). At the close of the chapter, Naomi will in turn echo Boaz's advice to Ruth to stay close to the young women rather than the young men while she is in the field. The result of this identification via speech patterns is a sort of alignment of Naomi and Boaz over against Ruth. This alignment may be, as Campbell suggests, an indication of generational differences—the more formal, elaborate speech of one generation in contrast to the informal, clipped speech of the next. It may also be an indicator of class or even of nationality—the polished speech of native, landowning Israelites versus the less polished speech of a foreigner. Or it may be the author's subtle way of affirming that even though Naomi and Boaz never meet in the book, they are nonetheless bound to each other.

The NRSV is right to distinguish between "young women" (*naʿᵃrôt*) and "young men" (*nᵉʿārîm*) in Boaz's speech, a distinction that is elided by many translations. But it seems clear, especially in light of Naomi's sounding of the same warning at the end of the chapter, that Boaz is expressing a concern for Ruth's welfare at the hands of the young male workers, and that this is probably a concern for a sexual assault or at least unwanted sexual attention (the same verb is used in Gen 20:6 to indicate such unwanted sexual advances). It is up to the reader to decide if Boaz thinks he is protecting Ruth from sexual advances that are unwanted from her perspective, or if he is trying to protect her from sexual advances unwanted from his perspective because he himself has a romantic or sexual interest in her. In either case, the foreman has noted that she is an unattached, Moabite woman and Boaz wants to make sure that any thoughts of sexual availability this fact might inspire among the young men are squelched by Ruth's constant presence

---

[15] Jacob Myers, *The Linguistic and Literary Form of the Book of Ruth* (Leiden: E. J. Brill, 1955), 20; Campbell, *Ruth,* 110.

among a group of other women. And the warning to her not to lift her eyes from the field may be a concession to his own preconceptions about Moabite women, as if to say "And don't be making eyes at the young men."

As a sort of afterthought or add-on to his elaborate advice to Ruth about gleaning and gender relations, Boaz does concede an opportunity for indirect contact with the young male workers, and he does so in a way that represents a quite fascinating reversal of a well-known betrothal type-scene in biblical narrative.[16] "If you get thirsty," he tells her, "go to the vessels and drink from what the young men *(nᵉˤārîm)* have drawn" (2:9b). The biblical type-scene evoked in the story is one in which a traveler from another country arrives at a well, women arrive in order to draw water, and the traveler ends up finding a spouse at the well. Now, in all other examples of the type-scene (e.g., Genesis 24; 29; Exodus 2) the traveler is a man who finds a wife at the well. In the book of Ruth of course, Ruth is the traveler from another country and it is the young men who are drawing the water. The question becomes then how to interpret this allusion to and reversal of the well/marriage type-scene. Perhaps it serves as a signal of Boaz's interest in Ruth and foreshadows their marriage, or perhaps it serves to heighten the tension with regard to the young men. Ruth, it seems, cannot avoid them all day and even if she is safe from unwanted sexual advances it may be that she will find a rival suitor to Boaz among the young men. But perhaps what is most interesting about the scene is the fact of its reversal of narrative expectations with regard to gender. For all her deference (or mock deference) and for all the inequality with regard to power and wealth between her and Boaz, Ruth is nevertheless the one cast in the role that, in the other well scenes, is played by Isaac, Jacob, and Moses. In that sense, perhaps the allusion is a signal that Ruth is more of an actor in the narrative than traditional gender roles would suggest.

Ruth, we are told, falls prostrate before Boaz in response. Though occasionally this action is used in the Bible as an expression of gratitude (Gen 48:12; 2 Kgs 4:37), most often it is a response to an encounter with God (Josh 5:14; Job 1:20). The primary sense of the action here is of course the former, but no doubt there is a secondary play on the latter (see the comment on 2:11-13 below). Ruth's reply to Boaz, though short, is carefully worded. Her question, "Why have I found favor in your sight?", recalls her earlier announcement to Naomi in verse 2 and the ambiguity there with what it might mean to find favor. The

---

[16] On type scenes in general, see Robert Alter, *The Art of Biblical Narrative* (New York: Basic Books, 1981), 47–62; see 58–60 on this scene in Ruth in particular.

Hebrew word for "why" (*maddûa⁽*) used here is a bit more specific as a
request for information than the more common *lāmâ*. Ruth is ensuring
that the conversation continue, and also seems to be pressing Boaz as
to his motives. This is made even more specific in the second half of
her question, "that you should take notice of me, when I am a foreigner." In Hebrew the phrase is only three words long and is a model
of assonance and consonance: *lᵉhakkîrēnî wᵉānōkî nokrîyyâ*. With the first
and third words Ruth makes a pun between two words with nearly
opposite meanings: *nākar*, usually meaning "to recognize" someone,
and here used in the sense of "paying attention to," and *nokrîyyâ*, a
"foreigner," precisely someone who would not be recognized.

Boaz responds as one might expect a pillar of the community to in
the face of a Moabite woman who is inquiring in public after his motivation for such a keen interest in her: his answer is all piety and altruism, though the reader could be forgiven for detecting a slightly
nervous tone. In fact, Boaz essentially avoids the question of his interest in Ruth and his motivation for wanting to keep her in his field and
away from the young men. It is worth noting that Boaz has not at this
point granted Ruth permission for anything she has not already been
doing, except perhaps to drink from the workers' water supply. What
he has done is to try to ensure her continued presence. Thus her question is not just (or perhaps even) a show of gratitude, but a genuine
question probing his motivations for showing her "favor" and for sin-
gling her out for "attention." We might rightly imagine Boaz speaking
a bit more loudly this time to be sure that everyone hears as he scuttles
the question and instead praises Ruth for everything he has heard
about her willingness to leave behind her father and mother and her
native land in order to accompany her mother-in-law to a strange land.
The language he uses is distinctly reminiscent of how Abraham's mi-
gration is described in Genesis 11 and 12 and, in combination with
Boaz's previous allusion to the betrothal type-scene, reinforces the
identification of Ruth with the patriarchs of Israel; a major difference
between Ruth and the patriarchs being, as Trible astutely points out,
that Abraham and the other patriarchs had a constantly reiterated
promise from God to reassure them while Ruth seems reliant on her
own wits and willpower.[17] Though Ruth herself has never and will
never make mention to Boaz of "the LORD, the God of Israel," Boaz
seems to feel the need to bring the LORD into the matter and to even
portray Ruth as seeking shelter under the LORD's wings. As Ruth herself will make clear, she has done no such thing, but Boaz at this point
seems intent on playing the pious, disinterested father-figure, so he

---

[17] Trible, *God and the Rhetoric of Sexuality*, 173.

loads his second speech with what Hubbard calls "poetic language and rhythm." Thus the concept of seeking shelter "under the LORD's wings" is found elsewhere only in the psalms (Pss 17:8; 36:8; 57:2; 61:5; 63:8; 91:4). The invoking of the LORD may also be a deflection of Ruth's distinctly "worshipful" posture toward Boaz.

In any case, attempts to deflect either Boaz's manifest interest in Ruth or Ruth's manifest lack of interest in the LORD do not work, for in Ruth's response in 2:13 she not only evokes the former in her hope that she "continue to find favor" in Boaz's eyes (the NRSV is right to read the verb as a cohortative here, thus implying a wish for the future), but she sharpens the latter even more by referring to Boaz as "my lord." The word is just one of Ruth's many carefully chosen words to Boaz that may be taken as a double entendre, for while "my lord" (*ʾădōni*) is often used as an indicator of social or class distance between humans it is also often used as a title for God. Ruth, by means of a pun on Boaz's pious words, places the focus squarely back on him. And while Ruth's statement that he has "comforted" her and "spoken to her heart" may be read (or heard by those round about within the story) as an innocuous statement of Boaz's altruism (thus the NRSV's "spoken kindly"), it may also be Ruth's tacit indication that she knows when someone is trying to sweet-talk her. While the idiom of speaking to someone's heart occurs only nine times in the Bible, fully one-third of those occurrences (Gen 34:3; Judg 19:3; and Hos 2:16) clearly have the meaning "to woo" or "to entice" a woman.

Ruth carries the potential double meanings through to her final statement of their first exchange, translated by the NRSV as "even though I am not one of your servants." Most translations, like the NRSV, use the present tense to translate Ruth's statement here and take it to be a statement of deference and humility indicating that she is lower than the lowest servant. But Bush is certainly correct in arguing that the grammar and syntax of the Hebrew phrase (with the imperfect form *ʾehyeh*) demand a future tense. The term she uses to refer to herself, *šipḥâ*, does indeed connote the lowest rung of the social world of servants and slaves and is associated with the most menial duties. Later, in 3:9, she refers to herself as an *ʾāmâ*, a word indicating a servant of a bit higher status and more importantly one who had the prospect of marrying into the family for which she labored. Bush retains the deference and renders Ruth's statement as "though I myself will never be the equivalent of one of your maidservants."[18] But in keeping with the tendency of Ruth's speech to have one meaning for the listeners in the field and another for Boaz and/or the attentive

---

[18] Bush, *Ruth, Esther*, 107.

reader, it is also possible to render her statement, following Fewell and
Gunn, as "and I [for my part] would not be [merely] like one of your
maidservants," with the implication that she hopes to be *more* than a
šipḥâ.[19] This connotation is then confirmed in 3:9 when Ruth unilater-
ally promotes herself from *šipḥâ* (and therefore ineligible for marriage
to Boaz) to *ʾāmâ* (and therefore eligible for marriage).

Whatever the implications of Ruth's statement concerning her status relative to Boaz and his servants, it is the final word in their initial
conversation. Most commentators recognize the dramatic effect of
breaking off the conversation with Ruth's words in verse 13 and take
it as emphasizing her deferential gratitude, thereby reinforcing the
portrait of the great and generous man looking out for the welfare of a
widow in need. But as I noted above, Boaz has in fact granted nothing
to Ruth that is not already her right. And if one is right in seeing Boaz
as more than a bit flustered by the ways in which Ruth seems to be
drawing attention to his thinly disguised interest in her, then it may be
that Boaz has simply decided that it is time to end this conversation
rather than give Ruth a chance to twist another of his pious sounding
declarations.

[14-17]

Boaz reinitiates the exchange once again at mealtime, when he invites Ruth to "draw near" *(ngš)* to share some of his bread and to dip
her morsel in the sour wine. Campbell notes that the Hebrew word for
"draw near" which Boaz uses occurs often in contexts of unequal social status and thus also expresses a slight distance between the two.
The nuance fits well with the narrative context, in which Boaz may desire to pursue the relationship with Ruth hinted at above, but feels the
need to do so in a more circumspect manner. In any case, his invitation
to her to join in a meal with himself and the reapers (as opposed to the
other gleaners, who are not part of the official work and would not
have access to the meal) serves both a practical and a symbolic function. Practically, it gives Ruth the sustenance she needs to continue her
gleaning. This is no small matter in the narrative, for she is attempting
to provide enough to support both her and Naomi. The narrative emphasizes this practical aspect of the invitation by noting that Ruth was
able to eat "until she was satisfied" (something we may imagine she
has not been able to do for some time), and that she also had some food
left over, which in verse 18 she will present to Naomi. Symbolically, the
scene moves Ruth out of the status of "gleaner" and into the community

[19] Fewell and Gunn, *Compromising Redemption*, 102.

of Boaz's farm workers. Sasson suggests that the gesture of presenting her with roasted grain may be "ceremonial, perhaps quasi-legal, in nature"; while there is no support for such a claim, it does capture the symbolism of Ruth's integration into Boaz's circle.[20] One might also detect here a further conflation between Boaz's public concern for Ruth's relationship to God and his and/or the narrator's private concern for Ruth's relationship to Boaz, for as Hubbard points out, in twelve other occurrences of the phrase "to eat until satisfied" God is always the provider of the food. Boaz steps into that role here.

When Ruth returns to her gleaning, Boaz instructs the young men (*n^eʿārîm*) directly—rather than through the foreman—to allow her to glean "even among the standing sheaves" and not to "reproach" her. The Hebrew verb translated by the NRSV as "reproach" often carries the meaning of "molestation" or "humiliation." The LXX emphasizes the undertone of sexuality by translating it as "shame, disgrace" (*kataischynēte*), though most modern interpreters argue for a non-sexual meaning of "rebuke" or "scold." But this is, once again, to misunderstand the function of allusion, in which one need not deny the primary sense of a word or phrase in order to see the hint of a secondary meaning. Thus Campbell is right to see here "a nuance which underscores Boaz' determination to protect Ruth from improper advances from the men."[21]

Though it is not clear what exactly is meant by Boaz's orders that Ruth should be allowed to glean "even among the standing sheaves," it is clear that he is for the first time in the narrative granting Ruth gleaning rights beyond those stipulated by law. He is granting her access to an area in which her gleaning will be more fruitful, and to multiply her productivity he even instructs the young men to "pull out handfuls [of stalks] from the bundles" for Ruth to glean. Boaz is clearly stacking the deck in favor of Ruth—a midrash comments with the analogy that "Rabbi Johanan used to scatter coins about in order that Rabbi Simeon b. Abba might acquire them, and Rabbi Judah used to leave lentils about in order that Rabbi Simeon b. Halafta might acquire them"—though as always his motives are left unclear. Whether it is his magnanimous "generosity and kindness," as Bush suggests, is debatable. We know from his advice to Ruth in 1:8-9 that Boaz desires to keep her from moving on to another field, and what better way of ensuring her continued presence in his field than by assuring a wildly successful day of gleaning?

---

[20] Jack M. Sasson, *Ruth: A New Translation with a Philological Commentary and a Formalist-Folklorist Interpretation* (2nd ed.; Sheffield: Sheffield Academic Press, 1989) 55.

[21] Campbell, *Ruth*, 103.

The final verse of the scene, verse 17, confirms Ruth's success in gleaning by reporting that when she had "beat out what she had gleaned" she had about an "ephah" of barley. We cannot know for sure exactly how much barley is represented by an ephah, but estimates based on a reconstructed system of weights and measures in the Ancient Near East range from between thirty and fifty pounds. In either case an ephah represents an extraordinary amount for one person to glean. As Sasson points out, Ruth is taking home after one day of work enough grain for several weeks' consumption[22]—we can presume that she will return to Boaz's field.

2:18-23

[vv. 18-20]

Verse 18 serves as a transition from the field to the town and from Boaz to Naomi. Ruth's coming *(bô')* into town recalls the earlier coming *(bô')* into town of Naomi and Ruth at the end of chapter 1. But, as the author begins to elaborate on the theme of the movement from emptiness to fullness, Naomi's earlier declaration of her emptiness (1:21) is matched here by her astonishment at the abundance of what Ruth has gleaned. Her astonishment is indicated not only by her wondering questions of verse 19, but also by the subtle switch in point-of-view from Ruth "picking up" her bundle and "coming" into town to Naomi "seeing" how much Ruth had gleaned. The brief change in subject mid-sentence is resisted by a few ancient versions (the Syriac and Vulgate read "she showed her mother-in-law") and some modern commentators, but the change serves to give a clearer picture to the reader of just how loaded up with grain Ruth is. On top of the sheer quantity of her gleanings, Ruth also "takes out"—apparently from underneath a fold of her garment—the leftovers of the prepared food (the "roasted grain") that she had eaten earlier in the day and gives them to Naomi. Not only has Ruth secured a veritable mountain of barley for them, but she has a portion of prepared food that Naomi can eat right away.

The portion of prepared food makes clear to Naomi that something more than just gleaning had been taking place. Thus her response, in a parallel structure that we have seen is typical of Naomi's way of speaking, inquires first as to the source of all this barley:

[22] Sasson, *Ruth*, 55.

A) Where have you gleaned today?

A¹) Where have you worked?

But in a third line—which supplements and moves beyond the scope of the first two in a rhetorical move common to Hebrew poetry but less frequent in prose—Naomi states, "Blessed be the man who took notice of you." The addition of the third line is interesting in that, first, it shows that Naomi recognizes that something other than a phenomenal luck in gleaning is at play here and, second, she employs the same verb *(nkr)* that Ruth used earlier when she spoke to Boaz of his "taking notice" of her (2:10). One does not simply come across large portions of cooked food while gleaning in a stranger's field, and Naomi rightly concludes that "a man" must have "noticed" Ruth.

When Ruth reveals to Naomi with whom she worked, she withholds the name of Boaz until the very end of the line. There is some dramatic import in the NRSV's rendering then, which reproduces well the effect of the Hebrew: "The name of the man with whom I worked today is Boaz" (2:19b). Ruth follows the narrator in this rhetorical technique of placing the name of Boaz at the end of long string of qualifying phrases. "The audience has known this all along, but the dramatic suspense lies with the recognition that Naomi has not."[23] There remains the question of whether or not Ruth has yet to discover the identity of Boaz, before informed of it by Naomi in v. 20, and thus whether the reader may assume that she is herself employing the dramatic effect or that it is the author's wink to the reader. The former may well be the case, since as we will see, Ruth is not above "teasing" Naomi with her report.

In either case, Naomi's reaction registers the desired surprise: "Blessed be he by the LORD, whose kindness *(ḥesed)* has not forsaken the living or the dead!" Her statement preserves a fundamental ambiguity that interpreters have been all too anxious to reduce to a single meaning: the antecedent for the phrase "whose kindness has not forsaken the living or the dead." Are we to understand that the LORD's kindness or Boaz's kindness is being referred to? Though grammatically either reading is equally possible, the consensus has been to see the Lord as the author of the kindness in question. But recently, Rebera has given new support for Glueck's earlier argument that Boaz is the antecedent and has been followed by both Hubbard and Bush.[24] The

---

[23] Campbell, *Ruth*, 106.

[24] B. Rebera, "Yahweh or Boaz? Ruth 2:20 Reconsidered," *The Bible Translator* 36 (1985) 317–27; N. Glueck, *Hesed in the Bible* (Cincinnati: Hebrew Union College, 1967) 41–2; Hubbard, *The Book of Ruth*, 186; Bush, *Ruth, Esther*, 134–7.

attempt to "prove" one way or the other seems misguided. The author has worked hard to establish a confusion, or at least an overlap, between the LORD and Boaz in the story, and will go on to make problematic the separation of human and divine activity. There is no need then to force a decision on the question of whether the LORD's or Boaz's kindness is at issue here; for the purposes of the narrative art of the story, *both* are. Boaz has tried to deflect attention from himself onto God with his formal theological talk, but Ruth kept it squarely focused on Boaz. Likewise, Naomi may employ a formal theological tone and subject matter in her statement of surprise, but she knows that without Boaz's interest in Ruth there would be no parched grain for dinner tonight.

Naomi goes on to specify in 2:20b that "the man is a relative *(qārôb)* of ours" (notice how closely identified she and Ruth are in this statement), and in her typical parallel way of speaking follows this with the statement that he is "one of our nearest kin" (NRSV). The word taken by the NRSV to mean "nearest kin" is the Hebrew *gōʾel,* commonly translated elsewhere as "redeemer." In continued good poetic fashion, Naomi's two statements about Boaz's relation to them move from the general to the more specific. *Qārôb* is a very broad term indicating a relative and even on occasion a "friend" (Lev 25:25; Pss 15:3; 38:11), whereas *gōʾel* is a much more specific term indicating a close family member who has some assigned role in family legal affairs. There are a number of such roles designated by the term in the Torah: (1) the buying back of land that has been sold outside of the family due to economic necessity (Lev 25:24-5); (2) the buying back of family members who have sold themselves into slavery (Lev 25:47-55); (3) the receiving of money paid as restitution for a wrong against a family member who is now dead (Num 5:5-8); (4) the avenging of the murder of a family member (Num 35:9-28; Deut 19:6-13). It is clear that "redemption" in these cases concerns primarily financial matters, though the term also is used in an expanded metaphorical sense—often applied to God—of rescue from any situation of distress or danger. Though the first of these roles will come up again in the story in chapter 4, at this point in the narrative it is tantalizingly unclear whether Naomi has a specific legal function in mind with regard to Boaz, or if she is referring to a general expectation of assistance, financial or otherwise, from this *gōʾel.* This is consistent with the storyteller's art throughout the book, leaving the reader to negotiate various levels of meaning but without giving one the information necessary to settle once and for all on a single reading. Commentators who insist on just such a single meaning betray the narrative art.

[vv. 21-23]

As noted above, Ruth's final line of dialogue in the chapter is introduced with the phrase, "Then Ruth the Moabite said" (2:21). The reference again to Ruth's nationality has seemed out of place to many interpreters. Thus the LXX, the Syriac, and the Old Latin all delete the phrase and are followed in this by some moderns (e.g., Juöun, Rudolph). But the designation seems quite intentional, both as a literary inclusio with 2:2, where Ruth's first line of dialogue is also introduced with mention of her nationality, and as a reminder that Ruth's Moabite origins are a genuine thematic concern to the narrator. I noted above that Hubbard is surely correct in identifying the cluster of references to her foreignness around the issue of her gleaning in the field, but that he does not pursue sufficiently the issue of her Moabite identity in the context of chapter 2, which is at issue here when Ruth says to Naomi that "He even said to me, 'Stick to my young men [*n^eʿārîm*], until they have finished all my harvest.'" One notes immediately that this is in fact not what Boaz told her; rather, Boaz instructed Ruth to "stick to my young women [*naʿ^arôt*]" (2:8), with a clear implication that she should avoid the young men, whom he had to warn against molesting her (2:9, 16). There are a number ways of taking Ruth's misquoting of Boaz. One is to simply deny that it is significant, that is, that the gender distinctions are unimportant for the story and that the masculine *n^eʿārîm* is simply used to indicate all workers, male and female. This seems to me to seriously under-read the narrative art of the story, however, and does not account for Naomi's response in 2:22, where she clearly takes *n^eʿārîm* as indicative of male workers. Another way is to attribute the misquotation to her foreignness, that is, that she does not quite catch the distinctions in the Hebrew between *n^eʿārîm* and *naʿ^arôt*. A third way is to see the change in gender as intentional on Ruth's part, that is, that she would prefer to stay with the young men (so Nielsen). The midrash combines these two possibilities with its terse comment, "Rabbi Hanin b. Levi said: In truth she was a Moabitess, for Boaz said to her, 'Abide here fast by my maidens,'" leaving open the possibility that Ruth, as a Moabite, misunderstood Boaz's instructions or that she willfully ignored them in her attempts to seduce Israelite men. A fourth way is more plausible and more interesting, but seems only to have been entertained by Fewell and Gunn, who write that Ruth "teasingly" reports the wrong words to Naomi.[25] In this reading, Ruth is prodding Naomi to express a concern

---

[25] Fewell and Gunn, *Compromising Redemption*, 98.

for her well-being (as a Moabite woman off in a field with a group of young men) and/or is hinting at the possibility of separation from Naomi if she ends up marrying one of these young men (recall that the verb "stick to" [dbq] is used this way in Gen 2:24).

Naomi in any case recognizes the danger or at least the undesirability of Ruth "sticking to" the young men in Boaz's field, and she immediately advises her (in words that echo Boaz) to stay close to the young women instead. She combines this advice, again just as Boaz did, with the cautionary statement that Ruth should not go looking to glean in any other fields now that she has done so well in Boaz's. The chapter closes with the narrator reporting that Ruth worked in Boaz's field, sticking close to the young women as instructed, through both the barley harvest and the wheat harvest, after which she stayed home with her mother-in-law. The final line of the chapter (v. 23) reminds the reader that this provision of grain, as abundant as it is, is strictly temporary. Ruth and Naomi have still not found a reliable way to provide for themselves. The plot has been advanced significantly in chapter 2, with the movement from emptiness to fullness and from lack to abundance provisionally completed, but only provisionally. More drastic action will be required to advance further both the plot and the two women's chances for security.

Chapter 3

AN AMBIGUOUS ENCOUNTER IN THE NIGHT

Chapter 3 of the book of Ruth is in many respects a counterpart to chapter 2. With regard to form, or structure, chapter 3 conforms to chapter 2 by opening and closing with an interchange between Naomi and Ruth, in the middle of which one finds a more extensive account of an encounter between Ruth and Boaz. And the encounter at the center of chapter 3 is built upon five primary narrative elements that mirror quite closely the five elements in chapter two identified above (pp. 23–24). Once again following Bertman, with some modifications, we may identify these elements as follows:[1]

a) Exchange between Naomi and Ruth (vv. 1-5).

b) Ruth goes to the threshing floor and meets Boaz (v. 6-7).

c) Boaz inquires as to Ruth's identity (vv. 8-9).

d) Boaz asks Ruth to stay, deems her worthy, gives her food and protection (vv. 10-15).

e) Ruth reports back to Naomi and receives counsel (vv. 16-18).

With regard to content, there is both similarity and difference between the two chapters. Similarity exists especially in the way the author chooses to describe the interaction between the two characters: in each case the dialogue as well as the narrator's reports are filled with double entendres. Differences between the chapters are manifested primarily in relation to the context in which the encounter takes place. In chapter 2 Ruth and Boaz meet in a public place and thus their exchange follows, at least on the surface, the social codes of disinterested magna-

---

[1] Bertman, "Symmetrical Design in the Book of Ruth," 165–8.

nimity (on his part) and fawning deference (on her part). In chapter three, by contrast, they meet in a private place under the cover of night; and without the necessity of following the social codes determined by gender, age, nationality, and class, they interact in a very different manner. As we will see, Ruth is clearly the initiator and Boaz is left to react to her.

In light of the fact that the two meet in a clandestine manner, the author has created an overriding sense of mystery, secrecy, and ambiguity, as Campbell has seen so well. Thus, the keyword for this chapter seems to be "to know" (*yd^c*). Occurring in verses 2, 3, 4, 10, 14, and 18, the leitmotif of knowledge serves to emphasize that one character (Ruth) knows much more than another (Boaz) and is able to capitalize on that. It also points up the fact that the reader often cannot know precisely what is happening, but must instead negotiate constantly the pervasive ambiguity.

3:1-5

[vv. 1-2a]

In the same way that chapter 2 closed with Naomi having the last line of dialogue and with Ruth living at home with her, chapter 3 opens with Naomi initiating an exchange with Ruth in their home. Reinforcing the identification of Naomi and Boaz by way of their speech patterns, the author once again has Naomi sounding very much like Boaz did in 2:8-9; while at the end of chapter 2 she echoed his warning from verses 8-9 about staying with the young women rather than the young men, here she echoes his pattern of his speech. Like Boaz she begins by addressing Ruth as "my daughter," which might certainly be taken as a simple term of endearment, but which also certainly works to establish an unequal power relationship. The latter is especially the case when followed by instructions, as it is in both cases here. And in both cases the instructions are couched in the form of questions, albeit questions that clearly function as emphatic statements (thus the NRSV's rendering of them without interrogative markers). Rendered literally, Naomi's questions in verses 1-2 read:

My daughter,

> Shall I not (*halo$^{>}$*) seek security for you, that it may go well with you?

> Is not (*halo$^{>}$*) Boaz one of our relatives, with whose young women you have been?

The parallelism of Naomi's speech, and its mirroring of Hebrew poetic patterns, is apparent in the way that each clause of the two questions correspond to each other. The two second clauses, regarding Naomi's wish that it go well (verbal form of *tôb*) with Ruth and her mention of the young women *(nᵉˁārôt)* with whom Ruth has been, are positioned to recall that in the previous chapter Naomi deemed it better *(tôb)* for Ruth to go out with the young women *(nᵉˁārôt)* rather than the young men. The narrative seems to be at pains to assure the reader that this is what happened, with the narrator confirming it in 2:23 and then Naomi confirming it again here. Naomi only now begins to make clear why it is "better" from her perspective for Ruth to have gone out with the young women rather than the young men, though of course it has become clear to the reader: by remaining eligible for marriage there is a chance that she will end up with Boaz. Glancing back at Naomi's parallel lines, we may note that the symmetry of the first two clauses functions to equate Naomi's seeking of security with Boaz. If lack of security is the problem, Boaz is the answer. We may also note that Naomi's reference to security *(mānôaḥ)* utilizes the same Hebrew root word that she used in 1:9 when she wished for Ruth and Orpah to find security *(menûḥâ)* in the house of a husband. Boaz has become for Naomi the potential husband in whose house Ruth might find security. The question now is how to make all this rhetoric into a reality.

[vv. 2b-5]

Naomi's plan, depending on one's perspective, is either "clever"[2] or "dangerous and deceptive."[3] Perhaps it is both. It is in any case bold, and it shows Naomi taking an initiative that she lacked in chapter 2. The plan is unfolded in verses 2-4, and as always with the characters' dialogue it is worth taking a closer look at the structure of it. Campbell has noted that Naomi makes use of a series of four verbs in the perfect tense ("wash . . . anoint . . . put on . . . go down"), followed by a negative imperative ("do not make known") and an imperfect ("when he lies down"), and then another series of four verbs in the perfect tense ("observe . . . go . . . uncover . . . lie down"). Enclosing these instructions are two references to Boaz's actions, flagged by the dual occurrence of the pronoun "he" *(hûʾ)*. The speech can thus be mapped out rhetorically as follows:

²Hubbard, *The Book of Ruth,* 196.
³Fewell and Gunn, *Compromising Redemption,* 99.

A) "He *(hûʾ)* is winnowing barley tonight . . ." (v. 2b)

   B) Series of four perfect verbs. (v. 3a)
     Wash
     Anoint
     Put on
     Go down

       C) "Do not make yourself known. . . ." (v. 3b)

       C¹) "When he lies down . . ." (v. 4a)

B¹) Series of four perfect verbs. (v. 4b)
     Observe
     Go
     Uncover
     Lie down

A¹) "He *(hûʾ)* will tell you what to do." (v. 5)

The form of Naomi's instructions to Ruth communicates a great deal to the reader even before looking closely at the content of the instructions. Boaz *(hûʾ)* is at the beginning and the end of the speech—clearly he is the focus of the machinations. At the center of these machinations (C and C¹) is an unequivocal deception, which involves both Ruth's concealing of herself and Boaz's lying down. Leading up to this act of deception is the preparation that Ruth is to undertake, presented in a series of symbolic actions that move from Ruth's uncovered body (while washing) to her anointed body to her covered body. It is under this literal and figurative "cloak" that Ruth is to approach the unknowing Boaz, at which point the scenario imagined by Naomi moves in the opposite direction of literal and symbolic "*uncovering.*" Though Ruth has been instructed not to make herself "known" (a form of the Hebrew word *ydʿ*) to "the man," she is nevertheless to make sure she "knows" (again a form of *ydʿ*, rendered by the NRSV as "observe") where he is lying down. The plan depends on Ruth having more knowledge than Boaz, who is to be literally and figuratively in the dark. But once the scenario turns to its second phase, Naomi assumes that Boaz will be the one with the knowledge—that is, he will tell (or "reveal to," *ngd*) Ruth what to do next. As we will see, however, Naomi has not quite got it right; for as the scene unfolds in the following verses it is Ruth who tells Boaz what to do.

It seems that whether or not the plan is clever, it is obviously dangerous and deceptive. Naomi is sending an unmarried Moabite woman out in the dead of night to lie down next to a (perhaps drunken) man, to uncover that man in some way, and then to wait and see what he

tells her to do. The plan just as obviously trades in a barely submerged
—if submerged at all—sexuality. The first clue, if the reader needs one,
is the setting at the threshing floor. If the reference to the threshing
floor in Hos 9:1 is any indication, the place is associated in Israelite
imagination if not in fact with illicit sexual activity. Whether this activity has to do with religious fertility rites or with the simple fact that
workingmen away from home for the harvest took the opportunity to
have sex with other women (perhaps prostitutes) is a matter of debate.
While the book of Ruth certainly makes no mention of fertility rites, it
does seem to play here on the image of fertility, with Boaz laying about
the heaps of harvested grain, perhaps a latent symbol of his potency.
As numerous commentators note, the scenario is laced with other sexually loaded terms as well. The verb *škb* "to lie down," occurs eight
times in the chapter, and while it often means in Hebrew simply to
sleep it also often has the explicit meaning of to engage in sexual intercourse. The verb *yd*ᶜ, "to know," occurs six times in the chapter and
is also a frequent term in Hebrew for sexual intercourse, as is the verb
*bo*ʾ, "to come to/go into," which is used three times in verses 4-14.

All of these possible double entendres and sexual allusions are centered around the crucial instruction of Naomi's that Ruth should "uncover his feet." It is difficult to know exactly what to make of the
Hebrew word *margᵉlôt*, commonly translated as "feet" or "the place at
the feet." The term is obviously related to the more commonly occurring word for foot, *regel*, which is a well-known euphemism in the
Bible for genitalia (cf. Judg 3:24; 1 Sam 24:3; 2 Kgs 18:27; Isa 7:20; Ezek
16:25), but in the present form it occurs only in Dan 10:6 where it
means "legs." It is possible that it also means legs here, but one of the
problems with the word is that it is used in 3:4 and 7 to indicate what
Ruth uncovers, while in 3:8 and 14 it seems to refer to the place that
Ruth spends the night (hence the translation "place at his feet").
Whether the word means "feet" in a quite literal sense," or "feet" in a
euphemistic sense, or "legs," or even "the place at his feet/legs" hardly
matters: any one or combination of the above meanings is equally
scandalous (for Boaz) and dangerous (for Ruth). Any of the actions—
done in the middle of the night, alone behind a pile of grain—would
imply the offer of a sexual encounter. In a situation like this, Naomi's
final words of instruction, "he will tell you what to do" (v. 4), presume
that Boaz will not refuse the offer. As Hubbard writes, albeit without
the irony I intend, Boaz will respond "with some instructions of his
own."[4]

---

[4] Hubbard, *The Book of Ruth*, 204.

Ruth's only response is to assent to Naomi's plan: "All that you tell me I will do" (v. 5). The response tells us nothing about Ruth's thoughts on the matter. She does not evaluate it as a good plan or a bad plan, she does not say whether or not she wants security in the house of Boaz, and she does not betray surprise at Naomi's willingness to put her at such risk. The great twelfth-century Jewish exegete Rashi, picking up on not only the doubts that a reader might naturally suspect Ruth to have about this plan but also apparently on the reference to the threshing floor and its possible association with prostitution, supplies a response on Ruth's part. He comments:

> She said to her: "Wash yourself and anoint yourself and put on your cloak and afterwards go down to the threshing-floor." She did not do this, for she said, "If I go down all dressed up, anyone who meets me and sees me will think I am a harlot." Therefore she went down in the first place to the threshing-floor and afterwards adorned herself as her mother-in-law had instructed her.[5]

The comment is interesting as much for what it inadvertently reveals as for what it intends to reveal. If Ruth does not perfume herself and get dressed-up until arriving at the threshing floor for fear that she will be mistaken for a prostitute on the way, the implication is that she does not mind being mistaken for one once there, that is, by Boaz. Indeed, it is possible that this is precisely what Naomi hopes will happen, and that if a child is conceived by the union then they may confront Boaz and force him to own up to it. Fewell and Gunn suggest this possible motivation on Naomi's part, and given the fact that this same basic plot line has been used by one biblical writer in Genesis 38, one cannot dismiss it out of hand.[6]

It is left to the reader, in the end, to supply her motivation for Ruth's assenting to the plan. Interpreters have typically supplied a motivation of self-emptying love for and/or mindless obedience to Naomi. We saw in 1:16-17 that she is certainly devoted to Naomi and committed to an unshakable solidarity with her, but as Fewell and Gunn point out, solidarity with another does not necessitate a lack of will or desires of one's own.[7] Moreover, the scene in the field in chapter 2 gave strong hints of Ruth's interest in Boaz, though whether this is a genuine romantic interest on her part or a further attempt to pro-

---

[5] Cited in D.R.G. Beattie, *Jewish Exegesis of the Book of Ruth* (Sheffield: JSOT Press, 1977) 107.

[6] Fewell and Gunn, *Compromising Redemption*, 78.

[7] Ibid., 98.

vide for Naomi and herself through this man who has first shown an interest in her is again impossible to decide.

3:6-15

[vv. 6-7]

The narrator informs the reader that Ruth went to the threshing floor and did "all that her mother-in-law had instructed her" (v. 6). In the Hebrew, the word for "all," *kol*, has the preposition *kᵉ*, "like/as," attached to it. This is often taken to emphasize that Ruth did *exactly* as Naomi had instructed (NRSV, "just as . . ."). In fact, the preposition often carries the connotation of "approximately"—as it does in 2:17 where Ruth beats out "about an ephah (*kᵉʾēpāh*) of barley"—and it is likely that this is the sense of the preposition here. As we will see, Ruth does not do all that Naomi instructs her, or perhaps it is better said that she does all that Naomi instructs her and more as well.

Ruth waits until Boaz has eaten and drunk, but the narrator adds a detail that was lacking (though perhaps implied) in Naomi's envisioning of the scene: "he was in a contented mood" (v. 7, NRSV). The Hebrew idiom *yatab lēb*, "the heart was good," often carries the sense of having drunk enough alcohol that one is incapable of making good decisions or is particularly vulnerable (1 Sam 25:36; 2 Sam 13:28; Esth 1:10; Judg 19:22). Other times the phrase indicates an exuberance that does not necessarily come from alcoholic beverages (1 Kgs 8:66; Prov 15:15; Eccl 9:7). Whether or not we are to assume Boaz to be drunk, perhaps indicating that it was a common occurrence at harvest-time on which Naomi had counted, or simply that he was, in Campbell's memorable phrase, in a "mellower-than-usual condition," the effect is the same: Boaz is primed for the plan.

Ruth is described as approaching the sleeping Boaz *ballāt*, a Hebrew word most likely derived from the root-word *lût* ("enwrapped") and connoting something done in secret or without someone else's knowledge. Thus, the primary sense here is not that she approached him quietly (contra Joüon and others who take the word as deriving from the Hebrew *ʾat*, "gentle"), but rather that he was blissfully unaware of what was taking place or about to take place. The word also has the distinct connotation of something not quite above board, of trickery (compare its use in 1 Sam 18:22 and 24:5). The closest parallel elsewhere in the Bible to the word's use in our scene is Judges 4, where Jael lulls a trusting Sisera with a skin of milk and then ap-

proaches him *ballā'ṭ* (4:21; a slightly different spelling) and drives a
tent peg through his mouth *(raqāh)*. The use of the word here indicates
not just the fact that Jael is sneaking up on a sleeping Sisera, as commentators virtually all assume. Rather, the point is that Jael is engaged in a subterfuge, having given Sisera the impression that she is
an ally, when in fact she is about to assassinate him. Likewise, Ruth is
engaged in the implementation of a plan of which Boaz has no knowledge and which depends on catching him unawares and in a vulnerable position.

The word *ballāṭ* is undoubtedly carefully chosen by the author,
likely intended to echo the story of Jael and Sisera (a story that is also
loaded with double entendres, like our scene) and perhaps even the
story of David catching Saul off guard in 1 Samuel 24 (where we find
not only the euphemistic use of *regel*, "foot," in the description of Saul
relieving himself, but also the word *kānāp*, a key word used by Ruth in
verse 9). Possibly there is another echo as well. The root word *lût* has,
in unpointed Hebrew, the precise lettering (that is, *lwt*) of the name
Lot. And with the preposition *ba* ("in/as") attached, there is a flicker-
ing pun: she approached him "as Lot," that is, as Lot's daughters approached him and lay with him when he was drunk. The pun, if
intended, is surely only at the second or third level of meaning; but it
is reinforced by the other intertextual connections that the book of
Ruth has with the story of Lot and his daughters, which is among
other things an etiology for the origins of Moab, and by more specific
verbal correspondences between the two scenes, including the Hebrew
words *laylâ* ("night"), *škb* ("lie"), *yd'* ("know"), and *bō'* ("go in"), all of
which are keywords for both stories. The allusion serves as one more
way, in addition to the double entendres, to flag for the reader both the
sexual ambiguity of the scene and the fact that sexuality is being put in
the service of a secret plan. Having approached Boaz, Ruth uncovers
his "feet" *(marg'lôt)* and lays down.

[vv. 8-9]

The turning point of the crucial scene at threshing floor comes, ap-
propriately, in "the middle of night." Rendered by the NRSV as "mid-
night," the term is used throughout the Hebrew Bible to indicate a
time of ambivalent destiny—the moment of both terror and exhilara-
tion, of promise and threat. It was "in the middle of the night" that the
Lord visited Egypt in order to kill all the Egyptian first born, an action
that had horrific consequences for the Egyptians but was perceived as
a moment of liberation for the Israelites (Exodus 11-12). It was also "in
the middle of the night" that Jacob wrestled with the mysterious fig-

ure at the Jabbok, a contest that resulted in both a permanent limp and a wondrous blessing (Genesis 32). The middle of the night thus certainly signifies a time of deadly peril (so Bush), but also a time that, if one can get through it, holds the promise of a reordered reality. At this time of ambivalent destiny, Boaz wakes up. The cause of his waking is not stated, and speculation that he was cold from having been uncovered (so Campbell and others)—and even that this was according to Naomi's plan (Hubbard)—are simply unjustified by the story. Nor does it seem, as Bush points out (contra Sasson), that Boaz is awakened by the presence of Ruth, since the syntax suggests that his noticing of her is temporally subsequent to his awakening rather than its cause. The impression given by the story is rather that it is the middle of the night *itself* that awakens Boaz.

As Campbell has astutely noted, the author creates in this chapter an ambience of profound mystery and secrecy, going so far as to keep even the names of the two protagonists under wraps, referring to them as "the man" and "the woman" or "he" and "she," with the exception of the singular moment of Ruth's revelation of her identity to Boaz in verse 9. Contributing to this sense that the reader, as perhaps the characters themselves, is not quite getting the whole story is the presence in verse 8 of two tantalizingly unclear verbs that describe Boaz's actions: *ḥrd* and *lpt*, translated by the NRSV as "the man was startled *(ḥrd)*, and turned over *(lpt)*." The first, *ḥrd*, is fairly common in the Bible and clearly carries the connotation of "trembling," "shuddering," or "quaking," usually because of fear. In this sense the meaning is not unclear at all; what is unclear is how the author means to use it in this context. What is the cause of Boaz's trembling? Of what is he afraid? The second verb, *lpt*, is obscure, occurring only in two other places in the Bible (Judg 16:29; Job 6:18). Based on the use of *lpt* in Judg 16:29 it would seem to mean "to grasp" in the Qal stem, but when used in the Niphal as it is here it likely carries a metaphorical sense of "being grasped/seized" by something involuntarily. The common translation of it here as "turned over" is based on an Arabic cognate word rather than on any evidence from the Bible itself. But this is too easy a way to settle what is obviously meant to be an unsettling situation, and for which the author has intentionally chosen an obscure word of uncertain meaning. I would argue that the entire verse is meant to be ambiguous and slightly disturbing, at least from Boaz's perspective. One should resist turning the episode into a prosaic description that could be deciphered if only one had the proper philological tools. Much is unclear, but what we can say is that Boaz, during the day a wealthy landowner in control of his immediate world, is at night transformed into a man who shudders and is seized by forces

54   *Ruth*

beyond his control. Given the double entendres that fill the chapter,
one also should not overlook the possible sexual connotations of shuddering and involuntary physical reactions.

Boaz's next action only reinforces the sense of his confusion and
fear. Using the Hebrew word *hinnēh* as an indicator of point of view,[8]
the narrative gives us Boaz's perspective upon awakening in a nameless fear and experiencing an undefined physical reaction beyond his
control: "there [*hinnēh*], lying at his feet [*margᵉlôt*], was a woman!"
(NRSV). His abrupt, fearful request for information contrasts with his
measured tones and archaic speech elsewhere in the book and conveys
the way in which this pillar of the community has been shaken. How
long has this woman been here? Why are his "feet" uncovered? What
was the cause of his shuddering and starting awake? Just how much
had he drunk? All of these questions make good candidates for what
is going on in Boaz's head. Fewell and Gunn suggest that perhaps
Boaz is wondering himself whether or not he has had sexual intercourse with this woman, and if so what the consequences will be.[9]
While the question is a clear parallel to his earlier seeking after Ruth's
identity in 2:5, the differences are telling. There, Boaz was the master
of the situation and speaks to his underling in the third person about
"to whom this girl (*naʕărâ*) belongs." Here, Boaz is on the defensive
and no longer has an intermediary; he must speak directly to the
"woman" (*ʔiššâ*) and ask who she is rather than to whom she belongs.
If the "girl" was able to fluster Boaz in the very public field by seeing
through his pious statements of altruism, the "woman" is able here,
alone in the dead of night, to erase for a moment the formality and
condescension of the prominent man.

Ruth's identifying of herself in verse 9b is the turning point of the
scene, which otherwise resists naming the characters. She refers to herself as "your servant" (*ʔāmâ*), in contrast to her earlier (public) identification of herself as a *šipḥâ*. As discussed above in reference to 2:13, the
difference is significant since *ʔāmâ* indicates an eligibility for marriage.
In contrast to Naomi's scenario, in which she imagines the older, more
powerful man instructing Ruth on what to do next, Ruth retains control of the situation and immediately tells the quaking Boaz what to
do. Whether or not her instructions to Boaz are a proposal for marriage
or an invitation to sexual intercourse is another of the central ambiguities on which the scene turns. By telling Boaz to "spread his 'wing'
(*kānāp*)" over her, she may well be invoking a rite of betrothal that is
perhaps alluded to also in Ezek 16:8. But as Beattie and Fewell and

---

[8] Berlin, *Poetics and Interpretation of Hebrew Narrative*, 91–2.
[9] Fewell and Gunn, *Compromising Redemption*, 96–7.

Gunn point out, this is not simply a given.[10] Nowhere is the term for "betrothal" (ˀeres) used in either of these texts, while both present an atmosphere of highly charged sexuality. Moreover, the word kānāp, which literally means an "extension" or "extremity," may itself, like "feet," be a euphemism for male genitalia. It is Saul's kānāp that David cuts off in a symbolic castration scene in 1 Samuel 24, which as I noted above takes place while Saul is relieving himself in a cave, and when the book of Deuteronomy (23:1) legislates against adulterous relationships it does so with the idiom "to uncover another man's kānāp" in a way parallel to the idiom in Leviticus "to uncover another man's nakedness [ˁerwat]" (18:7, passim; 20:17). It may be, then, that Ruth is offering herself sexually to Boaz. Protestations to this interpretation based on the assumed morality of the characters (so Bush) are simply circular in their arguments. Moreover, Boaz's relieved reaction to Ruth's statement can be cited in support of either. An invitation to sex would indicate that such has not already taken place, while an invitation to marriage would mean that even if it had he was being given the opportunity to cover the indiscretion in private rather than being accused later in public (as was his ancestor Judah in Genesis 38).

I would maintain, again, that the ambiguities present in the scene and reinforced by the author's choice of so many words with potential double meaning should not be reduced to one meaning above all others. Rather, these ambiguities are part of the narrative art and are what makes the story more than a simple morality tale. Fewell and Gunn put it well: "Ruth allows Boaz freedom to make a choice. See her as but an ephemeral sexual object ('extend your penis'), or see her as a person in need ('spread your wing/skirt'), a person who offers an enduring relationship, in which sexuality will have its home."[11] Thus, it is not just that the reader must decide what to make of Ruth's ambiguous invitation, but that Boaz must as well. In forcing Boaz to decide what to make of this woman lying at his feet, Ruth is also continuing to push him past his moral and theological platitudes, for we may recall that when they met in the field Boaz praised Ruth for seeking shelter under the LORD's "wing" (kānāp). Her reply then was to address him as "my lord" (ˀădōnî) and to wish for future "favor" in his eyes. By using the word kānāp here she makes even more explicit, via a shrewd wordplay, her resolve not to wait around for the Lord but to take a gamble on Boaz and his kānāp instead.

---

[10] D.R.G. Beattie, "Ruth III," *Journal for the Study of the Old Testament* 5 (1978) 43; Fewell and Gunn, *Compromising Redemption*, 128–29.

[11] Fewell and Gunn, *Compromising Redemption*, 102.

Ruth not only draws vocabulary from Boaz's earlier speech, but from Naomi's as well. Naomi informed her that Boaz was not only a "relative" of theirs, but a "redeemer" *(gōʾel)* as well. There, Naomi left it unclear as to what she meant by the term *gōʾel*. Ruth too leaves this unclear. Many interpreters have tried to link the duties of the *gōʾel* to the duties of the *levir*, the one responsible for marrying a dead brother's widow in order to continue the family line (see Deut 25:5). The institutions of the redemption and levitate marriage are never elsewhere linked in the Bible, however, and if they are linked here it is a linkage proposed by Ruth herself and not by social custom or legislation. And the fact that Ruth and Naomi have to resort to a nighttime seduction to convince Boaz to marry Ruth indicates that there is no expectation that he will do so as a part of his duties as a *gōʾel*. The question remains as to why Ruth links the two institutions here. It is possible that she does so by mistake, being a Moabite and not being fully aware of what being a *gōʾel* entailed but recognizing that Naomi thought it would offer them some assistance. Or it is possible that she links them intentionally, using the notion of "redemption" in its larger sense and thereby challenging Boaz to do more than the law required or was expected by him. Moreover, by linking their relationship with the institution of the *gōʾel*, Ruth has given Boaz the "cloak" he needs to pursue his interest in this Moabite woman and still maintain his public reputation. As we will see in chapter 4, Boaz's public concerns are very different than his concerns in private as expressed to Ruth.

[vv. 10-15]

In this section, having gotten over his fright, Boaz is allowed by the author to return to his familiar patterns of speech, full of redundancies, parallelism, and piety. His speech here thus mirrors in many ways his earlier speech to Ruth in the field. He once again refers to Ruth as "my daughter" (cf. 2:8), thereby bringing back into focus the social inequality that has been obscured momentarily on the threshing floor. He once again invokes the Lord's blessing on Ruth (cf. 2:12), thereby adding an element of religiosity to the whole affair, although given the easy way in which the name of the Lord appears on Boaz's lips (e.g., 2:4; 2:12) one is tempted to read it as saying no more than "Thank God!" And he evidences a curious sort of sputtering speech pattern especially at the beginning of verse 12, where as Campbell observes "there are simply too many introductory words."[12] Various proposed deletions to make the sentence more concise are all arbitrary, and they fail to recognize

---

[12] Campbell, *Ruth*, 125.

that Boaz is always a bit of a blowhard and that the only difference here is that he is a *flustered* blowhard, trying to maintain control over the situation but not quite succeeding.

That Boaz has been flustered by the whole experience would explain why his personal interest in Ruth gets expressed here in a very candid way that belies his outward concern for propriety. The phrase "this last instance of your loyalty [ḥesed] is better than the first" reveals more of Boaz's ulterior motives than most interpreters are comfortable with. If the "first" act of loyalty or kindness to which he refers is Ruth's solidarity with Naomi in order to provide for her, as virtually all commentators agree it is, then Boaz's statement that he would prefer her to be with him is hardly altruistic. Even those who assume a marriage proposal on Ruth's part, thereby tempering the scandal of the scene a bit already, see the problem if one is trying to preserve the characters as moral paragons. As Sasson puts it: "how could one not find fault with a man who chooses to value a marriage proposal over an act of mercy?"[13] Nor can one easily resort to the notion that Boaz sees Ruth's latest act of *ḥesed* to be a further way of providing for Naomi and/or preserving the name of her dead husband via levirate marriage, since Boaz never mentions Naomi or the duty of the *levir*. Either of these may in fact be what Ruth has in mind, the former more likely than the latter given her obvious commitment to Naomi, but it seems clear they are not what Boaz has in mind.

If one needs any more support for the argument that Boaz is expressing his gratitude for Ruth's interest in him—as Rashi puts it in his paraphrase of Boaz, "you desire an old man"—Boaz himself provides it with his next statement, which in fact provides the content of her latest act of *ḥesed:* "for you have not gone after the young men, whether rich or poor" (v. 10b). The Koehler/Baumgartner lexicon catches well the sense of the Hebrew word for "young men" *(baḥûrîm)* used here, describing them as "fully developed, vigorous, unmarried."[14] The idiom "to go after" often has the meaning of pursuing a sexual relationship (Prov. 7:22; Hos 2:7), though it is also worth noting that it also describes Rebekah's and Abigail's "following after" the messengers who represent their respective bridegrooms, Isaac and David (Gen 24:5-8; 1 Sam 25:42). The Targum obviously takes the first of these connotations to be intended and, eschewing understatement, adds the interpretive comment "to commit fornication with them." Modern

---

[13] Jack Sasson, "Ruth III: A Response," *Journal for the Study of the Old Testament* 5 (1978) 55.

[14] L. Koehler and W. Baumgartner, *Lexicon in Veteris Testamenti Libros* (Vol. I; Leiden: E. J. Brill, 1951) 116.

interpreters have tended to favor the second connotation, taking the phrase as referring to her other marriage options with no hint of sexuality involved (Campbell; Hubbard; Bush). At this point it hardly seems necessary to observe that the narrative is supple enough to carry both connotations at the same time, especially given the ambiguity of Ruth's invitation to Boaz to "extend his *kānāp*." In any case, it is clear that Boaz's thoughts are occupied not so much with Naomi's welfare, as so many interpreters want to suggest, as with his relationship with Ruth.

There is more than a little irony in Boaz's instructions to Ruth in verse 11, "do not be afraid," considering that he is the one who moments before was quaking in his sandals. And his statement, "I will do for you all that you ask," only reminds the reader that despite Naomi's expectations it is Ruth who tells Boaz what to do, not vice versa. In agreeing to carrying out Ruth's request, however Boaz sees that request, he labels her a "worthy woman." In Hebrew the phrase is *ʾēšet ḥayil*, the linguistic counterpart to the narrator's earlier labeling in 2:1 of Boaz as an *ʾîš gibbôr ḥayil*, which there referred to his social status. While commentators are certainly right that the phrase as used here does not refer to Ruth's wealth or social status, neither does it exclusively or unambiguously refer to "the quality of Ruth's person" (Campbell) or her "exemplary conduct" (Hubbard). While it may carry this latter connotation in the mouth of the character Boaz, for the reader it serves as one more marker of the ironic reversal between this supposed "mighty man of strength" (the literal meaning of the phrase in 2:1) and supposed lowly servant. It is a signal of a larger theme of the scene, which Trible has caught well with her argument that while Boaz possesses officially recognized social power *within* the story, he does not have power *over* the story.[15] Against Naomi's expectations Ruth is the one who tells Boaz what to do, and against the reader's expectations Ruth is the one who drives the plot of the story rather than Boaz.

Boaz's revelation in verse 12 that there is another "redeemer" (*gōʾel*) who is more closely related than he complicates the issue and keeps the tension of the plot from being resolved too easily. This complication is usually interpreted as being a threat to the relationship between Ruth and Boaz. This reading assumes that marriage and the duties of the *gōʾel* (primarily relating to land redemption) are either coterminous or bound together in some way, but this may not be the case. Indeed, as we will see below, the exchange between Boaz and the other redeemer in chapter 4 indicates that the two are separate issues except as

[15] Trible, *God and the Rhetoric of Sexuality*, 195–6.

linked together by Ruth in verse 9 and here by Boaz. Perhaps Boaz's sputtering speech in this verse is an indication that he is only belatedly realizing the import of Ruth's linking these two issues: if he wants the relationship/marriage with her, then he should also assume the role of *gōʾel* and do the duties of land redemption, thus providing not only for her but also Naomi (who, we only now learn, has available some land that can be used to support her). Boaz was so grateful that she showed up at his pile of grain in the middle of the night rather than at some younger man's that he missed this linkage. And while Ruth has stopped short of making herself strictly contingent on his performing the duties of the *gōʾel,* she has presented the two together, and now Boaz agrees that he will pursue both. Boaz promises to present the matter of redemption to this other *gōʾel* and if he will redeem the land well and good, Naomi will be provided for, but if he will not then Boaz will do it himself. The fact that Boaz so easily consents to the other redeemer's right and that Ruth raises no questions about it gives support to the idea that marriage and land redemption are separate issues in the book. On this reading, Boaz is not saying to Ruth "if he marries you fine, but if not I will," but rather assumes that he and Ruth will be together whether or not he redeems the land.

Ruth "lay at his feet until morning" and then, in keeping with the tenor of mystery, ambiguity, and hiddenness constructed by the storyteller, she got up "before one person could recognize another" and prepared to head back to Naomi. The verb *nkr* ("recognize") harks back to 2:10, where Ruth inquires as to why Boaz has "recognized" *(nkr)* her in such a special way. Ruth arrives at the threshing floor under the cover of darkness and leaves under the cover of darkness, and what exactly transpires between her and Boaz in between is only slightly less obscured. That Ruth has advanced the plot significantly through her initiative is clear. Indeed, the Syriac version recognizes the role reversal represented by Ruth's initiative by placing verse 14b in Ruth's mouth rather than Boaz's: "and she said to him, 'No one should learn that I came to you at the threshing floor." The reading is not supported in any other extant manuscripts, but it is an interesting extrapolation of the fact that it is Ruth who has to tell Boaz what to do.

Before leaving the threshing floor, Ruth receives an unspecified but clearly ample amount of barley ("six measures") from Boaz. Many commentators have recognized the symbolic value of both the heap of grain beside which Boaz reclines and the gift of grain with which he sends Ruth back to the city. They are the products of "seed," a word used in the Hebrew Bible in its literal sense as well as in a metaphorical sense of semen and by extension of offspring. Boaz, for all his fright and failure of nerve at the threshing floor, is the possessor of seed. It is the literal product of the seed that the two widows need to survive and which Ruth has secured by her gleaning; it is the metaphorical product of the seed that they need if they are to continue the family line and after the encounter at the threshing floor it seems that Ruth is on the verge of securing that as well. Rabbinic interpreters intuited the symbolic value of Boaz's gift of grain when they interpreted the six measures as representing six great descendants of Ruth. Porten's comment is a bit reductive, but he nevertheless captures the central meaning of the symbolism when he writes that "the seed to fill the stomach was promise of the seed to fill the womb."[16] The imagery is, of course, male-centered and biologically wrong—implying as it does that a woman contributes nothing to the pregnancy but a place for the man's seed to find purchase—but it is rather common in the Bible. It must be said however that the book of Ruth complicates the matter a bit, for as we will see below in 4:12 Ruth is also presented as giving "seed" or descendants to Boaz.

[vv. 16-18]

The chapter closes as it began, with Ruth and Naomi conversing and Naomi referring to her as "my daughter." The close of chapter 3 also mirrors the close of chapter 2, with Ruth handing over to Naomi the grain that she has secured from Boaz in both cases. The identification of Naomi with Boaz is reinforced here in Naomi's initial question to Ruth, "How did things go with you?" (v. 16; NRSV). In Hebrew the question literally reads "who are you" *(mî 'at)*, and is precisely what Boaz asked Ruth when he awoke in a fright and saw a woman at his "feet." There the phrase was meant as a question of identity, here it is a broader question seeking information, as indicated by the fact that Naomi addresses her as "my daughter," showing that she knows her identity, and by the fact that Ruth immediately begins to tell her of the encounter with Boaz rather than identifying herself. Thus the repeated phrase, used in two differing senses, is the author's way of tying the two scenes together and of further reinforcing the connection between Naomi and Boaz despite the fact that they are never described as meeting each other.

After reporting to Naomi "all that the man had done for her" and that he had given her "these six measures of barley," Ruth adds another statement: "He said, 'Do not go back to your mother-in-law empty-handed'" (v. 17b). Looking back a few verses to the scene at the

[16] B. Porten, "The Scroll of Ruth: A Rhetorical Study," *Gratz College Annual* 7 (1978) 40.

threshing floor, one notices that Boaz is never reported as saying any such thing and in fact never mentions Naomi at all. It may be that we are to assume that the storyteller simply waited to report these words of Boaz now, but it may also be that Ruth is not being completely truthful to Naomi, that she is putting words into Boaz's mouth for Naomi's benefit. This reading is supported by the fact that we saw Ruth do this already back in chapter 2. In a structurally parallel scene, Ruth returns from an encounter with Boaz and reports the events of the day to Naomi, then she added the statement that Boaz told her to "cling to his young men" (2:21) when in fact the reader knows the he warned her away from the young men and instructed her to "cling to the young women" (2:8-9). It seems likely too that in this scene Ruth adds something to her report that is more than a little misleading. It is also worth noting that Ruth does not tell Naomi how it was she who had to tell Boaz what to do, against Naomi's original plan. But why would the author have Ruth mislead Naomi in this way? One possibility is simply that Ruth is trying to make Naomi feel included in these proceedings, that she is keeping the older woman from feeling left out. But more specifically, we may recall that it is Naomi who in chapter 1 defined her self-worth in relation to her ability to produce (male) offspring (vv. 11-13), something that Ruth has never shown a concern for nor even alluded to. Rather, the one clear statement of Ruth's intentions, found in her extraordinary speech in 1:16-17, focused on her commitment to and solidarity with Naomi. Thus, the symbolism of Ruth handing over the "seed" of Boaz to Naomi and specifying that it is for her rather than for Ruth may be seen as another way of Ruth providing for Naomi. While Naomi saw herself as coming home "empty" (*rêqām;* 1:21) because she had no men left, despite the fact that she had Ruth with her, Ruth attributes to Boaz a desire to make sure that Ruth not return to Naomi "empty" *(rêqām).* If it is seed Naomi wants, then Ruth will make sure that she gets it.

There is something a bit melancholy about the fact that this is the last time that the character Ruth speaks in the book. From here until the end of the story she will only be referred to in the third person, and will be acted upon more than she acts. Chapters 2 and 3 are clearly Ruth's chapters—it is here that she is most fully developed as a character who acts and controls the narrative flow. But it is as if once she has performed her duty of securing the coveted "seed" she loses all subjectivity. The fact that this narrative development mirrors the actual course of many women's lives in the ancient world—and even, one supposes, today—in which procreation is thought to be the only worthwhile goal, makes it all the more poignant and disturbing. It is easy to feel ambivalent about a book that constructs such a strong and

shrewd female character, and which focuses so intently on her relationship with another woman, but that also ends up subsuming that
character and her interests into the goal of producing a male child;
though whether this is a fair characterization of the narrative must
wait until chapter 4 has played itself out.

Naomi's final line of the book is her response to Ruth's final line:
"Wait, my daughter, until you learn how the matter will turn out, for
the man will not rest, but will settle the matter today" (v. 18). The chapter ends as chapter 2 ended, with the two women waiting, and despite
the quick thinking and bold actions of the protagonist Ruth they are
still dependant on the actions of Boaz. They are two widows in a world
that does not value widows and in which public power, if not private,
is wielded in the square by "prominent rich men." There seems nothing they can do but wait and see whether Boaz is able to pull off his
part of the plan in the public sphere, before the town elders, as well as
Ruth was able to pull off hers under the cover of night, behind a pile
of grain.

Chapter 4

MAKING IT ALL LEGAL

Chapter 4 of the book of Ruth returns the reader and the characters to the light of day. The story is back to the public realm where social codes based on gender, nationality, and class determine to a large degree how one may act and what one may say. It is no surprise, then, to find that Ruth recedes as a character and Boaz comes to the fore. The primary concerns of the chapter are the legal issues raised by Ruth's proposal to Boaz on the threshing floor. Thus the key words are "to redeem" (gāʾal), "to acquire" (qānāh), and "inheritance" (naḥălâ).

The chapter may be divided into three main parts, which in the larger chiastic structure of the book correspond to the three main parts of chapter 1 (see the Introduction on this). In verses 1-13 we find the negotiation of kinship ties (cf. 1:6-18), followed in verses 14-17 by an exchange between Naomi and the women of Bethlehem (cf. 1:19-21). Finally, in verses 18-22 one finds the family history that closes out the chapter and the book (cf. 1:1-5). While cohering formally with chapter 1, the final chapter of the book nevertheless differs in fundamental and significant ways. A family history concerned with death in chapter 1 has given way to a family history concerned with life in chapter 4, and likewise Naomi's exchange with the women of Bethlehem has changed from lament over her emptiness to celebration over her abundance. The negotiation of kinship ties among women in a private setting has given way to the negotiation of kinship ties in the public realm solely among men. We will see that how one is to adjudicate these differences—whether one sees them solely as a positive culmination to the narrative—is not at all obvious. Formally, that is with regard to the tight structure of the book, the plot gets tied up neatly by the end; but ethically and theologically, one may well be left with more than a little ambiguity.

4:1-12

[vv. 1-2]

Chapter 3 concluded with Naomi predicting that Boaz would be anxious to finish what was begun on the threshing floor, and chapter 4 begins with Boaz doing exactly that. The narrator tells us in 4:1 that Boaz "went up to the gate and sat down there." At this point, with the use of the Hebrew word *hinnēh*, the point of view switches to that of Boaz. As Adele Berlin has seen, *hinnēh* does not indicate the simultaneity of the arrivals of Boaz and the nearer redeemer—thus the NRSV's "no sooner had Boaz gone up . . ." is misleading—but rather that now we are seeing the action from Boaz's perspective.[1] Boaz is waiting at the gate and as he looks up to see the nearer redeemer approaching, the reader looks up with him. As with camera shots in film making, the technique functions to recruit the reader subtly to Boaz's side in the transaction that is about to take place. We may note that in the Hebrew the name Boaz is the first and last word of the opening sentence: it is Boaz's interests that frame the exchange. Furthermore, Boaz is portrayed as sitting down and waiting in readiness, while the other possible redeemer is merely "passing by" (*'br*), with no inkling that a legal encounter with Boaz may be in the works; he is clearly at a disadvantage in the legal proceedings that will follow.

If Boaz was unsure of himself, more than a bit frightened, and—literally and figuratively—in the dark in his interaction with Ruth on the threshing floor, in this scene he is in his element. The "gate" in the Bible represents the place of public, male power; a place where legal decisions and economic transactions take place in the presence of other men who wield power in a patriarchal society. As Köhler puts it, writing in the early part of this century in a book entitled *The Hebrew Man* and thus with no trace of irony: "It is the meeting place of those who really matter."[2] This judgment is cited approvingly in Bush's recent commentary, but Trible catches better the nuance of the story's movement out from the threshing floor to the gate in her comment that "this is a man's world" and that "no women are present, even though their actions alone have made the occasion mandatory."[3] In this man's world Boaz, the "prominent rich man" (2:1), is able to operate with a confidence and surety of tone that was manifestly missing when he awoke to find a woman at his feet. The story establishes his effective-

---

[1] Berlin, *Poetics and Interpretation of Biblical Narrative*, 92–3.
[2] Ludwig Köhler, *Hebrew Man* (London: SCM, 1956) 153.
[3] Trible, *God and the Rhetoric of Sexuality*, 188.

ness in this realm by two parallel commands in 4:1-2, each of which is immediately carried out. First, Boaz hails the other redeemer and tells him to turn aside from his path and to "sit down here," and, the narrator informs us, "he went over and sat down." Likewise Boaz gathers a group of elders and tells them to "sit down here," and, the narrator informs us, "they sat down." Boaz's status and authority go unchallenged and rather than *telling* the reader this, the narrator *demonstrates* it by the efficacy of Boaz's commands.

When Boaz hails the other redeemer—who is in fact repeatedly designated simply as "the redeemer [*gōʾel*]" in this chapter—he calls him by a rhyming Hebrew nonsense phrase, *pᵉlōnî ʾalmōnî*. The phrase is probably best translated as "so-and-so," or when used in reference to a place rather than a person, "such-and-such" (cf. 1 Sam 21:3; 2 Kgs 6:8). The fact that it is obviously not a proper name has caused a good deal of consternation among interpreters who cannot imagine that Boaz would not know the name of a relative from the same small city or that if he did know it he would not use it. This is too literal a reading of what is another example of the storyteller's flair. As I noted above in commenting on chapter 1, the designation *pᵉlōnî ʾalmōnî* serves as a rhetorical and thematic counterpart to the names Mahlon and Chilion, another rhyming pair of words which, though functioning as proper names, also indicate a secondary character status. Moreover, by refusing to give this character a name, the author uses *pᵉlōnî ʾalmōnî* as an ironic contrast to Boaz's pledge to "maintain the name" of Mahlon via his marriage to Ruth.

[vv. 3-4]

Having set the scene for a legal exchange, Boaz presents a case to the other redeemer, with the ten elders as witnesses. Nowhere in the Bible is ten prescribed as a quorum for such proceedings, but it seems to represent a round number as well as an irrefutable witness. The number ten also resonates with the ten years spent in Moab in the opening verses of chapter 1 and the ten generations of descendants recounted at the end of chapter 4. Boaz is staking everything on this exchange, which clearly will be binding however it turns out.

Having arranged a controlled environment in a way he was unable to do at the threshing floor, Boaz launches into his presentation with his usual stylized manner of speaking, making use again of both parallelism and repetition. Note for example, with the Hebrew word order restored in a literal rendering, the structure of his first sentence to the other redeemer:

A) The portion of <u>field</u> *(śādeh)*

   B) belonging to our relative <u>Elimelech</u>

     C) is being sold

   B¹) by <u>Naomi</u> who returned

A¹) from the <u>field</u> *(śādeh)* of Moab.

At the center of the legal transaction is the action of selling a field, which is of course what bears the most relevance to the role of the redeemer to whom Boaz is speaking. The transaction turns, both literally and rhetorically, on this proceeding; it is the central legal issue in the exchange and is the central term of Boaz's opening statement. Surrounding this act of selling are two proper names of family members, Elimelech and Naomi (labeled B and B¹). The order is not accidental, Elimelech's name comes first both because he is the blood kin of Boaz and the redeemer and thus the necessary hook for the case, but also because he represents the past and must give way to the present, represented by Naomi. This transition is also implied by the modifiers attached to each of their names: Elimelech is "our relative" while Naomi is the one who has "returned" and is now being reintegrated into the extended family. Framing both the act of selling and the two references to family members is a wordplay on the word "field" *(śādeh)*, in the first instance referring to the portion of land being sold by Naomi and in the second instance referring to the country from which Naomi has returned.

While Boaz's opening statement to the redeemer is brief and tightly structured, his elaboration of the case in verse 4 is less tightly structured but makes even greater use of repetition. He uses some form of the word *gāʾal* ("redeem") four times in this verse, beginning with the positive conditional statement to the other redeemer, "if you will redeem it, redeem it." The NRSV, along with most commentators, emends the negative conditional statement that follows from the MT's third person to the second person, so that Boaz continues to address the redeemer. But the Hebrew presents it almost as an aside to the elders and watchers around them, "but if he will not redeem it," before turning back to the other redeemer to present the second half of the conditional statement, "tell me, so that I may know; for there is no one prior to you to redeem it, and I come after you." Sasson is correct I think in arguing that we ought to retain the MT's third person, thus making the scene a more vivid portrayal of Boaz's working not only the other redeemer but also the elders and the crowd which has apparently gathered (note Boaz's reference to "those sitting here," which seems to indicate another group of onlookers in addition to the elders).[4]

The brevity of the redeemer's response, "I will redeem it," contrasts with Boaz's prolixity. The redeemer, led by Boaz's repeated emphasis on the act of redeeming and by the focus of his opening statement on the act of selling land, assumes that this is a simple matter of land redemption, of acquiring from Naomi a piece of family land that she has inherited upon the death of her husband and that she is unable to work herself but from which she would benefit by selling. It is intriguing that the reader has not yet heard a word about this piece of land. The story has proceeded on the assumption that Naomi and Ruth have returned to nothing. One wonders why Naomi has not mentioned the field earlier or tried to sell it upon their return, but rather has counted on Ruth's gleaning and constructed an elaborate plan for her to convince Boaz to marry her as a means for providing for them. Furthermore, there is no report of Naomi giving Boaz the right to arrange for the land's purchase by the other redeemer or even an indication that she wanted to sell the land, and there is simply not time in the narrative flow of events to imagine an unreported conversation between Boaz and Naomi taking place before the scene at the gate. Though interpreters have tended to take Boaz at his word, it is quite possible that the reader is meant to wonder if he has fabricated the story of the field and its imminent sale entirely. If this is the case, it gives him the cover he needs to pursue in public his desire to marry Ruth: while everyone is focused on the noble duties of land-redemption, Boaz can slip in the fact that he is also "acquiring" Ruth. It is quite a risky venture, if indeed Boaz is resorting to this sort of fabrication, for it depends on the other redeemer ultimately giving up his right of redemption; otherwise, when it comes time to produce the field in question, Boaz's lie will be revealed. Alternately, one may imagine that Boaz is in fact telling the truth, that there is a field that belongs to Naomi and is available for redemption. In this case, the presentation to the other redeemer in verses 3-4 is straightforward enough, and it is only when we move on to verses 5-6 that things begin to get tricky.

[vv. 5-6]

In verse 5, Boaz adds a stipulation to the redemption of the field (whether real or fabricated) that will throw a wrench into the legal works. What this stipulation is remains a matter of debate. A majority of interpreters, assuming that the duties of the *gōʾel* include a version

---

[4] Sasson, *Ruth*, 118.

of levirate marriage, read Boaz's next statement to the other redeemer as follows: "The day you acquire the field from the hand of Naomi, you are also acquiring Ruth the Moabite, the widow of the dead man, to maintain the dead man's name on his inheritance" (NRSV). This rendering results from choosing the *qere* (the marginal notation in the MT on how one should read the word) over the *ketiv* (the actual written consonantal text of the MT). If one reads the consonantal text as it is written, however, Boaz informs the would-be redeemer that, "the day you acquire the field from the hand of Naomi, *I* am acquiring Ruth the Moabite, the widow of the dead man, to maintain the dead man's name on his inheritance." In either of these readings, Boaz is springing a trap of sorts on *pᵉlōnî ʾalmōnî*, who has been thinking only of adding to his landholdings, but the second of the readings is the more likely. The first would involve Boaz taking an extraordinary risk with his relationship with Ruth; he could not be sure that the redeemer would reject the stipulation that he acquire Ruth. Moreover, the redeemer's concern for damaging his own inheritance would simply not obtain if he acquired Ruth as well as the land. Any child resulting from the man's marriage to Ruth would, even though "maintaining the dead man's name," remain the child of *pᵉlōnî ʾalmōnî*. Rather, it is Boaz's assertion that he is himself acquiring Ruth in order to maintain the name of Mahlon upon the land that threatens the other redeemer's inheritance. For if a child results from the marriage of Ruth and Boaz, a child whom Boaz explicitly names here as an heir to Elimelech's holdings, then this child will end up with a legal claim to land that the redeemer had purchased for himself.

The question remains as to why Boaz raises the issue of the sale of the field at all, if in fact the two issues—land redemption and marriage —are legally separate as they appear to be. If one takes the position that Boaz has invented the field, then the answer is simple: he does so in order to cover his desire to marry Ruth. But if one reads this offer of land redemption to *pᵉlōnî ʾalmōnî* as genuine, then Boaz's motivation may be found in Ruth's linking of the two at the threshing floor, which in turn may be motivated by her desire to remain with Naomi even while providing security for both of them with Boaz. In other words, it seems likely that Naomi and the field are seen as bound up with each other legally or at least by custom in a way that Naomi and Ruth are not. Only by convincing Boaz to attempt to hold on to the land of Elimelech can Ruth assure that once she is married to Boaz she will be able to maintain her close connection with Naomi. Once again, we find that the structure of Boaz's statement in verse 5 reflects the way in which the plot turns on the linking of Naomi, the field, and Ruth. Thus the three main clauses of the verse lie in a complex interlocking pattern. The first two display a familiar chiastic pattern:

A) On the day <u>you acquire</u> the field

    B) from the hand of <u>Naomi,</u>

    B¹) <u>Ruth</u> the Moabite,

A¹) the wife of the dead, <u>I acquire</u>.

The outside terms (labeled A and A¹) match each other in their focus on "acquiring," even as they contrast the subject of the verb "acquire" (in Hebrew, *qnh*). Matching up as the two middle terms are the two widows, Naomi being identified with the field in question and Ruth being identified with the dead man and presented as the object of Boaz's acquiring. As it stands, the two acts of acquiring remain separate rhetorically, but with the third clause of Boaz's statement in v. 5, we see how they are subtly linked. By adding a description of his intent in marrying Ruth—"to maintain the name of the dead upon his inheritance"—Boaz has not only justified his relationship with Ruth by couching it in terms of levirate marriage (despite the fact that it is not legally such a marriage), but has also effectively linked the land with Ruth, both rhetorically for the reader and in the mind of the other redeemer. Thus we may note that the third clause takes the concept of "the name of the dead" from A¹ above ("wife of the dead") and combines it with "his inheritance," taken from A above ("the field"). The field, of course, is the dead man's inheritance, and by linking it to his marriage with Ruth he is also linking Ruth with Naomi, just as Ruth intimated he should do as he lay on the threshing floor with his feet uncovered. There is, of course, no way of getting around the offensiveness of this idiom of "acquiring" a woman (and the Hebrew word for "acquire" elsewhere means "to buy"), even if it is simply a shorthand phrase for marriage.

As we have seen, Boaz has never expressed an interest in the welfare of Naomi, nor has he seemed concerned to redeem the field on her behalf before now (assuming it existed). In this light, Boaz's offer of land redemption to *pelōnî ʾalmōnî* is not so risky after all—if the other man accepts, Boaz still has Ruth and he can claim to have at least attempted to keep Ruth, Naomi, and the family land together. As it turns out, however, Boaz's linkage convinces *pelōnî ʾalmōnî* to give up his right of redemption in verse 6. The author seems to delight in the ironic wordplay in which a character repeatedly called "redeemer" (*gōʾel*) here declares twice—at the beginning and ending of his speech and thus framing the response to Boaz—that his is unable to redeem (*gāʾal*). And between this frame in which he categorically states his inability to redeem lies his request that Boaz should "redeem" the man's "right of redemption." In the end, the man is not a redeemer at all, but simply *pᵉlōnî ʾalmōnî*, "Mr. So-and-so." It is Boaz who fills the role of redeemer.

[vv. 7-8]

Verse 7 reads as if it were an aside to the audience, as if a storyteller is taking a break from the real action of the story in order to explain a custom that is no longer in practice for the audience. Scholars have generally taken this as a genuine aside, as a description of a real legal practice that was part of the original story and that now (i.e., the time of its being written down) needs explaining in order to make sense. For example, Campbell assumes a change in circumstance from the time being described in the book and the author's own time: "Altered circumstances require some altered modes—together with explanation and instruction."[5] And Nielsen adds that in her opinion, "the author may be employing traditions that not even he can grasp the full meaning of."[6] But there is no need to see this seeming "aside" as any less a part of the "real" story, or the storyteller's art, than what surrounds it in the narrative. Nor must one presume a genuine custom here that has been lost but that might be recovered with enough comparative legal material from other ancient near eastern civilizations.[7] Rather, I think that Hubbard is imaginatively correct in his assertion that "the remark serves more literary than historical purposes."[8] We may note that the "aside" clearly makes use of the same sorts of rhetorical patterns that our author is shown to be fond of elsewhere, especially repetition and assonance. In a repetition that serves to frame the verse with an inclusio, the author begins and ends with nearly identical phrases: "this was the custom previously in Israel . . .," and "this was the custom of attesting in Israel." The sentence also employs three rhyming legal words: *haggᵉʾûllâ*, *hattᵉmûrâ*, and *hatteʿûdâ* ("redeeming," "exchanging," and "attesting," respectively). And given the ambiguity of the remark—Who removes whose sandal? Why a sandal?—it does not function well as an attempt to make a previously practiced custom clear.

---

[5] Campbell, *Ruth*, 148.

[6] Nielsen, *Ruth*, 89.

[7] For attempts at such recovery, see E. A. Speiser, "Of Shoes and Shekels," *The Bulletin of the American School for Oriental Research* 77 (1937) 15–20; and D. Thompson and T. Thompson, "Some Legal Problems in the Book of Ruth," *Vetus Testamentum* 18 (1968) 79–99.

[8] Hubbard, *The Book of Ruth*, 248.

If the remark does serve a literary rather than a genuine historical (or explanatory) purpose, then, what might that purpose be? The simplest answer is that it injects a bit of "historical color" into the narrative. That is, our author has a penchant for archaizing, for making use of words or syntax that appear to be ancient and thus give the story an ancient feel. The remark in verse 7, like the remark in the opening sentence of the book, "Back in the days of the judges," may also function this way. In this case, the fact that the author has sent modern scholars scurrying to find evidence for such a practice is a tribute to the storyteller's art: he or she has convinced them that some genuine custom is being referred to. Moreover, as Hubbard points out, by interrupting the flow of the scene, the "aside" allows a narrative pause at a critical juncture, allowing the reader to absorb all that has happened to advance the plot in the last few verses. Finally, one cannot overlook the resonance of this sandal ceremony with the strikingly similar ceremony in the context of levirate marriage. There, when one refuses the duty of taking the widow of his brother in marriage and raising a child to continue the name of the dead man (and by implication provide for the widow), the following ceremony obtains:

> But if the man has no desire to marry his brother's widow, then his brother's widow shall go up to the elders at the gate and say, "My husband's brother refuses to perpetuate his brother's name in Israel; he will not perform the duty of the husband's brother [*levir*] to me." Then the elders of his town shall summon him and speak to him. If he persists, saying, "I have no desire to marry her," then his brother's wife shall go up to him in the presence of the elders, pull his sandal off his foot, spit in his face, and declare, "This is what is done to the man who does not build up his brother's house" (Deut. 25:7-9).

Because the book of Ruth is not dealing strictly with a case of levirate marriage, the scene is obviously not precisely the same as that imagined in Deuteronomy: the other redeemer is never publicly condemned for his refusal to take Ruth as a wife, nor does Ruth herself play any part in the symbolic act of sandal removal as she would in the case of a levirate marriage. Rather the official legal issue is that of land redemption and the transferring of the right (or duty) of redemption. But by importing elements from the public shaming of the reluctant *levir* into this scene at the gate in Ruth 4, the author must surely mean to allude to the ceremony described above. Allusion to the ceremony of levirate marriage in the context of a transaction regarding the rights of land redemption serve to reinforce in the reader's mind the connections between the two that have been forged by Ruth and accepted by Boaz, but not by the other redeemer. The connections are not officially recognized or legally binding, but have been bound together in the plot of the book by the desire of Ruth to maintain her relationship with Naomi.

[vv. 9-12]

With the other redeemer having ceded over his right of redemption, Boaz is in the clear to make an official declaration of his acquisition of the field as well as an official announcement of his marriage to Ruth. Boaz's words, in the context of a legal transaction, seem to carry a perlocutionary force, with his stated intentions becoming reality at precisely this point. Boaz plays the scene for all it is worth, loading his final speech of the book with legal language and a concern for social propriety befitting a pillar of the community. This public male forum is the place that Boaz knows well and is able to manipulate to his own ends, and thus his final speech finds him returning unequivocally to his formal, repetitive mode of speech. In the same way that the other redeemer's speech in verse 6 was framed with his repeated declaration that he was "unable to redeem," and the narrator's statement in verse 7 was framed with the repetition of "this was the custom . . . in Israel," so too Boaz's final speech in verses 9 and 10 is framed with the phrase "today you are witnesses." Boaz's business with the other redeemer is finished and now has only to be ratified by the assembly at the gate. Mapping out the rhetoric of the verses shows again the stylized way of speaking characteristic of Boaz.

A) Today you are witnesses,

>   B) that I have acquired (*qānîtî*) all that belonged to Elimelech
>   and to Mahlon and Chilion
>
>   C) from the hand of Naomi,
>
>   C¹) and also Ruth the Moabite the wife of Mahlon
>
>   B¹) I have acquired (*qānîtî*) as wife in order to maintain the
>   name of the dead on his inheritance, so that the name of
>   the dead will not be cut off from his kindred and from
>   the gate of his native place;

A¹) today you are witnesses.

The speech mirrors quite closely the structure of his previous statement to the other redeemer in verse 5. In both cases at the heart of the statement is the pairing of the two widows, and in both cases the mentioning of Ruth and Naomi is surrounded by the interests of male property-holders and their inheritance (signaled by the repetition of the verb *qnh*, "acquire."). A major difference hosted by these similarly structured statements is that in the previous statement the two widows were split by the splitting of land-redemption and marriage, while here Boaz has consolidated the two legal issues and so has also ensured that Ruth and Naomi will not be parted.

Focusing on Boaz's stated motivation (labeled B¹ above) for acquiring Ruth as wife, we may note that it differs significantly from his earlier exchange with Ruth at the threshing floor. Phyllis Trible has noted this shift in the content of Boaz's speech: "In a private conversation with Ruth, Boaz made her welfare the sole object of his concern, but in a public discussion with men he makes Ruth the means for achieving a male purpose."[9] Trible saw, earlier and better than anyone, the conflict between what characters in the book of Ruth say in one scene and what they say in the next, but here even she stops short of noting the full dissonance between Boaz's private and public concerns. For as we may recall from chapter three, Boaz's main reaction to Ruth's nocturnal visit was gratitude that she had not "gone after young men" (3:10). Ruth's welfare, far from being the sole object of his concern, seems to arise secondarily from his own desire for her. This, naturally, will not do at the gate in front of the elders and the gathering crowd, so Boaz switches into the socially acceptable rhetoric of which he seems to be a master.

After declaring their assent to the scenario of acquisition just proposed by Boaz by repeating the single word "Witnesses!" (*ʿēdîm*), and thus serving their legal purpose, the crowd of people along with the elders pronounce a blessing upon Boaz. One at first might think to say that they pronounce a blessing upon Boaz and Ruth or upon the marriage, but on closer inspection it becomes clear that the blessing, in keeping with the concerns of this public, male realm, is strictly for Boaz. Again, the form of the blessing reinforces the meaning. It may be outlined as follows:

A) May the Lord make *the woman* who is coming into <u>your house</u> like <u>Rachel and Leah</u>, who together built up the **house of Israel**.

B) Thus you will prosper in *Ephrathah*!

B¹) Thus you will make a name in *Bethlehem*!

A¹) May <u>your house</u> be like the **house of Perez**, whom <u>Tamar</u> bore to **Judah**, through the seed that the Lord will give you by *this young woman*.

---

[9] Trible, *God and the Rhetoric of Sexuality*, 192.

The blessing is balanced both syntactically as well as in vocabulary and content. The syntactic pattern matches two extended sentences in the jussive mood (A and A¹) with two shorter sentences in the imperative (B and B¹), which are themselves result clauses dependant on the preceding jussive. With regard to content, the two central elements are parallel in their use of place names and in their wish for Boaz's prosperity and posterity. The phrase "thus you will prosper" (*ʿāśâ ḥayil*) elsewhere in the Bible means "to acquire wealth" (Deut. 8:17-18) as well as "to father children" (Joel 2:22), and it serves here as a play on the earlier designation of Boaz as a "prominent rich man" (*ʾîš gibbôr ḥayil*). The idiom "make a name" (*qārāʾ šēm*) occurs only here in the Bible, and while it is close to a common naming formula for a newborn child, "to call a name," it is not precisely the same. No doubt the author means the reader to catch this nuance and thus to foreshadow the imminent birth of a child, especially given the concern in the context for fertility, but just as its parallel blessing in the phrase labeled B above carries both the meaning of prosperity and success for Boaz personally as well as the birth of children, so this phrase in B¹ also seems both to allude to a child and to express a wish for the establishment of Boaz's name as a man of continued importance in his hometown. Thus Boaz's well-being, reputation, and posterity are at the center of the chiastic structure of the blessing pronounced upon him by the crowd.

The irony of this focus on Boaz and his prosperity, intended perhaps by the author but surely not by the crowd pronouncing the blessing, is that it is entirely dependant upon the fertility of the woman Ruth. This is acknowledged subtly by the very syntax, in which the imperatives at the center are subordinate to the jussive of the initial sentence concerning "the woman who is coming into your house." It is made more explicit by the content of the blessing found in A and A¹. We may note first the parallel constructions that follow the jussive verb with dual mention of "your house" and "the house of Israel/Perez" and that focus so intently on women. In each blessing Ruth is being compared to a figure or figures from the ancestral narratives of Genesis. In the first she is compared to Rachel and Leah, "who together built up the house of Israel." Rachel and Leah, along with it must be said their servants Bilhah and Zilpah, were the mothers of the twelve sons that became the ancestors of the twelve tribes of Israel. Thus, the blessing carries connotations of progeny both numerous and distinguished. It may also, given the legal fiction in Genesis whereby sons born to Bilhah and Zilpah were considered descendants of Jacob, allude to the notion that the child born to Ruth would continue the line of Mahlon. The second framing blessing, labeled A¹ above, exemplifies a focusing move typical of Hebrew rhetoric: while its counterpart in A compared Ruth to the ancestors of all of Israel, this line compares her more specifically to Tamar, the ancestor of the tribe of Judah, that is, Boaz's own tribe. It also begins to focus the ending of our story ever so slightly toward David, the most renowned of all Judahites.

I have called this focus on women and children which surround the portrayal of Boaz as the great man in B and B[1] ironic, in the sense that what prominent rich men in the ancient world (as perhaps the modern) often value most can only be had through a woman. Children, or to be more precise in this context, *male* children, are necessary for such important men both to pass on their wealth they have so assiduously acquired and to guarantee a semblance of immortality through posterity. Although this fact is certainly not in and of itself subversive of patriarchy and in reality has been a primary factor in valuing women's worth in relation to their ability to bear children—as they say in England, "the heir and the spare"—it does perhaps introduce just enough male insecurity to take the wind out of any imagined self-sufficiency of a man like Boaz. In this particular scene, its irony consists in the tacit acknowledgment that even in this utterly male, public realm concerned with male property holders and the continuance of a male name, the future depends on the bodies of women. The acknowledgment becomes more than tacit in the final line of the blessing in verse 12, when the crowd states the wish that the Lord will give Boaz "seed" (i.e., "descendants") from Ruth. Throughout the story, Boaz has been the possessor of seed, both in the literal sense of the grain that the women need to survive and in the sense of the semen that is necessary to produce progeny. Boaz has given Ruth seed in the first sense twice already in chapters two and three and has given at least an indication of his willingness (perhaps overwillingness!) to do so in the second sense. Yet here the terms are reversed and it is Ruth who will "give seed" to Boaz.

Now, if the author intends the reader to catch this irony of male interests dependant on women, it is curious that with as much focus as the blessings place on the person of Ruth they never actually mention her name. The crowd refers to her as "the woman" (ʾiššâ) in verse 11 and as "this young woman" (naʿărâ) in verse 12. It is perhaps possible to read this as the irony of ironies, as pointing up the insecurity of a patriarchy that cannot bear to acknowledge the name of this (Moabite) woman who is so necessary to the greatness of Boaz. I would like to read it this way, but my sense is that such a reading is a stretch, the more likely explanation being that Ruth has at this point become reduced to the role of child-producer, that she has been summarily re-defined as no more than a womb. This second reading does seem to be supported by the final scene that follows in verses 13-22, which focuses so squarely on the newborn child. Still, the more subversive reading gets support from the names that *do* get mentioned by the storyteller: Rachel, Leah, and Tamar. For not only are these women renowned ancestors of Israel and Judah, they also share an identity as what James Black has called "brides-in-the-dark."[10] That is, all of them, like Ruth, have been able to manipulate the sexuality of men toward their own interests either under the cover of night (with Rachel, Leah, and Ruth) or under the cover of a veil (with Tamar). One may add to this list the daughters of Lot, whom Black considers to be a part of this category. Indeed, the midrash makes explicit their presence, which has seemed to hover over the book in the repeated references to Ruth's Moabite identity, in its brief comment on this blessing:

> R. Hunya said: It was as a result of the blessings of those women that the line of David was not cut off entirely in the days of Athaliah. R. Tanhuma said in the name of R. Samuel: Elsewhere it is written, "That we may preserve seed of our father" (Gen 19:32).

To be sure, the interests of the women dovetail all too easily with the interests of patriarchy in all these stories, yet all remain compelling characters with an independent agency that is not so easily absorbed. Subversion never happens totally and without remainder, but often by incremental dislocations and usually by partly compromised actions and pacts. It is up to the individual reader to decide how much has been compromised in our story.

[vv. 13-17]

In Bertman's chiastic outline of the book of Ruth, which for the most part I have followed in this commentary, verse 13 is placed with the previous section (vv. 1-13) on kinship ties. Indeed, its placement there is quite justifiable, since it represents the culmination of the theme of kinship ties at they relate immediately to Ruth, Naomi, and Boaz. Yet it also serves as the beginning point of the final scene of the book and is thus, beginning with the MT itself, most often set off with what follows rather than what precedes. As I noted with regard to 1:6, which is also a similar sort of liminal verse, this is the nature of transitional episodes in narrative.

Quite a bit gets said in this single verse. Ruth and Boaz are married and have sex, and Ruth conceives and gives birth in only thirteen He-

---

[10] James Black, "Ruth in the Dark: Folktale, Law and Creative Ambiguity in the Old Testament," *Literature and Theology* 5 (1991) 20–35.

brew words! The story does not linger over the episode, but moves quickly to its importance for the denouement which is narrated in the verses that follow. It is worth noting that a boy is born to Ruth and Boaz, which the reader could have guessed ahead of time. The Bible unfortunately almost never narrates the birth of girls since, as we have seen, birth stories tend to concern themselves with male property rights. It is also worth noting that in this concisely told episode, the author takes pains to point out that "the LORD allowed her to conceive." Smack in the middle of this cozy romantic scene between Ruth and Boaz one finds the LORD. As one might expect, interpreters typically wax eloquently about God's role here. Hubbard writes: "For a brief instant, Yahweh stepped from the shadows to center stage. By granting Ruth motherhood, he finally paid the 'full wages' which her devotion to Naomi, both earlier and later (2:11; 3:10), had earned."[11] Never mind that God is "granting" Ruth something that she has never requested nor shown any interest in. Unlike Hannah, who prays fervently for a child in 1 Samuel 1, Ruth's most fervent commitment in the book has been to Naomi. Commentators have for the most part simply not addressed the question of Ruth's own desires in relation to childbearing, but have rather taken this verse as not only the glad fulfillment of everyone else's desires. Consider, for example, Nielsen's comment: "Chapter 4 can thus be read as a fulfillment of Naomi and Boaz's prayers as well as the witnesses' prayers for fertility and procreation for both Ruth and Boaz. All three parties are rewarded with what they have prayed for when Boaz marries Ruth and Yahweh enables her to conceive and bear a son."[12] Noticeably missing from this reading is any concern for Ruth's thoughts on the matter. Such consideration is easily left behind in interpreters' eagerness to develop a theology of providential guidance based on the narrator's comment here.

The phrase "the LORD allowed her to conceive" may well be no more than a stock way of saying "she became pregnant." While there is a midrash that expands the phrase to mean, "She lacked the main portion of the womb, but the Holy One, blessed be He, shaped a womb for her," there is no explicit reference in the book to Ruth being barren and thus needing divine intervention to conceive. Nor does the fact that she was married ten years to Mahlon without conceiving mean that we are to assume she is portrayed as infertile, for while the Bible nearly always blames the failure to conceive on the infertility of women it does on occasion entertain the possibility that men are somehow the problem. For example, the story of Tamar in Genesis 38 does

[11] Hubbard, *The Book of Ruth*, 267.
[12] Nielsen, *Ruth*, 30.

not (contra Nielsen) assume that she is infertile but rather makes clear, in a notoriously graphic way in the case of Onan, that it is the male characters who are at fault. Moreover, even if one takes this phrase in verse 13 as a genuine indication of divine intervention, it simply does not bear the weight of a full-blown theology of divine providence. It is the only place in the book that God is described as taking direct action—despite attempts to see 1:6 as another example, it remains simply a description of what Naomi has "heard" God did—and one could argue that it is the one place where God is needed least. And even this opportunity to act would never have been given to God had not Ruth convinced Boaz to take a more active role in the welfare of herself and Naomi. If there is someone acting throughout the story from behind the scenes or in the shadows, we must conclude that it is Ruth.

Verses 14-17, constituting the final scene of the narrative before the genealogy of verses 18-22, continue to exhibit an ambiguity between celebrating the welfare and the ingenuity of the book's female characters and coopting them in the service of male interests. On the one hand, we have returned to a nearly entirely female cast of characters (with the exception of the baby boy). The scene consists of a group of women addressing another woman, celebrating her well-being. In this respect it matches up in the larger structure of the book with 1:19-21 (see the Introduction for the chiastic structure of the book). There Naomi is also portrayed in relation to the women of Bethlehem, but there it is Naomi who does the talking as she describes her state of emptiness and abjection resulting from the deaths of her husband and two sons. Here, of course, it is the women who address Naomi and celebrate her present fullness, with the birth of the child to Ruth as a counterpart to the death of her two previous children. The new child is in a very real sense a *literal* replacement for Naomi's two sons, in the sense that he is the one who will "nourish her old age." That is, as a male child who now has inheritance rights he will assure that Naomi not fall back into destitution late in her life. For this reason the boy is called a *gōʾel*, or redeemer, as the author plays one last time on this key word. The boy is also a *symbolic* replacement for the two dead sons as the narrative plays out its movement from death to life, from emptiness to fullness. The new life at the end of the book balances the loss of life at the beginning. In a very striking way, the women also counterbalance Naomi's earlier refusal to recognize Ruth as a significant presence in her life. In 1:19-21, Naomi evaluated her life as empty, even though Ruth had just made her extraordinary statement of solidarity with Naomi. In 4:15, the women modify their celebration of the child with the phrase, "for your daughter-in-law who loves you, who is more to you than seven sons, has borne him" (NRSV). The women not only value Ruth as better than seven sons, let alone the two that Naomi has lost, but they also base their evaluation of this new son on the fact that Ruth is his mother. As Bush puts it, "It is because of Ruth's proven commitment and fidelity that Naomi can count on this child to redeem her old age."[13]

On the other hand, despite the strong female presence in the scene, its concern for Naomi's welfare, and its obvious valorizing of Ruth, the end of the story cannot seem to shake the bias—found both in the Bible and elsewhere—toward the "great man" tendency in storytelling. That is, for a story to really "count," to be worth preserving, it must finally have to do with a great man. And so, the women's speech in this final scene gives way to the statement of the narrator: "They named him Obed; he became the father of Jesse, the father of David" (v. 17). It is common among interpreters to gush with delight over this culmination to the story. What could a woman hope for, this line of thinking contends, then to be the ancestor of Israel's most renowned king? To be sure, there is something satisfying subversive about the claim that David was descended from a Moabite woman, given the xenophobic law that "No Ammonite or Moabite shall be admitted to the assembly of the LORD" (Deut 23:4). But there is something equally dissatisfying about the fact that the story of Ruth and Naomi seems to be usurped by the same old story of royal (male) succession.

[vv. 18-22]

This dissatisfaction is only reinforced by the coda to the book, the genealogical list running from Perez, the son of Tamar and Judah, to David. What the reader is left with, after a story that has focused so intently on the triumph of two women in a world constructed around and favoring male concerns, is a list of ten men. Not a single woman shows up in the genealogical list. While it is unusual to find women listed in such genealogies it is not without precedent (cf. Gen 11:27-30), and where better than the book of Ruth to emphasize the obvious yet repressed role that women play in the generation of a family line? Whether or not the genealogy is original to the book or the addition of a later hand—and scholars are very much divided on the question— hardly makes a difference, since even verse 17 gives essentially a truncated version of this genealogical concern. In any case, it seems likely that verses 18-22 are original, given that they serve to balance the "family history" of 1:1-5. While the family there was characterized by death and the threat of extinction, here the genealogy, with its regular

---

[13] Bush, *Ruth, Esther*, 255.

and formulaic expression of one generation yielding to the next, conveys fecundity and permanence. And it seems likely that the ten generations, besides being a typically round number in the Bible, function as a counterpart to the ten years of sterility in Moab mentioned in 1:4. Ten years of emptiness, which seemed a long time to endure in the beginning of the story, suddenly seems much less consequential when compared with ten generations of life in its fullness. So the author begins the story with the death of all the male members of a family, which as we saw opened up a space to develop more fully the characters of Ruth and Naomi and to accord these women an unusual narrative importance; and the author ends the story by recounting the births of ten generations of men in this same family, a structural and thematic inclusio that seems to close off that space that had been opened and usher the reader back into a mind set in which only the names of men deserve to be preserved.

There is, however, another way to read the ending of the book. As I noted in the introduction to this commentary, the book opens with the phrase "In the days when the judges ruled" (NRSV), and it ends with the name of David. The reader has moved, in the space of four chapters, from the period of the judges to the period of the monarchy, making the book of Ruth a natural connector between the book of Judges and the books of Samuel. If the author in fact intended the book to serve as such a connector, that is, the author knew these other books or some versions of them (and I argue in the Introduction that this is plausible), then one can begin to imagine a more ironic tone to the ending, a tone that is not so wholly positive toward David or toward the institution of monarchy. The ending of the book of Judges is the culmination of the disintegration of Israel into inter-tribal warfare and into random murder, kidnapping, and rape. The narrator rarely condemns these actions directly, but does make use of a repeated refrain to end the book, "In those days there was no king in Israel; all the people did what was right in their own eyes" (21:25; cf. 17:6; 18:1; 19:1). The statement indicates that part of the reason for the lawlessness and chaos of the time was that there was no centralized authority such as the monarchy to keep people in line. It encourages the reader to look ahead to the time of the monarchy as a time of potential tranquility and order. The books of Samuel, however, are profoundly ambivalent about the merits of kingship, and in particular the merits of David the ideal king. Decentralized chaos gives way to centralized bureaucracy and exploitation, with its own fair share of murder, rape and kidnapping. This negative view of the monarchy is stated most clearly by Samuel, who represents the last of the judges, in 1 Samuel 8, but is echoed by the structure of the books and their movement from David's success in obtaining the kingship from Saul and in unifying the tribes to God's condemnation of the Uriah/Bathsheba incident, God's refusal to allow David to erect a temple, and the decline of his house in the later chapters.

What has all this to do with the book of Ruth? It raises the distinct possibility that the author of the book of Ruth had a less than ideal portrait of David and of kingship in mind when he or she composed the ending of the book. If this claim is correct—and it is supported by the way in which the chiastic structure of the book mirrors in striking ways the chiastic structure of 2 Sam 5:13–8:18, the section of the books of Samuel that narrate the shift from a positive view of David to a negative view (see the Introduction above)—then one has a warrant for an ironic reading of the culmination of the story in the figure of David. It becomes not a culmination to be celebrated, but a usurpation to be resisted. On this reading, the parallel between the family history in 1:1-5 and the genealogy of 4:18-22 is not only antithetical but synonymous as well. The sections are antithetical in the sense that the blessing of fecundity has replaced the curse of death, but they are synonymous in that both represent failures to establish a just governance in Israel. The fact that those who tended to be at the mercy of men wielding power and thus most vulnerable to exploitation and violence in these stories are women—one thinks of Jephthah's daughter (Judges 11), the levite's concubine (Judges 19), and the young women of Shiloh (Judges 21), as well as Michal (2 Samuel 6), Bathsheba (2 Samuel 11), and David's daughter Tamar (2 Samuel 13)—makes the story of Ruth and Naomi especially poignant. Emerging out of the chaos of the "days of the judges" and the violence against women narrated in the book of Judges, these two women forge a relationship of commitment and solidarity with each other independent of men and manage to hold on not only to each other but also to their family's land, before slipping back into the dominant story of male power and prerogative and being absorbed into the story of the monarchy.

And yet, if "the days of the judges" and "David" together present bookends of failure, then the book of Ruth, framed by and connecting the two yet not wholly invested in either, becomes a moment of possibility, perhaps even of grace. It is not the grace of a providential God all-consumed with manipulating the characters in order to produce God's favorite king, as most commentators suggest, but rather the grace manifested in the persistence of two women, who manage to secure their own survival against the odds, and in the persistence of their story, which in the end is perhaps—just perhaps—not about some king after all.

FOR FURTHER READING

The following list of resources on the book of Ruth is by no means exhaustive, but represents a beginning point for serious exegesis of the narrative. Some of the works will be stronger on issues such as the dating of the book, the textual traditions, philological arguments, etc., while others will be stronger on literary, rhetorical, or theological issues. All contribute in substantial ways to our understanding of Ruth. I have concentrated (though not exclusively) on English-language works.

COMMENTARIES

Bush, Frederic W. *Ruth, Esther*. Word Biblical Commentary. Dallas: Word Books, 1996.

Campbell, Edward F., Jr. *Ruth: A New Translation with Introduction and Commentary*. The Anchor Bible. Garden City, NY: Doubleday, 1975.

Hubbard, Robert L., Jr. *The Book of Ruth*. The New International Commentary on the Old Testament. Grand Rapids, MI: Eardmans, 1988.

Joüon, Paul. *Ruth: Commentaire philologique et exégétique*. Rome: Pontifical Biblical Institute, 1953.

Nielsen, Kirsten. *Ruth*. The Old Testament Library. Louisville: Westminster John Knox, 1997.

Rudolph, Wilhelm. *Das Buch Ruth, Das Hohelied, Die Klagelieder*. 2nd ed. Kommentar zum Alten Testament. Gütersloh: Gerd Mohn, 1962.

MONOGRAPHS AND EDITED VOLUMES

Beattie, D.R.G. *Jewish Exegesis of the Book of Ruth*. Sheffield: JSOT Press, 1977.

Brenner, Athalya, ed. *A Feminist Companion to Ruth*. Sheffield: Sheffield Academic Press, 1993.

Fewell, Danna N. and David M. Gunn. *Compromising Redemption: Relating Characters in the Book of Ruth*. Literary Currents in Biblical Interpretation. Louisville: Westminster John Knox Press, 1990.

Gow, Murray, D. *The Book of Ruth: Its structure, theme and purpose*. Leicester, UK: Apollos, 1992.

Kates, Judith A., and Gail Twersky Reimer. *Reading Ruth: Contemporary Women Reclaim a Sacred Story*. New York: Ballantine Books, 1994.

Myers, Jacob M. *The Linguistic and Literary Form of the Book of Ruth*. Leiden: E. J. Brill, 1955.

Sasson, Jack M. *Ruth: A New Translation with a Philological Commentary and a Formalist-Folklorist Interpretation*. 2nd ed. Sheffield: Sheffield Academic Press, 1989.

ARTICLES AND OTHER STUDIES

Alter, Robert. "Biblical Type-Scenes and the Uses of Convention." *The Art of Biblical Narrative*. 47–62. New York: Basic Books, 1981.

Berlin, Adele. "Poetics in the Book of Ruth." *Poetics and Interpretation of Biblical Narrative*. 83–110. Sheffield: Almond Press, 1983.

Bertman, S. "Symmetrical Design in the Book of Ruth." *Journal of Biblical Literature* 84 (1965) 165–68.

Black, James. "Ruth in the Dark: Folktale, Law and Creative Ambiguity in the Old Testament." *Literature and Theology* 5 (1991) 20–35.

Fisch, Harold. "Ruth and the Structure of Covenant History." *Vetus Testamentum* 32 (1982) 425–37.

Gunkel, Hermann. "Ruth." *Reden und Aufsätze*. 65–92. Gottingen: Vandenhoeck & Ruprecht, 1913.

Landy, Francis. "Ruth and the Romance of Realism, or Deconstructing History." *Journal of the American Academy of Religion* 62 (1994) 285–317.

Levine, Amy-Jill. "Ruth." *The Women's Bible Commentary*. Ed. Carol A. Newsom and Sharon H. Ringe, Louisville: Westminster John Knox, 1992.

Ostriker, Alicia S. "The Redeeming of Ruth." *The Nakedness of the Fathers: Biblical Visions and Revisions*. 169–75. New Brunswick: Rutgers University Press, 1994.

Ozick, Cynthia. "Ruth." *Metaphor and Memory*. 240–64. New York: Alfred A. Knopf, 1989.

Trible, Phyllis. "A Human Comedy." *God and the Rhetoric of Sexuality*. 166–99. Overtures to Biblical Theology. Philadelphia: Westminster John Knox Press, 1978.

GENERAL INDEX

INDEX OF SCRIPTURAL REFERENCES

Esther

Timothy K. Beal

for my parents,
Clay G. Beal
and
Geraldine Kandler Beal

CONTENTS

ACKNOWLEDGMENTS

I am indebted to many wonderful people. Many thanks to the spring 1998 students in the Hebrew Readings course at Eckerd College, some of whose comments and suggestions on the Hebrew text of Esther have been incorporated directly into my commentary here; to faculty colleagues at Eckerd College, especially Carolyn Johnston, Jim Goetsch, Gary Meltzer, Martha Nichols-Pecceu, and other members of the Unbearable Lightness of Discussion Group, whose close and curious readings of my earlier book on Esther, *The Book of Hiding,* opened new possibilities for me as I returned to the text once more; to Shirley Ruggles for administrative assistance again and again; to David Cotter, the senior editor of this commentary series, for critical reading and careful prodding; to true friends Deb Krause, Tod Linafelt, Sue Fendrick, and Bill Perman for taking me not too seriously while engaging me and my writing on more levels than I realize; to senior professor-colleagues, especially Walter Brueggemann, Rebecca Chopp, David Gunn, Carol Newsom, Gene Tucker, and Elie Wiesel for their dedication to teaching and for giving of themselves as mentors, models, and believing critics; and to Clover Reuter Beal for long-time love, friendship, and collegiality.

Finally, I dedicate this commentary to my parents, Geraldine Kandler Beal and Clay G. Beal, who have instilled in me an abiding love for the biblical text, even while we each wrestle relentlessly with it in very different ways. I am grateful for their love, their faith, their patience, and their exasperation. They are my first readers.

INTRODUCTION

A Strangely Familiar Fragment

Some ancient works of literature have survived in such fragmented form—bits and pieces of papyrus or pottery, a few words here, a few lines there—that it is difficult to imagine them as ever having been whole. Such is the case with many of the Dead Sea scrolls, for example, and with the work of the ancient Greek poet Sappho. Some have argued that this is also the case with certain biblical texts, including the book of Job and the prophet Micah. When reading such fragmented ancient texts, one is often powerfully aware of the *distance* between the reader and the text, between the contemporary and the ancient. The ancient text appears incommensurably strange.

In other cases, however, the ancient fragment appears so complete, so whole, that it is difficult to imagine it as a fragment. In these cases, one experiences a sense of nearness to the text and its ancient context, as though the historical differences between reader and text are insignificant. Such is the case for many reading Esther. On first reading it appears so simple, so whole, and its meaning so completely self-evident. Yet the closer one gets to this text, the more perplexing it becomes. Questions lead not to answers but to more profound questions, and a certain distance begins to open between reader and text. Rather than becoming more familiar upon further reading, it appears more and more strange, in some sense unknowable, like a letter fragment which arrives to us from a world that is otherwise inaccessible. That world is the world of the Jews in Persia during the time of the Diaspora, after the Babylonian Exile and before the Hellenistic period. Indeed, it is the only surviving work of literature from that context.

Esther is indeed strange and unfamiliar, a fragment lifted from the illegible ruins of a lost world. In another sense, however, it is profoundly familiar, even uncannily so. Long before Christian anti-Judaism and modern anti-Semitism, Esther tells a story of (among other things) anti-Judaism, of the survival of the Jewish people in the face of a government-supported attempt to project them as quintessentially other, or "not us," and to annihilate them as such. It also a story of sexism, in which the projection of women as other parallels the projection of Jews as other. As such it raises strikingly contemporary questions concerning relations between sexism, ethnocentrism, and national identity.

The Esther scroll is, moreover, the centerpiece of the Jewish festival of Purim.[1] At Purim, children and adults gather together, many in costume, to hear the scroll read aloud—indeed, to *participate* in its reading, as actors in a *Purimspiel* ("Purim play") or as an audience of fantastically noisy interpretation, jeering at Haman, cheering for Esther and Mordecai, and so on (others, such as the king and Vashti, often get mixed reviews). And of course drinking has traditionally played a major part in the celebration. In fact, in the Talmud (Megilla 7b), Raba says that one "should mellow oneself [with wine] on Purim until one cannot know the difference between 'cursed be Haman' [the anti-Jewish enemy in the story] and 'blessed be Mordecai' [one of the story's heroes]."

Indeed, the wild, carnivalesque festival of Purim, as a living, communally embodied interpretation of Esther, may be the most appropriate way to acknowledge both the wonderful strangeness and the troubling familiarity of this ancient text. It is a time when the familiar becomes strange and the strange becomes familiar, a time when distinctions between self and other blur, as do the rules of social hierarchy that normally guarantee those distinctions.

Method (Commentary Is Pointless)

If festivals and plays are perhaps the best interpretive approaches to Esther, what is the point in a commentary like this? Precisely. Commentary is pointless.

---

[1] From earliest Jewish tradition until today, Esther is commonly referred to as a "scroll," Megillah, rather than as a book, especially in the context of Purim (on which see below), when the story is read aloud from a traditional hand-written scroll version. However, the Talmud (Megillah 19a) also indicates that early on it was also called a "book" (*sēper*) and a "letter" (*ʾiggeret*). This commentary will refer to it as the Esther scroll when discussing it in its liturgical context of Purim, and will refer to it as the book of Esther when referring to it in its biblical context.

The word "method" comes from a Greek compound of *meta*, "with," and *hodos*, "way" or "road." Therefore a method in literary study is, most basically, the path one takes into a text and its various contexts. Some methods are largely excavative, aimed at revealing or extracting layers and infrastructures by digging, constructing inroads through unknown regions and thereby urbanizing them. This sort of excavative method (archeological, with plans for construction of a tourist information center on the site) has been typical in modern biblical studies as in literary studies more generally. Without dismissing the value of such methods in Esther studies, this commentary will attempt to make its way into the text more tentatively and (to carry the metaphor further) in a more environmentally sensitive manner. Leaving the bulldozers behind, it will attempt to find its way into the thickets of meaning; to explore textual spaces in ways that will not reduce them or close them off to subsequent explorers; to ask questions without assuming that there must be answers; to assume complexity, perplexity, and the importance of accidents; to approach in a way that does not close textual spaces off to other readers or reduce them to a single point.

Herein lies the value of commentary as a genre for literary analysis of Esther. Commentary is pointless; that is, insofar as it demands careful analysis of as much detail as possible, including those details in the text that do not necessarily "fit" into one's overall reading of the book as a whole, commentary works against the interpreter's desire to make a single point about the text as a whole. Commentary steers one's attention away from the general and toward the particular, away from the overall and toward the discontinuous. Although very traditional—indeed, one of the most ancient genres of biblical interpretation—it is not very wholesome. It works against building a whole interpretation, a total vision of the meaning of a text. Commentary is thus an important predecessor to contemporary literary theory and criticism, although it has received far less attention in this regard than its close cousin, midrash.[2]

The approach of this commentary is most closely identified in with rhetorical criticism, a trajectory of biblical criticism which was inaugurated in Hebrew Bible studies by the work of James Muilenburg.[3]

---

[2] On midrash and contemporary poststructuralist literary theory, see esp. Daniel Boyarin, *Intertextuality and the Reading of Midrash* (Bloomington: Indiana University Press, 1990).

[3] Esp. James Muilenburg, "Form Criticism and Beyond," *Journal of Biblical Literature* 88 (1969) 1–18. See also Phyllis Trible, *Rhetorical Criticism: Context, Method, and the Book of Jonah,* Guides to Biblical Scholarship (Minneapolis: Fortress Press,

Although it has taken on many different literary and form-critical nuances over the years since Muilenburg,[4] rhetorical criticism is fundamentally concerned with the particulars of the text, and thus runs counter to those approaches that aim to give a broad overview, presuming that you see more when you pull back from the text and view it from a distance. Rhetorical criticism presumes that the closer you look the more you see.

For Muilenburg, the aim of rhetorical criticism was to return scholarly focus to the particular details of the text in order (a) to better identify the boundaries of a particular textual unit (esp. in poetry as a form of speech) and (b) to recognize the intentionality of that particular textual unit. Muilenburg clearly saw rhetorical criticism as integrally related to form criticism, which had been inaugurated at the turn of the century by Hermann Gunkel but which Muilenburg and others believed had gotten lost in the work of categorizing and cataloguing various forms to such an extent that the particularities of the texts themselves were being ignored. In reemphasizing the particular details of particular texts, moreover, Muilenburg's rhetorical criticism also contributed to the rise of literary critical approaches in biblical studies.

In some respects, Muilenburg's rhetorical criticism pushed beyond Muilenburg's own understanding of its purpose in biblical criticism. For in its insistent and steadfast attention to textual details, rhetorical criticism not only identifies the boundaries and intentionality of a text, but also those elements that *blur* its boundaries and *split* its intentions. When practiced within the genre of commentary, these blurs and splits emerge all the more prominently.

Rhetorical criticism presumes that every detail is significant, including those details that may work against larger intentions within a particular text or a particular reading. Rhetorical criticism attends to tensions and ambivalences in the text, to what is said as well as what is not said. It considers how meanings are developed, and how these developments can build toward a whole narrative; but it also considers how this development is undermined, how the text doubles over its own intentions, how it fissures, how the dynamics of language and writing do more than what may be intended.[5] Rhetorical criticism,

---

1994); and Walter Brueggemann, *Theology of the Old Testament: Testimony, Dispute, Advocacy* (Minneapolis: Fortress Press, 1997) 54–60.

[4] For discussion of many of the different scholarly studies that have been carried out recently in the name of rhetorical criticism, see Phyllis Trible, *Rhetorical Criticism*, 25–87.

[5] One might describe these tensive dynamics as phenomena of deconstruction as described by Jacques Derrida. Contrary to many academically and intellectually

thus construed, is obviously compatible with the genre of commentary. Without reducing the text to a single point, rhetorical criticism allows a reader to follow movements as well as countermovements, to make connections, to draw parallels, and to look for structuring principles within the text without glossing over those particularities that introduce tension, anomaly, and blurring.

By describing my approach as emphasizing the particular over the general, and the tensive over the continuous, I am not altogether dismissing the importance of broader, overall interpretations of the book of Esther, especially those focusing on narrative structure. Michael V. Fox, for example, has shown convincingly how the series of reversals within the Esther narrative function like Aristotelian *peripety*, in which the result of an action turns out to be the exact reverse of what was expected (summarized with regard to Mordecai and the Jews in 9:1).[6] Fox has also shown how these reversals play out through a series of five interrelated pairs of banquets, or drinking parties.[7] Drawing from Fox's earlier work on *peripety*, furthermore, Sandra Beth Berg has argued that the entire narrative is structured as a chiasm, the center of which is the royal procession of Mordecai (to Haman's shame) in chapter 6.[8] Yet no structural interpretation comprehends every element or every interconnection within the narrative. Indeed, there are other interconnections within the narrative that appear to work against reading Esther entirely in terms of reversals, let alone as a chiasm. In the present

---

irresponsible caricatures, deconstruction is not an iconoclastic method. Indeed, as Derrida has made clear on numerous occasions, it is not a method at all, but rather a phenomenon of textuality and writing; that is, deconstruction happens. See esp. Jacques Derrida, "Letter to a Japanese Friend," *Derrida and Différance*, ed. D. Wood and R. Bernasconi (Coventry: Parousia Press, 1985). For a clear and accessible introduction to Derrida, see John D. Caputo, ed., *Deconstruction in a Nutshell: A Conversation with Jacques Derrida. With a Commentary by John D. Caputo* (New York: Fordham University Press, 1997).

[6] Michael V. Fox, "The Structure of the Book of Esther," *Isac L. Seeligmann Volume*, ed. A. Rofé and Y. Zakovitch (Jerusalem, 1983) 291–304, cited in Michael V. Fox, *Character and Ideology in the Book of Esther* (Columbia: University of South Carolina Press, 1991), 159 n. 13. For a summary and further development of Fox's earlier structural analysis, see his discussion in *Character and Ideology*, 157–63.

[7] See esp. Fox, *Character and Ideology*, 157.

[8] Sandra Beth Berg, *The Book of Esther: Motifs, Themes, and Structure* (Missoula: Scholars Press, 1979) 103–13; and "After the Exile: God and History in the Books of the Chronicles and Esther," *The Divine Helmsman*, ed. J. L. Crenshaw and S. Sandmel (New York: Ktav, 1980) 115–8. Berg refers to a prepublication copy of Fox's 1983 essay. These and other overall structural interpretations of the narrative will be discussed in the commentary as they are relevant to the discussion.

commentary and in an earlier study, for example, I identify a strong literal and thematic relationship between the story of Vashti's refusal of the king's command in chapter 1 and the story of Mordecai's refusal to honor Haman in chapter 3.[9] These parallels suggest a certain solidarity between Vashti and the Mordecai over against the royal order of things, along with the collective identities represented by them, as those who have been marked off as "other" in order to shore up a certain construal of national identity. Once this narrative parallel is recognized, a larger series of convergences emerge involving Vashti as "other woman," Mordecai as "other Jew," and Esther as both "other woman" and "other Jew," so that it is no longer possible to read the story of Vashti's banishment in chapter 1 simply as a preface to the "real" story concerning Jewish identity, necessary primarily in order to make space in the royal court for the new Queen Esther.

The book of Esther is richly complex with interconnections between scenes, relational dynamics, words, phrases, and narrative patterns. These interconnections must be allowed to stand in tension with one another. To claim that it is organized around any single motif, theme, or set of connections is to lose this rich and complex textual interplay within the narrative.

History-Likeness

Although this commentary attends primarily to the literary details of the text, it is neither ahistorical (unconscious of historical particularities of the text and of the reader) nor antihistoricist (unwilling to recognize the importance of such historical differences). At the same time, while conscious of the historical differences that separate readers today from Esther and its contexts, we must be extremely tentative concerning what we know and what we *can* know about the worlds behind this text. In fact, the book of Esther often appears to be less a resource than a problem for historical research into Second Temple Judaism and the Persian period.

As mentioned earlier, the Esther narrative is set in the context of the Jewish Diaspora in Persia, after the Persians under Cyrus defeated the Babylonians in 539 B.C.E., and after many Jews had returned to Judah with Cyrus's support (Ezra 1-3). As such it is our only surviving text from the eastern Diaspora during the early Second Temple period.

---

[9] Timothy K. Beal, *The Book of Hiding: Gender, Ethnicity, Annihilation, and Esther* (London and New York: Routledge, 1997) esp. 54–9, 112–4.

Ahasuerus in the book of Esther can be positively identified as the Hebrew name for Xerxes I, son of Darius, who ruled Persia from 485–465 B.C.E. (see the commentary on 1:1-4). Given those dates, the events in the book of Esther are set in the middle of his reign, roughly between 483 and 474 B.C.E. (cf. 1:1; 2:16; 3:7). However, although the narrative is set in this context, the Hebrew text as we have it now was not written at that time. It took something close to its final form at a much later date, probably in the later Persian period during the fourth or third century B.C.E.[10]

In many respects, the narrative is historically realistic, given what we know of Persian history from other sources, especially the Greek historian Herodotus. For example, many of the practices and features of Persian government depicted in the narrative are compatible with what we know from extrabiblical sources, including the king's reliance on royal advisors (1:13-15), his honoring of those who help him (esp. ch. 6), feasting while lounging on couches (7:8), and the well-organized and efficient postal network (3:13-15; 8:10-14; 9:20, 30). Moreover, the narrative draws frequently from Persian vocabulary, including *partĕmîm*, ("nobles," 1:3), *bîtan* ("palace" or "pavilion," 1:5), *pitgān* ("edict," 1:20), *ginzîm* ("treasuries," 3:9), *ʾaḥašdarpĕnîm* ("satraps"?, 3:12; 8:9), and *ʾaḥaštĕrānîm* ("royal horses," 8:10). All of the names of the king's eunuchs and advisors (1:10, 14), as well as the names of Haman's sons (9:6-9), are believable as Persian names, and some have been found in extra-biblical documents.[11] Finally, although its style is certainly farci-

---

[10] Most scholars today consider the latest possible date for the composition of the Masoretic text (MT) to be before or during the Maccabean period (167–135 B.C.E.). It certainly dates earlier than the LXX, which is a translation of it (on which see below, "The Three Esthers"). The complete lack of Greek words in the MT text, along with the presence of many Old Persian and Aramaic words and constructions, moreover, probably indicates a pre-Hellenistic date (i.e., before Alexander the Great conquered Persia in 333 B.C.E.); Hans Striedl, "Untersuchung zur Syntax und Stilistik des hebräischen Buches Esther," *Zeitschrift für die Alttestamentliche Wissenschaft* 55 (1937) 73–108. For a clear and concise discussion of the date(s) of composition, see esp. Carey A. Moore, "Esther, Book of," *Anchor Bible Dictionary* 2 (1992) 641; see also Jon D. Levenson, *Esther: A Commentary*, Old Testament Library (Louisville: Westminster John Knox Press, 1997) 26–7.

[11] On the historicity of events and the late Hebrew vocabulary of MT Esther, including a catalog of purported Persian names and vocabulary in the book of Esther, see esp. Paton, *Esther*, 62–71; see also H. S. Gehman, "Notes on the Persian Words in the Book of Esther," *Journal of Biblical Literature* 43 (1924) 321–8; the discussion is updated in A. R. Millard, "The Persian Names in Esther and the Reliability of the Hebrew Text," *Journal of Biblical Literature* 96 (1977) 481–8; and briefly summarized and supplemented in Moore, "Esther," 638.

cal, the portrayal of King Ahasuerus in the book of Esther as insecure, impulsive, and prone to fits of rage bears a striking resemblance to extra-biblical depictions of him. Note, moreover, that Xerxes's actual reign ended when he was assassinated by his own palace officials (compare the attempted assassination in Esth 1:21-23).[12]

In other respects, however, the narrative is quite unrealistic, ranging from the unlikely to the outrageous. It seems unlikely, for example, that the king would have appointed two non-Persians, Haman the Agagite and Mordecai the Jew, to the position of prime minister (3:1; 10:3), and even less likely that a non-Persian named Esther would have been made queen.[13] Nor is there any precedent for royal decrees such as those in chapters 1, 3, and 8 being issued in multiple languages and multiple scripts (Aramaic was the common language of the Persian empire, and certainly would have been used universally for issuing such decrees). And of course the content of the decrees themselves—one announcing the dethronement of a queen for refusing to come when called and thereby enforcing a patriarchal sexual politics (1:19-22), one calling for the annihilation of all Jews on a single day (3:12-15), and one calling for the annihilation of all those who would have annihilated all Jews (8:9-14)—are each quite outlandish. Likewise, that the Jews could kill over seventy-five thousand people without suffering a single casualty of their own (9:1-19), and without this mass slaughter being mentioned in any other ancient text, is beyond credible.

Indeed, the amount of blood spilled in the story is matched only by the amount of wine poured. The king's half-year-long party for all his officials (1:1-4), not to mention a week-long party for all the people of Susa (1:5-8) is beyond exorbitant, as is the pageant-like selection process for replacing Vashti, involving every beautiful young woman in the empire (as many as one thousand four hundred sixty before Esther's turn comes, depending on when the pageant started)[14] in a full year of cosmetic treatments (2:12-14).

Clearly, then, although there are elements within the text that are historically realistic, what we are reading here is not historiography in anything close to a modern sense of the term. Granted, the elements of

---

[12] Lewis Bayles Paton, *The Book of Esther*, International Critical Commentary XX (New York: Charles Scribner's Sons, 1908) 121. Depending on how one translates 2:5-6, there may also be a serious chronological error which would put Mordecai at over one hundred years old. See the commentary on those verses.

[13] Herodotus (3:84) indicates that the Persian king would have been allowed to marry only the daughters of seven noble families. Elsewhere (7:114; 9:112), Herodotus gives Amestris as the name of Xerxes's queen during this time.

[14] Paton, *Esther*, 183.

historical realism give the narrative a sense of "history-likeness," to borrow from Hans Frei's description of biblical narrative. Yet this likeness serves to set off its more outrageous, even carnivalesque dimensions all the more.[15] Indeed, to call these claims within the narrative "literary embellishments" is to understate things almost as radically as the text overstates them. This is a boldly excessive, sometimes enchantingly and sometimes horribly unbelievable narrative, in which history-likeness blends with outlandishness in truly remarkable ways.

The Three Esthers

The story of Esther has survived in three distinct but related ancient versions: two of them, the Septuagint (LXX) and the Alpha Text (AT) are Greek, and the other, the Masoretic text (MT), is Hebrew.[16] The MT is the basis for most English translations (including the NRSV) and is the canonical Esther for Protestant and Jewish traditions. The LXX, which is most basically a translation of the MT text (or of an ancient Hebrew text very close to it) to which six additions (A through F) have been made, is the canonical Esther for Roman Catholic and Orthodox Christian traditions. The AT, which also includes additions A–F but which differs significantly from LXX and the MT in other respects, does not hold canonical status in a surviving religious tradition.

[15]On Esther and the literary carnivalesque, see esp. Kenneth Craig, *Reading Esther: A Case for the Literary Carnivalesque,* Literary Currents in Biblical Interpretation (Louisville: Westminster/John Knox, 1995) and the discussion of that work in the commentary on Esther 9. Note that categorizations of the book of Esther according to the genre of "diaspora novella" tend to disregard the centrality of this text for the establishment and annual celebration of Purim—despite the numerous ways in which this narrative obviously lends itself to public reading and festal, participatory interpretation.

In a recent and highly insightful study, "The Book of Esther and the Festival of Purim: A Megillah Provides an Avenue for Social Change," presented at the XVIth Congress of the IOSOT, Oslo, August 2–7, 1998, Heather McKay relates Esther and Purim to anthropologist Victor Turner's account of how social groups address issues of marginality and liminality through the celebration of festivals. She shows how celebrations of Purim and the book of Esther "address, and allow room for fresh thought about, some of the most disturbing questions in modern Jewish life," including the transgression of traditional gender roles.

[16]There are also two Esther Targumim (Targum Sheni and Targum Rishon), which are Aramaic translations and renarrations of a text very close to the Hebrew MT.

Thanks to the careful researches of David J.A. Clines and Michael V. Fox, the genealogical relationships between these three versions and their literary traditions have emerged quite clearly.[17] Although there are significant differences between Clines and Fox, both scholars provide much data indicating that, while the LXX is basically a translation of MT Esther, the AT (less the six additions) is closer to MT Esther, and both the AT and the MT derive more or less directly from a Hebrew *Vorlage*.[18] The additions A–F were added to both the LXX and the AT at a much later date, and both Greek texts were then reworked in order to incorporate those additions smoothly.[19]

The result of this complex literary history is three very different stories. Insofar as the AT and MT derive from the same *Vorlage* ("proto-Esther"/"pre-MT"), they are more closely related to one another than either one is to the LXX. Insofar as the AT and the LXX are both Greek texts, and insofar as both incorporate the six additions which are not included in the MT, they are more closely related to one another than either one is to the MT. The fact is that they are all interrelated but nonetheless, in their "final" forms (i.e., in the forms we now have), significantly different from one another. These differences demand that each text be treated as a separate work of literature.

Although there are significant differences within the narrative materials held in common by these three texts, the most radical differences between them are found in the six additions to the LXX and AT. Perhaps most significantly, these additions give the story of Esther overriding theological and religious dimensions that are altogether absent from the MT text, which makes no mention whatsoever of either God or Jewish religious practice (see the subsequent discussion). As I have argued elsewhere, moreover, Addition A, which includes Mordecai's dream and his warning to the king about the eunuch's planned assassination, changes the beginning of the Esther story quite radically,

---

[17] David J.A. Clines, *The Esther Scroll: The Story of the Story* (Sheffield: Sheffield Academic Press, 1984); and Michael V. Fox, *The Redaction of the Book of Esther: On Reading Composite Texts* (Atlanta: Scholars Press, 1991). See also the pioneering study by Charles C. Torrey, "The Older Book of Esther," *Harvard Theological Review* 37 (1944) 1–40.

[18] Called "proto-Esther" in Fox, *Redaction,* 9; and "pre-MT" in Clines, *The Esther Scroll,* 140. Less than a century ago, the dominant scholarly view was that the AT was the Lucianic recension of the LXX (e.g., Paton, *Esther,* 37–8). Major differences between these two texts were considered to be a result of the poor source copy Lucian was using.

[19] See also Carey A. Moore, "On the Origins of the LXX Additions to the Book of Esther," *Journal of Biblical Literature* 92 (1973) 382–93; and *Daniel, Esther, and Jeremiah: The Additions,* Anchor Bible (Garden City: Doubleday, 1977).

making it impossible for readers to identify with Vashti as heroine, and impossible to draw parallels between, on the one hand, Vashti's refusal and the subsequent decree against the woman-as-other in chapter 1, and, on the other, Mordecai's refusal and the subsequent decree against the Jew-as-other in chapter 3.[20] This radical change in narrative beginning is accomplished by Addition A's alignment of Mordecai with the king (who is presented as far cooler and nobler in both Greek versions), and thus over against Vashti, who in turn ends up associated with the plotting eunuchs and Haman.

Needless to say, although the three versions of Esther are related to one another genealogically, it is a mistake to try to analyze them together (unless, of course, one's interest is in the redaction history of the literature). Each tells a different story—not only through the additions or lack thereof, but throughout their texts—and each deserves to be attended to on its own. It must be emphasized, therefore, that this is a commentary on the MT Esther,[21] and the particulars of the two Greek versions will be consulted primarily in reference to issues of textual criticism and translation of the MT text.[22]

Hiding God, God Hiding, Hiding God Hiding (Until One Cannot Know)

Remarkably, God is never mentioned in MT Esther. Indeed, it and the Song of Songs are the only two texts in the Hebrew Bible that never mention God. In the narrative of Esther, this absence appears to be part

---

[20] Timothy K. Beal, "Tracing Esther's Beginnings," *A Feminist Companion to Esther, Judith and Susanna*, ed. Athalya Brenner (Sheffield: Sheffield Academic Press, 1995).

[21] This commentary is based on the Hebrew text as presented in the standard critical edition, *Biblia Hebraica Stuttgartensia*. Unless otherwise noted, English translations will be from the New Revised Standard Version (NRSV).

[22] For a well intended, responsible, genuinely interfaith attempt at presenting a commentary on both the MT and the LXX simultaneously, see Levenson (1997), in which analyses of the Greek Additions are inserted where they would appear in the LXX version of the narrative. Admittedly a compromise, this approach necessarily confuses the two very different Esther narratives, creating a new bilingual hybrid. A (much needed) commentary on the LXX should include commentary on the entire Greek text, not just the additions, insofar as there are major differences between the LXX and the MT even in the narrative material that they have in common. By inserting analyses of the Greek additions into the commentary on MT Esther, moreover, the continuity of that narrative is broken.

of its craft. That is, it is not simply that there was no appropriate place to include mention of God, but rather that God was intentionally written out, or perhaps veiled, from the story world of the text.

As will be clear throughout this commentary, the book of Esther is in subtle dialogue with many other biblical texts, including the Joseph narratives, Samuel, and Deuteronomy, as well as, to some extent, wisdom literature and the Exodus/Passover traditions. These intertextual dimensions integrate the book of Esther within the larger dialogical space of canonical Scripture. Given these connections between Esther and other Scriptures, the absence of any reference to God, or to anything that can be clearly identified with Jewish religious practice, is all the more remarkable. Indeed, it would require a concerted effort to avoid theological issues while remaining in conversation with these other biblical texts, for in these other texts God is invariably acknowledged to be present and active.

The fact that God is under erasure in MT Esther is further indicated by recent scholarship on the relation of this text to the AT and their shared *Vorlage*, as discussed above. Apart from the later Greek additions, Clines identifies nine religious references (to God or gods) that are present in the main body of the AT but not in the MT.[23] Clines argues convincingly that at least some of these religious "pluses" in the main body of the AT reflect religious elements that were present in the earlier Hebrew *Vorlage* for both the AT and the MT. He concludes, therefore, "that MT represents a systematic attempt to remove religious language."[24] Thus our text appears to be *hiding God*.

What is the theological significance of hiding God in Esther? In the Talmud, this question is addressed through a reading of the name Esther (*ʾstr* without vowel points) as a first person imperfect form of the verb *str*, "hide." Thus in Talmud Hullin 139b the question is asked, "Where is Esther [*ʾstr*] indicated in the Torah?" The answer is a quotation from Deuteronomy 31:18, where God declares, "And I will surely hide [*hstr ʾstr* without vowel points] my face [or 'presence'] from them."[25] In this passage from the Talmud, then, the Esther scroll is read as a story of *divine* hiding. That is, Esther's name conveys the message, via Deut 31:18, that God is hiding from the Jews in this story. Thus *hiding God* in Esther suggests *God hiding*.

---

[23] Clines, *The Esther Scroll*, 107–12.

[24] Ibid., 113.

[25] See also Talmud Megilla 13a, in which Rabbi Judah says that, although Esther's actual name was Hadassah, she was called Esther "because she hid facts about herself" (referring to the fact that she "did not reveal her people" to the king initially [2:10, 20]).

Given the connection of Esther to Deuteronomy 31, however, this assertion in the Talmud that God is hiding in the story of Esther is far from reassuring. In fact, it assures *divine unavailability* as a consequence of divine judgment. In the passage from Deuteronomy, God is telling Moses that after he dies, the people of Israel

> will forsake me, breaking my covenant that I have made with them. My anger will be kindled against them in that day. I will forsake them and *hide my face* from them; they will become easy prey, and many terrible troubles will come upon them. In that day they will say, "Have not these troubles come upon us because our God is not in our midst?" On that day *I will surely hide my face* on account of all the evil they have done by turning to other gods. (Deut 31:16b-18)

Certainly any allusion to this passage offers little comfort or reassurance to a Jewish community in Diaspora. In relation to the story of Esther, it would only suggest that they will find no divine deliverance from the "terrible troubles"[26] they are facing. Indeed, as an intertext for Esther, this passage would suggest the absence of God and that their troubles are their own fault. The fact that this passage from Deuteronomy is typically interpreted as a reference to the Babylonian Exile as divine punishment would certainly add salt to the wound.[27] There is no blessed assurance in this rabbinic interpretation of God hiding.

By contrast, many modern scholars find the hiddenness of God to be, paradoxically, a clear and undeniable reference to the veiled presence of God in this story world. One might describe this interpretive stratagy as *hiding God hiding*. That is, the absence of any explicit reference to God is taken, by those who have eyes to see and ears to hear, to be a clear affirmation of God working providentially on behalf of the Jews throughout the story. Most recently, for example, Frederic W. Bush believes that divine providence is affirmed in two ways: (a) in the denouement of the narrative (9:6-32), especially in the joyful celebration that "they gained relief from their enemies," assuming that this language of relief or deliverance subtly implies a divine reliever or deliverer; and (b) in the problem-based plot of the story, in which deliverance is accomplished by the complimentary efforts of Mordecai,

---

[26] It is striking to note that "terrible troubles" is a translation of two words, *rāʿôt* ("evils," "calamities") and *ṣārôt* ("enemies"), both of which are used in the book of Esther (in singular rather than plural forms) to describe Haman (see esp. 7:6).

[27] Compare also Gen 4:14, in which Cain, in a state of terror after being cursed by God, says to God, "I will be hidden [*ʾessātēr*; unpointed *ʾstr*] from your face/presence."

Esther, and God.[28] Similarly, while recognizing that the text stands at a "considerable distance from the sacral institutions of ancient Israel, especially as they were developing in the Second Temple period," Levenson agrees with Berg that the narrative implies "a hidden causality behind the surface of human history."[29]

This commentary will neither affirm nor deny such theological claims on the text, but it will problematize them. The text certainly allows for such a theological hermeneutic. At the same time, however, it allows equally for a reading that makes no recourse whatsoever to God-talk of any kind. Nothing is obviously or necessarily theological about this story. But neither is there anything obviously or necessarily atheological or atheistic about it. To borrow Abraham D. Cohen's well-known description of *Purim*, we might say that, with regard to theology, the entire book of Esther stands within the canon of Scripture as *"the appellation of a problem . . .* Do chance and determinism rule supreme in the universe, or does God?"[30] We might also want to distinguish between chance and human determinism. At any rate, the narrative does not demand an either/or answer to such questions. Rather, it seems to insist on the survival of the question over any and every answer—to borrow again, this time from Raba, "until one cannot know."

[28] Frederic W. Bush, *Ruth, Esther,* Word Biblical Commentary (Dallas: Word Books, 1996) 327–35.

[29] Levenson, *Esther,* 18, 21; Berg, *The Book of Esther,* 178.

[30] Abraham D. Cohen, "'Hu Ha-goral': The Religious Significance of Esther," *Judaism* 23 (1974) 94.

Chapter 1

BEGINNING WITH THE END OF VASHTI

Esther 1:1-22

Too often Esther 1, the story of Vashti, is treated simply as a preface to the "real" story of Jewish survival in the face of attempted nation-wide genocide. That is, the main purpose of Vashti's story is often seen as stage-setting: it introduces the character of the king and it opens up a spot in the palace for Queen Esther. But such prefatory readings miss the many important ways in which this narrative opening will trace its way through the rest of the story, making the book of Esther not simply a story concerned with issues of Jewish identity and anti-Judaism, but also a story profoundly concerned with issues of gender identity and sexism, and with the interrelations between the "othering" dynamics of sexism (which projects women as other) and anti-Judaism (which projects Jews as other).[1]

What becomes especially clear as the political space takes shape in chapter 1 is that the political ordering of the king's nation and of national identity implicate and are implicated by the political ordering of the sexes and sexual identity. This interrelationship between sexual politics and national politics—as well as the unstable and problematic ways by which "us" and "them," self and other, are constructed and reconstructed in terms of gender and ethnic identities—will be very significant as the story develops.

---

[1] This interrelation is analyzed in detail in Timothy K. Beal, *The Book of Hiding: Gender, Ethnicity, Annihilation, and Esther* (London and New York: Routledge, 1997). See also Beal, "Tracing Esther's Beginnings," 87-110, which compares this opening to MT Esther with the openings of the LXX and the AT.

Chapter 1 can be divided into two parts: (a) 1:1-4, the first drinking party, hosted by King Ahasuerus;[2] and (b) 1:5-22, two simultaneous drinking parties, one hosted by the king and the other hosted by Queen Vashti (v. 9). The king's first party (vv. 1-4) lasts for 180 days, and his second party (vv. 5-8, 9-22) lasts for seven days. The length of Vashti's party (v. 9) is not specified, but it obviously ends, along with her queendom, on the seventh day of the king's second party. The narrative moves quickly through the first party of 180 days. It then slows down on the second, seven-day party, dwelling especially on the seventh day (1:10-22). Narrative pace thus runs opposite to the chronology it presents: 180 days get a few verses (really just vv. 3b-4), the first six days of the second party get four verses (vv. 5-8), and the seventh day of the second party gets thirteen verses (vv. 10-22). Within the flow, moreover, note that the narrative pace slows down most dramatically immediately following mention of Vashti's party in verse 9. She stops the flow of time, and she will stop the flow of the wine, too—at least temporarily.

All the events in chapter 1 are set in the context of drinking parties (NRSV "banquets"). Like the book of Esther as a whole, the story of Vashti's refusal and subsequent ostracization begins and ends with drinking. In the middle, we find more drinking. The fact that drinking—indeed, lots of drinking—is what these "banquets" are all about is clear not only from the word designating them (*mišteh*, which is a noun form of the verb *šātah*, "drink"), but also from the details that are given to describe them: the different kinds of drinking vessels used (vv. 7-8); the great potency and quantity and of the wine (v. 7); the manner of drinking ("without restraint") that the king wants his guests to enjoy (v. 8); and the description of the king as "merry with wine" (v. 10).[3]

It would be a mistake, however, to divorce drinking from politics in the story world of Esther. Indeed, in the book of Esther nearly all major political determinations are made around wine and under its influence. The place and time for drinking is also often the place and time for defining "us" over against "them," and for consigning "them" to oblivion.

---

[2] These verses also include a brief sketch of the historical setting of the story (1:1-3a). Contrary to the impression given by the NRSV translation, however, this sketch does not constitute a stand-alone division within the chapter, insofar as it is presented as a lead-in to the focus of vv. 1-4, namely, the first drinking party. See the discussion of these verses below.

[3] For these reasons, this commentary will translate *mišteh* as "drinking party" throughout the narrative.

THE FIRST DRINKING PARTY (1:1-4)

The opening words in the opening verse, "this happened in the days of . . ." (*wayhî bîmê;* more literally, "and it was in the days of"), set the story in the distant past, giving the introduction to this narrative the quality of a legend. The NRSV translates verse 1 as a stand-alone sentence: "This happened in the days of Ahasuerus, the same Ahasuerus who ruled over one hundred twenty-seven provinces from from India to Ethiopia." When rendered thus, these opening lines are made to focus on the political setting of Ahasuerus's reign over Persia. But the more common sense of the opening verb, *wayhî* ("and it happened . . ."), and *bayyāmîm hāhēm k–* ("in those days when . . .") which introduces verse 2, would suggest translating the opening two verses as incomplete, leading one to skip quickly over the background given there and on into the main focus of the action in verse 3a, namely that the king gave a drinking party (on which see below). Although cumbersome by today's standards for English narrative style, these opening verses might be better translated as follows: "*And it happened in the days of* Ahasuerus, who ruled over one hundred twenty-seven provinces from India to Ethiopia, *in those days when* King Ahasuerus sat on the throne in the citadel of Susa, *in the third year of his reign,* that he gave a drinking party. . . ." Thus the brief sketch of the historical context is presented mainly as a lead-in to the primary royal subject of the story, namely King Ahasuerus as a literary character, and his actions, namely partying.[4]

It is interesting to note that this opening phrase ("and it was in the days of . . .") is identical to the opening phrase of Ruth 1:1 (see also the same opening in Gen 14:1; Isa 7:1; and Jer 1:3). In Ruth this phrase

---

[4] The name Ahasuerus can be positively identified with Xerxes I, son of Darius, who reigned over the Persian empire from 485 to 465 B.C.E. Given his character in the Esther narrative, it is interesting to note that this king was known for his "weak and passionate disposition" and that his rule was ended by assassination (Paton, *The Book of Esther,* 121). For problems in locating this story within that historical period, see the introduction. The qualifier in verse 1a, "the same one who ruled over . . ." (lit. "that is, Ahasuerus who ruled . . ."), probably serves to distinguish this Ahasuerus from the Ahasuerus mentioned in Dan 9:1 who may have been the father of Darius the Mede. Concerning the significance of the time of this narrative beginning, "in the third year of his reign" (v. 3a), Midrash Esther Rabbah suggests that this refers to "the third year of making [or working on] the throne," that is, he threw this party for his officials once he had secured his reign. This would add to the sense of security and stability with regard to the king's reign as the story begins.

introduces a story that takes place "in the days of the judges who judged" over Israel (before being unified as a nation under a monarch) during a time of "great famine" (Ruth 1:1). In Esther, by contrast, these words introduce a story that takes place centuries later, after the northern kingdom (Israel) and southern kingdom (Judah) have been destroyed, "in the days of Ahasuerus, that is, Ahasuerus who ruled" over Persia during a time of great security and prosperity.[5] Ruth begins in the land of Israel during a time of lack, whereas Esther begins outside the land of Israel during a time of plenitude.

That this is a time of prosperity and security for Ahasuerus's kingdom is emphasized by the two verbs identified with this subject: the participle *hammōlēk* ("who ruled") and the infinitive *kěšebet* ("when he sat" or "rested"). The territory governed by the first verb, "one hundred twenty-seven provinces from India to Ethiopia," expresses the vastness of his dominion. Indeed, following the lead of Talmud Megillah 11a, many scholars take the number 127 to be a symbolic rendering of the entire known world. For example, Paton suggests that the number is a combination of three numbers—*twelve* times *ten* plus *seven*—each signifying totality, completeness, rest, and/or security in other Hebrew texts.[6] Given this context, the second verb, *kěšebet*, carries the sense of "resting securely" (thus Talmud Megilla 11b).

The term for "province" *(mědînâ)* is probably not synonymous with "satrap" *(ʾaḥašdarpěnîm)*,[7] which was the standard governmental division within the ancient Persian empire. It appears from other ancient sources (esp. Herodotus's history and inscriptions from the King Darius of Persia) that the Persians claimed, at most, just over thirty satraps—at any rate, nowhere near one hundred twenty-seven. Therefore either the number in 1:2 is way off or *mědînâ* should be understood as a further subdivision of the empire into still smaller regions, perhaps based on ethnic identity or common language.[8] In support of this interpretation, see Esth 3:12, which refers to "the king's satraps

---

[5] The parallel between these two narrative openings is further developed by the use in both texts of Qal participles to describe the leadership of the respective rulers: "judge[s] judging *[haššōpṭîm]*" in Ruth 1:1a, and "Ahasuerus ruling *[hammōlēk]*" in Esther 1:1a.

[6] Paton, *Esther*, 123.

[7] This is the plural form, which occurs in Esth 3:12; 8:9; and 9:3. It appears to be closely related the Persian word *Khshatařpâvan* (cf. the Greek transliteration *exatrapēs* or *satrapēs*), as well as to the name Ahasuerus. Compare Ezra 8:36; and see Paton, *Esther*, 123–24.

[8] Cf. the use of *mědînâ* to describe Judah as a "province" during the Persian period in Ezra 2:1; Neh 7:6; and 1:3.

[*ʾaḥašdarpĕnîm*] and . . . the governors over all the provinces [*mĕdînôt*]." As discussed in the introduction, whether or not these terms can be made to jibe with what we know from others sources about the expanse and structure of the Persian empire during the fifth century B.C.E., it is a mistake to assume that this opening context establishes the Esther narrative as an historical record in any modern sense. On the other hand, insofar as it engages history, it may also blur the lines we so often assume to divide history and literature, record and recollection.

As mentioned earlier, the historical background in verses 1-3 is not presented for its own sake but is given as context for the main action, namely that the king "threw a drinking party [NRSV 'gave a banquet,' on which see above] for all his officials and ministers" (1:3a). The guests at this party are further specified in the next part of the verse: the "army [*ḥêl*, 'might'] of Persia and Media and the nobles and governors [*śārê*, 'officials'] of the provinces"(1:3b). The precise sense of these terms is not clear, especially when considered in relation to the previous references to "officials" (*śārîm*, the same word translated as "governors" in v. 3b) and "ministers" (or "servants"). In the Hebrew text it is not clear whether this is a continuation of the list begun in verse 3a, or whether these new terms are subcategories under the general categories "officials and ministers," as the NRSV translation suggests. Moreover, several scholars doubt whether the whole army would have been invited. Thus Moore, following the LXX, suggests that *śārê*, "officials of," be inserted before "army," making the text of verse 3b read that "all the *officials of* the army of Persia Media . . . were present."[9] As another alternative Bush, following Gerleman, suggests reading *ḥêl* not as "army" but as "nobility" or "aristocracy."[10] Given other uses of this term in similar contexts, however, it appears unlikely that it would have nothing to do with the military. Indeed, given the extravagance of the king's party in other respects, why not read it as indicating that the entire army (or at least all its leadership) is present for this party?[11] That is, the text claims that *everyone that is anyone* in the Persian empire is present—leaving the rest of the empire without leadership or protection. After all, the duration of this party is also excessive: one hundred

---

[9] Carey A. Moore, *Esther* (AB; Garden City: Doubleday, 1971) 5.

[10] Frederic W. Bush, *Ruth, Esther,* Word Bibiblical Commentary (Dallas: Word Books, 1996) 347; Gillis Gerleman, *Esther,* BKAT (Neukirchen-Vluyn: Neukirchener Verlag, 1982) 54-5.

[11] Along this same interpretive line, I have suggested elsewhere (*Book of Hiding,* 126) that the term might be read most literally as "might" or "strength," thus indicating that all the primary representatives of the Persian power structure are present. Cf. 8:11, which can be read similarly.

and eighty days (1:4)! In every respect, then, this party is extravagant to the point of logistical impossibility. This may be taken as indication of the king's excessive (if not exactly wise or prudent) confidence in the security of his empire.

These subordinate guests in verses 3-4 are described as being "in his presence" *(lĕpānāyw)*, or more literally, "to his face." The phrase "in the presence of" (the construct *lipnê* or something closely related) occurs nine times in chapter 1 alone, all in reference to the king. Here, and throughout the subsequent narrative, it connotes control: to be in the king's presence is to be under his control—at least by all appearances. The hierarchical social order, on top of which the king appears to be "resting securely" (1:2), is maintained so long as other subjects within that order remain "in his face," or at least so long as they can be brought there easily. As Vashti will make clear, simply refusing to be brought into the king's presence can introduce a profound sense of royal insecurity.

The king's objective in hosting this first party (and by extension the second as well) is made clear in verse 4, namely, to "display the great wealth of his kingdom and the splendor [or 'honor'] and pomp of his majesty." The term translated in the NRSV as "splendor" *(yĕqār)*, but which is normally translated "honor," deserves special attention. It occurs 10 times in the book of Esther alone (1:4, 20; 6:3, 6 [2x], 7, 9 [2x], 11; and 8:16)—more than anywhere else in the Hebrew Bible—and it is frequently associated with "greatness" or "majesty" *(gĕdûlâ)*, as it is here in 1:4.[12] Invariably in Esther it refers to the *public display and consolidation of power over against another's humiliation and/or subordination*, in much the same way as developed in recent anthropologies of honor and shame.[13] Thus in 1:20 it refers to the subordination of women by honoring their husbands (or "lords"); in chapter 6, it will be used to describe Mordecai's public honor over against Haman's shame; and in 8:16 it will refer to the honor of the Jews collectively, whose public exaltation at that point is linked to fear and emulation of them among

[12] The next most frequent usage is in the Aramaic material of Daniel (2:6, 37; 4:27, 33; 5:18, 20; 7:14), where it is likewise best translated in terms of honor.

[13] See esp. Lillian R. Klein, "Honor and Shame in Esther," *The Feminist Companion to Esther, Judith and Susanna,* Athalya Brenner, ed. (Sheffield: Sheffield Academic Press, 1995) 149-75. For background on honor-shame anthropology, see Julian Pitt-Rivers, *The Fate of Shechem or The Politics of Sex: Essays in the Anthropology of the Mediterranean* (Cambridge: Cambridge University Press, 1977); and J. G. Peristiany and Julian Pitt-Rivers, *Honour and Grace in Anthropology* (Cambridge: Cambridge University Press, 1992). On relations between honor, patriarchal domination, and other socio-economic hierarchies of power, see especially Jane Schneider, "Of Vigilance and Virgins," *Ethnology* 9 (1971) 1-24.

non-Jewish Persians (8:17). To have honor, then, is to have publicly recognized status and power over against another's public subordination. The king's aim for the parties in chapter 1 is to "display" his
honor and greatness "in the presence of" those under him.

THE SECOND AND THIRD DRINKING PARTIES (1:5-22)

"When these days were completed, the king gave for all the people
present in the citadel of Susa, both great and small, a drinking party
[NRSV 'banquet'] lasting for seven days, in the court of the garden of the
king's palace *[bîtan]*" (1:5).[14] The king thus turns his attention from the
upper echelons of his royal order to the whole range of his public, from
the greatest to the least within the city of Susa. Again, the aim of this
party is clearly related to that of the first, namely to display and
thereby secure his honor and greatness over the entire social order.

The first party was described as though by an outsider: only those
present and the duration were given. The second party, by contrast, is
described from an insider point of view:

> There were white cotton curtains and blue hangings tied with cords of
> fine linen and purple to silver rings and marble pillars. There were
> couches of gold and silver on a mosaic pavement of porphyry, marble,
> mother-of-pearl, and colored stones. Drinks were served in golden gob-
> lets, goblets of different kinds, and the royal wine was lavished accord-
> ing to the bounty of the king. Drinking was by flagons, without restraint;
> for the king had given orders to all the officials of his palace to do as each
> one desired. (1:6-8)

In a narrative that is otherwise quite sparse with regard to descriptive
details, these three verses are remarkable. Although the precise meanings of several of the Hebrew words used to describe the colors, textures,
and furnishings are uncertain, the general impression of spectacular
lavishness is overwhelming. Fox comments, "The exclamatory listing
creates a mass of images that overwhelm the sensory imagination and
suggest both a sybaritic delight in opulence and an awareness of its excess."[15] The extravagance of the first party was expressed through high

---

[14] While clearly related to "house" *(bayit)*, *bîtan* occurs only in Esther (see also
Esth 7:7-8). The Akkadian *bitānum* and related words suggest "palace" as the least
problematic translation here (cf. "pavilion" in Moore [1971: 7], following Oppen-
heim).

[15] Michael V. Fox, *Character and Ideology in the Book of Esther* (Columbia, SC: University of South Carolina Press, 1991) 16.

numbers and might: all the powerful were there for 180 days. The extravagance of this second party is conveyed through particulars: the
palace cosmetics and the drinking.

Every man is, by law, required to drink as he desires (1:8). This is
an interesting spin on freedom under the law if there ever was one.
Each man's fulfillment of his own desire is by law. Lack is against the
law. Plenitude and fulfillment are the orders of the week.

Although "both great and small" (v. 5) covers several classes of
people within the social order, it does not appear to include women.
This is confirmed in verse 9, as the narrative turns attention away from
the king's party and onto another party taking place within the palace:
"Furthermore, Queen Vashti gave a banquet for the women in the
palace of King Ahasuerus." In the otherwise all-male (i.e., "homosocial")[16] series of events described in the other two parties, Vashti's
party stands in sharp relief, insofar as it takes place elsewhere and is
thrown by and for the other sex. It is introduced with the particle *gam*
("furthermore"), which marks a turn of attention within the story
while maintaining an association with the previous material; that is, it
both separates and associates. As such, it draws attention to a new
royal subject, Queen Vasthi, while suggesting that this new subject has
everything to do with the royal subject of the other two parties. Up to
this point, every active verb has had the king as its subject. He has
"displayed" his honor and greatness (1:4), "ordered" his officials (1:8),
and twice "given" (or "thrown" [ʿāśâ]) drinking parties. Now, attention
suddenly turns to a new subject, whose actions are much like the king's:
she "throws [or 'gives'] a drinking fest" (ʿāśtâ mištēh).

Although Vashti and the other women are in the king's house (v. 9b),
furthermore, they are not quite "in his presence." Neither fully outside
nor fully inside, both inside and outside, they are not entirely under his
control. Exclusion is a common means of controlling and subordinating
women within patriarchal social structures. Yet to exclude is also, paradoxically, to lose control of the individual or group being excluded.
What might they be doing? Drinking, obviously. Beyond that, however,
the text does not say. Where exactly in the palace are they? What might
they be talking about? Indeed, this brief, laconic verse has elicited a great
deal of male interpretive anxiety over the centuries. For example, Targum Sheni, an early Aramaic renarration of the Hebrew text of Esther,
imagines that during Vashti's party she takes her guests into the king's
bedroom and answers all their questions about his private life.

---

[16] On the dynamics of male homosocial desire in literature, see esp. Eve Kosof-
sky Sedgwick, *Between Men: English Literature and Male Homosocial Desire* (New
York: Columbia University, 1985).

After this brief but important turn to Vashti and her party, narrative attention returns to the king's second party. "On the seventh day, when the king was merry with wine, he commanded [*ʾāmar l–*, 'said to'] Mehuman, Biztha, Harbona, Bigtha and Abagtha, Zethar and Carkas, the seven eunuchs who attended him, to bring Queen Vashti before the king, wearing the royal crown, in order to show the peoples and the officials her beauty; for she was fair to behold" (1:10–11). Whether out of insecurity or a desire to show off to the other men or some combination thereof, the king tells his seven eunuchs "to bring" (*lĕhābîʾ*)—as though an object—Vashti the queen "into the presence of" (*lipnê*) the king. The king's explicit motivation is "to show [*lĕharʾôt*] the peoples and the officials her beauty, for she was fair to behold [lit., 'pleasurable to look at,' *ṭôbat marʾeh*]" (v. 11). Just as his explicit aim in throwing parties was to "display" (*bĕharʾōt . . . ʾet*) his honor and greatness (1:4), so now he intends to "display" (*lĕharʾôt . . . ʾet*) his queen's good looks. This close textual parallel between the king's desire to display his honor and greatness in verse 4 and his desire to display Vashti here suggests that this new request is likewise aimed at securing his own honor and greatness. He considers her to be excellent display material, sure to reflect well on his own subjective status. In other words, he considers her to be an ideal object of exchange between himself and the other men. He wishes to share her good looks with them. Indeed, as will soon become clear, the maintenance of his patriarchal dominance within his own household is integrally bound up with the maintenance of his dominance in the larger order of things. Sexual politics and national politics, in this story world as in our world today, are inseparable.

The place and function of the eunuchs (*sārîsîm;* castrated personnel)[17] in this objectification of Vashti is also significant. Here, as in subsequent episodes, the eunuchs function as mediators between women and men. Ambiguous with regard to their own sexual identity—both physically (being castrated) and socially (being without wife, occupying women's quarters, etc.)—they occupy the physical and symbolic space between the sexes. Thus, paradoxically, their mediation in this

---

[17] It is doubtful whether *sārîs* (related to cognate verbs meaning "to castrate") always refers in Hebrew Scriptures to castrated personnel. In some cases, it simply refers to a kind of officer or servant (e.g., 2 Kgs 22:9, where it refers to an errand runner; and Gen 37-38, where it appears to refer to a high foreign official). On the discussion concerning eunuchs, see Robert North, "Postexilic Judean Officials," *Anchor Bible Dictionary* 5 (1992) 87; and E. M. Yamauchi, "Was Nehemiah the Cupbearer a Eunuch?," *ZAW* 92 (1980) 132-42. See also the earlier discussion in Paton, *Esther,* 148; and Herodotus viii.105.

episode and throughout the narrative guarantees separation of the sexes as part of the social and symbolic order within this story world. Ambiguity guarantees definition. As we shall soon see with Bigthan and Teresh in chapter 2, their ambiguous in-between location also carries potential for subversion of that order.

The fact that *seven* eunuchs are sent for her on the *seventh* day—the last day of the second party—suggests that this showcasing of Vashti will serve as the impressive finish to the king's second party, and will conclusively confirm his secure resting place on the throne. At the same time, the state of the king as he issues his command is "merry with wine" (*ṭôb lēb . . . bayyāyin;* v. 10a). A more literal translation of this would be "the heart of the king was good [or 'pleased'] with wine," suggesting a state of well-pleased drunkenness. In calling for Vashti to be brought in for a shared ogling, the aim is to add pleasure to pleasure: he is "pleased" or "good" (*ṭôb*) with wine, and she is "pleasing" or "good" (*ṭôbâ*) to look at.

The king's pleasure is immediately frustrated, however, by the queen's response: "Queen Vashti refused to come at the king's command conveyed by the eunuchs" (1:12a). Interestingly, the text gives no reason for her refusal. Perhaps she is insulted by his demand to be brought in and objectified by an all-male ogle. Along this interpretive line, Targum Sheni describes the queen lecturing the king about her higher nobility, and scolding him for suggesting that she be degraded by displaying herself naked before a party of drunken men (assuming that "wearing her royal crown" in 1:11 means wearing *nothing but* her royal crown). Perhaps, on the other hand, she was busy with other matters concerning her own party, and could not come at that time. Or perhaps she simply did not wish to be bothered. And what about the role of the eunuchs as mediators of the king's orders? How did they convey those orders? Was her response to them as blunt as the response they gave to the king—a simple refusal?

At any rate, this message of refusal sends the king into a rage: "The king was enraged, and his anger burned within him" (1:12b).[18] The text has already hinted at the king's dependence on Vashti to reflect well on his own character as a grand finale to his display of honor and greatness (vv. 4, 11). That is, his status as subject depends on her status as

---

[18] The LXX and AT convey two different emotions in the king at this point: "grieved" (*elupēthē*) and "angered" (*ōrgisthē*), rather than the double rage conveyed in the Hebrew text's "enraged . . . his anger burned within him." This variation should not influence our reading of the Hebrew text, however, since the two Greek versions often take a more sympathetic stance toward the king (whom Mordecai saves in Addition A). See Beal, "Tracing," 108-10.

object. At this point, as she refuses to be brought "into his presence," this dependence comes to the fore. She was to be the king's "privileged Other," to borrow from Simone de Beauvoir: "through whom the subject fulfills himself: one of the measures of man, his counterbalance, his salvation, his adventure, his happiness."[19] Of course, the irony in this dynamic of othering is that it reveals the male subject's special and highly problematic dependence on her as fixed object. As Luce Irigaray writes, within this dynamic the woman appears as "a bench mark that is ultimately more crucial than the subject, for he can sustain himself only by bouncing back off some objectiveness, some objective."[20] Since verse 10, Vashti has been the king's objective, the object that defines his status as subject, that is, his "benchmark." Her refusal, then, is radically disruptive: its bad reflection on the king as patriarch ruptures the very structure of the patriarchy she is expected to ground. It is a disruption of the world as the king is trying to construct it, and as such it elicits burning rage.

To say this is not, of course, to deny the farcical character of the king's response. Indeed, from here out, not only will the king be farced, but so will the sexual politics that is being introduced. The response to Vashti's refusal, here and in the verses to follow, is presented as at once both dead serious and comically overblown.[21]

As his pleased drunkenness turns suddenly into burning rage, the king turns to "the sages who knew the laws [lit. 'the times'] (for this was the king's procedure toward all who were versed in law and custom, and those next to him were Carshena, Shethar, Admatha, Tarshish, Meres, Marsena, and Memucan, the seven officials of Persia and Media, who had access to the king [lit., 'who look upon the king's face'], and sat first in the kingdom)" (1:13-14). Note how the text emphasizes the close proximity of these "sages" or "wisemen" in relation to the king:

---

[19] Simone de Beauvoir, *The Second Sex*, trans. H. M. Parshley (New York: Vintage, 1989) 248.

[20] Luce Irigaray, *Speculum of the Other Woman*, trans. G. G. Gill (Ithaca: Cornell University Press, 1985) 133. For an introduction to and critical analysis of Beauvoir and Irigaray in relation to biblical studies generally and Esther specifically, see chapter 5, "Finding Oneself Signed Up," in Beal, *Book of Hiding*, 60–74. For a recent series of engagements of Irigaray in relation to many different fields of study, see the articles in the special issue of *Diacritics*, "Irigaray and the Political Future of Sexual Difference," edited by Cheah and Grosz (1998), esp. the interview with Cornell and Butler, 19–42.

[21] On the comical in Esther, see esp. Yehuda T. Radday, "Esther with Humour," *On Humour and the Comic in the Hebrew Bible*, Yehuda T. Radday and Athalya Brenner, eds. (Sheffield: Sheffield Academic Press, 1990).

they are "next to him" (*haqqārōb ʾēlayw*); they "look upon the king's face" or "see to the king's presence" (*rōʾê pĕnê hammelek*); and they "sit first" (*hayyōbît rîʾōšnâ*) in his kingdom. These men are inside and up close, well-versed in the order of things, and therefore expected to know what will reestablish that order in the current crisis brought on by Vashti's refusal.

The king asks them, "According to the law, what is to be done to Queen Vashti because she has not performed the command [*maʾămar*, 'saying']²² of King Ahasuerus conveyed by the eunuchs [lit. 'by the hand of the eunuchs']?" (1:15). Note the play on words: the king asks what ought "to be done" (*laʾăśôt*) with Vashti on account of her "not doing" (*lōʾ ʿāśtâ*, NRSV "not performing"). In other words, what can be done to undo what she did not do? On the one hand, the king's desire to *do something* with her reveals his desire to reassert her status as object. On the other hand, his description of her "not doing" what he said acknowledges her status as acting subject.

What follows in 1:16-20 is an extended speech from Memucan, the seventh of the seven "sages" named in verse 14.²³ Delivered "in the presence of [*lipnê*] the king and his officials" (1:16a), Memucan's speech can be divided into two main parts: (a) verses 16-18, in which he describes the broader sexual-political crisis introduced by Vashti's transgression; and (b) verses 19-20, in which he recommends a royal order to undo that crisis by undoing her.

First, Memucan presents what he sees as the full scale of the Vashti catastrophe (1:16-18). In this outlandish, panicked description of the broad political ramifications of Vashti's transgression, verse 16 serves as a sort of thesis statement, and verses 17-18, introduced by *kî*, "for," serve to explicate how these broad ramifications will be realized.

His thesis: "Not only has Queen Vashti done wrong [*ʿāwtâ*] to the king, but also to all the officials and all the peoples who are in all the provinces of King Ahasuerus" (1:16). The opening declaration serves two rhetorical functions. First, it redefines what Vashti has done: whereas the king had called it "not doing" what the king said, which could suggest a fault of omission, Memucan describes her action in terms of crooked perversion. The verb he uses, *ʿāwtâ* (from *ʿwh*), is somewhat uncommon in Hebrew narrative, and thus striking in this instance. Its basic sense is to "bend," "make crooked," or "pervert," and is usually used in reference to perverting or troubling the estab-

---

²²The king does not literally issue a "command" (*ṣwh*) to bring Vashti, but rather "says" (*ʾmr*) to the eunuchs to bring her (cf. 1:10). The verb "command" (*ṣwh*) is used in Esth 2:10, 20; 3:2, 12; 4:5, 8, 10, 17; and 8:9.

²³Reading the Qere to agree with v. 14.

lished social and/or theological order (e.g., Isa 24:1; Job 33:27; Dan 9:5; Lam 3:36; often with God as the subject, e.g., Lam 3:9; Ezek 21:32 [ET 27]; cf. Job 8:3; 19:6; 34:12; Eccl 7:13). Memucan's use of the term here is certainly the only Scriptural instance in which it is used to convey the subversion of the established sexual-political order. It not only redefines Vashti's refusal as something more than simple omission ("not doing," as the king put it); it makes the stronger claim that what she has committed is downright subversive.

The second rhetorical function of Memucan's opening statement in verse 16 is to shift the crisis introduced by Vashti's refusal from the personal to the executive to the national level. The queen's subversive action, he declares, is not only "against the king" (*ʿal – hammelek*) and his own household order, but it is also "against all the chiefs" (*ʿal – kol – haśśārîm*), and also ultimately "against all the people" (*ʿal – kol – hāʿammîm*) throughout the kingdom.[24] Sexual politics and national politics are inseparable. An offense against the royal patriarch is an offense against the patriarchy.

Following the thesis (v. 16), verses 17-18 explain how the effects of Vashti's subversion will infiltrate the empire:

> For *[kî]* this deed [or 'word'] of the queen will be made known to all women, causing them to look with contempt on their husbands [or 'lords'], since they will say, "King Ahasuerus commanded Queen Vashti to be brought before him ['into his presence'], and she did not come." This very day the noble ladies of Persia and Media who have heard of the queen's behavior will rebel against [or 'talk to'][25] the king's officials, and there will be no end[26] of contempt and wrath! (1:17-18)

It is this Persian patriarch's nightmare. The king and his officials had been planning to ogle Vashti in her crown, "for she was good looking"

---

[24] In keeping with the logic of this sentence, and with the use of "all the people" in 1:5 to refer to all men in the city, "all people" here should be taken as referring to all men.

[25] As it stands in the Hebrew text, verse 18 has the noble women "talking *[tōʾmarnâ]* to all the king's officials about what they heard concerning the queen." It has been suggested, however, that the verb here be emended to "rebel" (*timrênâ*, as in NRSV), so that the noble women are depicted "rebelling against all the king's officials on account of what they heard concerning the queen." Weak support for this emendation comes from the LXX and Vulgate. Moreover, as noted by Levenson, *Esther*, 50, this verb (*mrh*) takes either a direct object or the preposition *bet*, but never *lamed*, as would be the case in this verse.

[26] One might also translate this phrase as "there *is* [already] enough." Given that it appears at the conclusion of Memucan's depiction of what he imagines *will* happen, however, the future sense given by the NRSV is preferable.

(1:11). Instead, when word of Vashti "gets out" (*yēṣēʾ*, NRSV "will be made known") to all the women (*ʿal – kol – hannāšîm*, v. 17; cf. v. 16), these same men will find *themselves* being looked over by their wives "with contempt."

Interestingly, at the center of his depiction of the wide-reaching subversion which Vashti's refusal threatens, we find Memucan imagining women *speaking*. Thus far in the narrative, no one but the king and Memucan have been quoted saying anything (*ʾmr*; vv. 10, 13, 15, and 16). Women, including Vashti, have been given no voice. It is ironic, then, that at the center of Memucan's speech, which aims ultimately to reestablish the subordination of women to their "lords," male anxiety about their power to speak finds its way into the discourse.[27]

In the end, according to Memucan, Vashti's perversion of the right sexual-political order will have no end. That is, there "will be no end of contempt and wrath" (v. 18b). The word translated here as "contempt" is a noun form of the verb used in the earlier phrase "look with contempt" or "despise with their eyes" (v. 17), and thus reiterates the anticipated general contempt of all women towards their "lords." The word translated as "wrath" (*qṣp*) also has been used in the text already—not to describe the women, however, but to describe *the king's* initial rage at Vashti's refusal in 1:12. The sense is that if Vashti's refusal goes undisciplined, its subversive effects could lead ultimately to a reversal of wrath: from the wrath of one lord against his subversive woman to the wrath of all subversive women against all their lords.

Next, Memucan makes his recommendation for a royal order that will undo the catastrophe he has just imagined before it is ever realized:

> If it pleases the king, let a royal order [lit. 'word'] go out from him, and let it be written among the laws of the Persians and the Medes so that it may not be altered, that Vashti is never again to come before ['into the presence of'] King Ahasuerus; and let the king give her royal position to another who is better than she. (1:19)

Memucan proposes that "word of the queen" (*dĕbar – hammalkâ*), which "will go out [*yēṣēʿ*] to all women" (v. 17) be followed closely by

---

[27] Irigaray, *Speculum*, 135, writes: "But what if the 'object' started to speak? Which also means beginning to 'see,' etc. What disaggregation of the subject would that entail?" To be sure, in this passage in Esther, the 'talk' is a projection by the self-same male subject, a 'specula(riza)tion,' to borrow again from Irigaray, but not an altogether comforting or 'pleasant' one. Rather, it is a projection of the male subject on trial, on the verge of instability.

a "royal word" or "word of the kingdom" *(dĕbar – malkût)*, which "will go out *[yēṣēˀ]* . . . from his [the king's] presence." Word of the queen, which Memucan imagines undoing the male domination on every level of the empire ("against all the chiefs and against all the people," v. 16), must be trailed by another word—a word of the kingdom, a word from the patriarch himself—which would undo what the word of the queen threatens to do.

Memucan then presents the content of this recommended word of the kingdom: first, Vashti (no longer referred to as "Vashti *the queen*") "will never again come into the king's presence"; second, her status shall be given to another who is "more pleasing than her" *(haṭṭôbâ mimmennâ;* cf. 2:2-4). The phrase "more pleasing than her" harkens back to Vashti's description as "pleasing *[ṭôbat]* to look at" in 1:11, suggesting that her replacement will be even better looking than she is. The phrase also recalls the king's happy state before Vashti's refusal and his rage, when he was "pleased *[ṭôb]* with wine" in 1:10, suggesting that a more pleasing replacement might be his ticket back to such drunken happy times. (He will finally get there, at least for a while, at the drinking party for his new queen, Esther, in 2:17-18).

Memucan concludes, in verse 20, with what he imagines will be the result of his recommendation: "when the decree[28] made by the king is proclaimed [or 'heard'] throughout all his kingdom, vast as it is, all women will give honor to their husbands [or 'lords'], high and low alike." Thus the catastrophe imagined in verses 16-18—endless contempt and wrath of women against their lords—will be put into reverse. As women hear this word of the kingdom, the potentially subversive word of the queen will be drowned out, and all women throughout the empire will *"give honor [yqr] to their lords."* As discussed earlier in relation to 1:4, honor is an important means of consolidating power and maintaining social order within the story world of Esther. Here in 1:20, Memucan is effectively linking the honor of every man, as lord of his own little household patriarchy, to the honor of the king, which Vashti's refusal has threatened.

[28] Note that the word translated here as "decree" *(pitgān)* is different from the word translated as "decree" *(dat,* also "law") in the subsequent narrative (2:8; 3:14-15; 4:3-16; 8:13-17; 9:1, 13-14). Given the present context, in which the royal word is to follow on the heels of the word of the queen, it is interesting to note that *pitgān* is best translated as "answer" in Ezra 4:17 and 5:11. Compare also Eccl 8:11, in which this word refers to a "sentence against an evil deed." In every case, the word appears to refer to *content* rather than to *form.* Thus here it should be understood not as a term for the formal decree itself, but as referring to the content of the decree.

Recall that Memucan had introduced his recommendation with "if it pleases *[ṭôb]* the king." The king's response is affirmative, as is the response of the other officials: "The word [NRSV 'this advice'] pleased the king and the officials, and the king did as Memucan proposed; he sent letters to all the royal provinces, to every province in its own script and to every people in its own language, declaring that every man should be master in his own house" (1:21-22). Thus the king's pleasure, which was frustrated by Vashti's refusal, returns. It is interesting to note that the details of Vashti's banishment and replacement are not included in this summary of the issuing of the decree (cf. 3:13-14; 8:11-13), but only the declaration "that every man should act as master." The verb here is *śōrēr*, a participle form of the title for the king's "officials" throughout the preceding narrative. Recall that in Memucan's speech the status of the king as patriarch over his household was closely related to the status of every royal official as patriarch over his household. The use of *śrr* here establishes a similar association between officials and other men. Clearly, the aim of this decree against Vashti is less a response to her action and more a response to what these men imagine will otherwise be its subversive effect in the realm of sexual politics.

What kind of a narrative beginning is this? On the one hand, it introduces the world of gender politics that Esther is about to enter. This world is both rigorous and ridiculous, dead serious and over-reactive. On the other hand, Vashti has also exposed the vulnerabilities and fragile dependencies of this patriarchal order.

Moreover, as will become clear in chapter 3, the dynamics of othering in terms of gender (projecting women as other) within this narrative world are closely paralleled by the dynamics of othering in terms of ethnicity (projecting Jews as other). Both dynamics are revealed as weak and unstable projections, open to radical subversion.

Chapter 2

REMEMBERING TO FORGET

Esther 2:1-4

This brief episode begins with a king still troubled by Vashti and concludes with a happy king. As in chapter 1, the turn from kingly displeasure to kingly pleasure is brought about by the recommendation of advisors. Thus the episode may be outlined as follows: (a) 2:1, which presents the problem, namely that king remembers Vashti; (b) 2:2-4a, the servants' recommendation of a procedure for replacing and thereby forgetting Vashti; and (c) 2:4b, stating that the king was pleased by the recommendation, and followed it.

The opening phrase in 2:1, "after these things," simultaneously links what follows in chapter 2 with the preceding story of Vashti in chapter 1 and marks a certain distance from it (cf. the identical opening phrase in 3:1). On the one hand, time has passed, and the king has settled down some—his "anger . . . had abated"—and most of the characters from the opening story in chapter 1 (all but the king) have disappeared; in fact, none of them will appear again in the story. On the other hand, Vashti remains present *precisely in her absence*, as the king continues to obsess over her: "he remembered Vashti and what she had done and what had been decreed against her."

The king remembers three things: "Vashti, what she had done, and what had been decreed against her" (2:1b). In the Hebrew text, these three objects of memory, each introduced by *ʾet* (the marker for a direct object), are presented poetically in a series that is necessarily lost in English translation: first one word, then two words, then three words, with each new object depending on the previous one:

King Ahasuerus remembered   *ʾet – waštî* (Vashti)

ʾet – ʾăšer – ʿāśâtâ
(and what she had done)

ʾet – ʾăšer – nigzar ʿālêhā
(and what had been decreed against her)

The sense of the king's remembering here is somewhat ambiguous, and one's interpretation of it depends on how one understands these particulars that are being remembered about Vashti. On the one hand, many commentators argue that the king remembered Vashti *unfavorably*. This interpretive tradition is long-standing, going all the way back to the two Targums. On this interpretation, the king continues to be agitated by memory of her; "what she had done" would refer to her refusal to come, which had enraged the drunken king; and "what had been decreed against her" has left him only more frustrated as he has sobered up.[1]

On the other hand, there is a long-standing interpretive tradition (found, for example, in Rashi and Ibn Ezra) which suggests that, now that the king's anger has abated, he remembers her fondly, regrets what had been decreed against her, and misses her. Thus, for example, Rashi writes that he remembered "her beauty and he was saddened." Along the same lines, the Midrash Esther Rabbah says that after the king's anger (which had been stirred up with all the wine) had begun to abate—"yet not wholly abated"—the king "began to feel remorse, for 'what she had done' was proper, and 'what had been decreed against her' was improper" (XXXII:ii; Neusner's translation).[2] This reading is followed by most modern commentators. In support of it is the fact that the verb "to remember" *(zkr)*, as Levenson notes, "often carries with it a note of compassion (as in Gen 40:14; Lev 26:42, 45; Jer 2:2): one 'remembers' someone to the latter's advantage. The implication of 2:1 is that Ahasuerus has become melancholy in the absence of his wife and regretful of the severity of her punishment."[3] Relatedly, as Clines points out, the verb "to abate" *(škk)* is also used in Gen 8:2 in reference to the abatement of the flood waters after God "remembered Noah" in 8:1.[4] It has been suggested further by Susan Niditch that this remembering contains "an erotic suggestion. 'The king remembered what Vashti used to do' (2:1), presumably 'for him.' He does not miss a person or a personality but a function."[5]

[1] So Paton, *Esther*, 164.

[2] Paton, *Esther*, 163–4, claims that Midrash Esther Rabbah recalls her unfavorably, as "a basis for the idea that he inflicted further punishment upon her." On the contrary, in this Midrash, it is assumed that by the time he remembers her in 2:1 he has already, in a drunken rage, had her killed (XXXII:i).

[3] Levenson, *Esther*, 54; see also Fox, *Character*, 26.

[4] David J. A. Clines, *Ezra, Nehemiah, Esther*, The New Century Bible Commentary (Grand Rapids: Eerdmans, 1984) 285. Note further that later, in Gen 8:21, God regrets that violent action and promises not to do it again.

[5] Susan Niditch, *Underdogs and Tricksters* (San Francisco: Harper & Row, 1987) 133–34.

Although there is certainly a sense of regret in the king's remembering here, it is less clear that compassion is operative, let alone affection or sexual attraction. Indeed, to read "what she had done" with an erotic connotation is to read this phrase without reference to the previous story and to dissociate it from the next phrase, "what had been decreed against her." Both of these phrases refer directly to the action narrated in chapter 1. The phrase "what she had done" (*ʾăšer – ʿāśātâ*) is very close to the king's request for legal advice in 1:15: "According to the law, what is to be done to Queen Vashti because she has not performed [lit. 'on account of what she did not do'; *ʾăšer lōʾ – ʿāśtâ*) the command of King Ahasuerus conveyed by the eunuchs?" The second phrase obviously refers to the action taken against her by the king and his advisors (and, ultimately, the nation) on account of "what she had done." Although he had obviously been aroused by her in the past, as a pleasing object who secured his own royal masculine subjectivity, there is no allusion to that here. On the contrary, what is remembered here is the fact that her actions jeopardized his own identity and subjective stability. Ironically, as he remembers "what she had done," he continues to remember his own vulnerability to her—not as lover but as insecure patriarch.

The verb used in the last phrase to describe Vashti's official banishment (*gzr* in passive form; translated here as "had been decreed") is particularly interesting. Elsewhere in Hebrew Scripture this verb is most commonly used in reference to "cutting off" (e.g., Hab 3:17; 2 Chr 26:21; Ps 88:6), and it occurs with the preposition *min*, "from" (but cf. Isa 53:8). In our passage, however, the verb is followed not by *min* but by *ʿālêhā* (a preposition plus an feminine objective suffix; thus "against her," "over her," or "concerning her"). In this passage, with this preposition, the verb has a nice double meaning, indicating both the official written "decree" against her and the fact that this decree actually "cut her off" from her status as queen and from the king's presence.[6]

Indeed, the decree was aimed to cut her out of the story itself—that is, precisely, to forget her, her offense, and the male subjective vulnerability it exposed. If there is any regret in the king's remembering her here, then, it is his regret that the problem introduced by her refusal has not been entirely resolved. Thus Vashti's initial refusal in 1:12

---

[6] Note also that this same verb is used frequently in Leviticus to refer to the portion of the sacrifice that should be set aside for the Levites, as well as to the Levitical cities. In a sense, Vashti, too, can be seen as a sacrifice—in this case, a sacrifice "cut off" from the royal domain in order to secure patriarchal rule over women, "from greatest to least" (see the previous discussion of chapter 1).

(which is "what she had done") becomes, in this passage, her refusal to be forgotten. In both cases, moreover, her refusal means that the king's "good pleasure" is deferred.

Verses 2-4a then present the recommendation offered by the "servants of [*naʿărê*, lit. 'young men of'] the king," whose function in the narrative is much like that of the advisors in the previous episode concerning Vashti's transgression. Note that this recommendation is different from that given by Memucan in chapter 1, in that it is given collectively by the servants and in that it is given without solicitation. The king does not identify the problem and ask what ought to be done; rather these attendants recognize that he still remembers Vashti, they percieve that his memory of her is a problem, and they recommend a way of forgetting:

> Let beautiful young virgins [*nĕʿārôt bĕtûlôt*] be sought out for the king. And let the king appoint commissioners in all the provinces of his kingdom to gather all the beautiful young virgins to the harem in the citadel of Susa under custody of Hegai, the king's eunuch, who is in charge of the women; let their cosmetic treatments be given them. And let the girl who pleases the king be queen instead of Vashti. (2:2-4a)

Thus the "young men" *(naʿărîm)* of the king recommend a gathering of "young women" *(nĕʿārôt)* for the king, in order to find a replacement for Vashti.

This recommendation recalls Memucan's in many important respects. As already discussed, Memucan's recommendation served both to officially reinscribe the objectification and subordination of women and to remove the problem presented by Vashti's refusal of that role. This recommendation serves basically the same purpose. There is, for example, a persistent objectification of the young women. Syntactically, they are not the subjects of verbs, but objects; they are to be "sought," "gathered," and "given" their preparatory beauty treatments. Although less clear in the NRSV, moreover, in the Hebrew text they are "kept" by Hegai, "the king's eunuch who keeps the women" (v. 3). In all this, they are exchanged among, or passed between, men: from their father's house to the king's. (Note, too, that here, as in 1:10, the primary mediator between the women and the king will be a eunuch.) Visually, moreover, their status as good-looking objects of the pleased male ogle is emphasized, almost to the point of excess: they are described as "pleasing to look at" twice; they will be given "cosmetic treatments" by Hegai; and the one "pleasing in the eyes of the king" will be given the highest regard, by being made queen. Indeed, passive looks appear to be the only criterion.

Beyond this common rhetoric of objectification, the recommendation of 2:2-4a is also linked to Memucan's earlier recommendation by shared rhetorical form and content. Both speeches, for example, use jussive verb forms ("let beautififul virgins be sought," "let the king appoint," etc.), as will all subsequent recommendations made to the king. Like Memucan's recommendation, moreover, which calls for elaborate and extensive publication of the decree against Vashti, the servants here devise an extravagant bureaucracy to carry out the search, including the appointment of commissioners in every province and a cosmetic processing plant in the central harem at Susa. Furthermore, both speeches are focused on *pleasing* the king (Hebrew words related to *ṭôb*, "pleasing," are used three times in 2:2-4a), whose good pleasure continues to be disturbed by Vashti. Relatedly, the phrase *ṭôbat / ṭôbôt marʾeh*, translated as "beautiful" in the NRSV but most literally "pleasing to look at," which is used twice in this speech, was likewise used to describe Vashti in 1:11; and the speech itself concludes with anticipation that this new royal selection will "be queen instead of Vashti" (compare 1:19, "let the king give her royal position to another who is better [lit. 'more pleasing'] than she"). This will be accomplished, according to the recommendation, by finding another good-looking object to take Vashti's place and thereby to cover up the insecurity she brought to light. This advice readily acknowledges, on the one hand, that the replacement must be like Vashti (i.e., "pleasing to look at"), and yet, on the other hand, that it is the intransigent memory of Vashti's *refusal*—indeed, it is the *refusal itself*—that must be overcome.

The aim of this recommendation is basically the same, then, as the one given by Memucan in chapter 1, namely, to cut off and to forget Vashti, who slipped out of her position as object for securing male subjectivity. Both recommendations speak to the king's desire to forget his own insecurities and to replace them with the good looks of another. Thus here, as before, the advice "pleases" the king and he follows it precisely (2:4b). Yet just as "what had been decreed against her" recalled "what she had done" even while its aim was to dismiss it, so this new recommendation for a pageant search acknowledges memory of Vashti in an effort to replace her. The work of forgetting is a kind of recollection.

Here, as elsewhere in the book of Esther, intriguing questions emerge with regard to writing, the written law, and remembering. In this episode, memory appears to be working against the written law by recalling that which the written law aims to write off, to forget. The king's memory is drawn to that which has been cut off or written out, that is, to what exceeds the law, both the written law and the laws of patriarchy—"that every man should be master in his own house"

(1:22)—which that written law aims to shore up. In what sense does writing serve memory and in what sense does it serve forgetting? In what sense is writing *inscription*, "writing in," and in what sense is it *exscription*, "writing out"?[7] Does writing work against itself by recalling that which it writes out, that which exceeds its boundaries?

[7] This notion of inscription as exscription is borrowed from Jean-Luc Nancy's *é(x)criture* as discussed in his explication of Georges Bataille in *The Birth To Presence*, trans. Brian Holmes *et al.* (Stanford: Stanford University Press, 1993) 333–40. The dynamic of inscription as exscription is also explored in relation to the "writing out" of Vashti in Beal, *Book of Hiding*, 23–5. The use here is not closely related to the use of the term by Nancy in relation to Bataille.

Chapter 3

NEW FAMILY DYNAMICS

Esther 2:5-18

The next two episodes, 2:5-11 and 2:12-18, are continuations of 2:1-4, insofar as they narrate the implementation and completion of the pageant search recommended and approved in that passage. As Bush makes clear, moreover, 2:1-18 is held together as a coherent literary whole by numerous word and phrase repetitions.[1] At the same time, we have already noted similar word and phrase interconnections between 2:1-4 and the previous story of Vashti's refusal and banishment, indicating that 2:1-4 can be read as a continuation of chapter 1. Indeed, any careful reading of the book of Esther reveals numerous word and phrase interconnections throughout, making clear that the book as a whole has such strong literary coherence that it works against the sectioning work that is a mainstay of biblical criticism on narratives such as Genesis, with its long and complex literary and editorial history which invites the identification of literary seams, formal distinctions, and generic classifications. The book of Esther does not read well in chunks, and the lines of division we draw within the story for the purpose of commentary will always appear very fuzzy on closer inspection.

ENTER MORDECAI AND ESTHER (2:5-11)

Granted the interconnections within 2:1-18 (not to mention between 2:1-4 and chapter 1), 2:5-11 is marked off from 2:1-4 by its shift

---

[1] Bush, *Ruth, Esther*, 359–60.

away from the king and his advisors in order to introduce two new characters, Mordecai and Esther, whose social location as exiles with broken families is in sharp contrast against the extravagant luxuries of the king's court. This material is also distinguished from what precedes it chronologically, in that the king's order for the pageant search has by this time been widely published and the young women are already being gathered in Susa (2:8).

This shift to new characters is in fact very abrupt in the Hebrew text—most literally, "A Jewish man there was [*ʾîš yĕhûdî hāyâ*] in Susa the capital, and his name [was] Mordecai . . ."—and the insertion of "Now" at the beginning of this verse in the NRSV translation appears to be aimed at smoothing it out. With or without the addition of "now," this verse appears to be making a new, almost legendary beginning. Compare, for example, the beginning of Job: "A man there was [*ʾîš hāyâ*] in the land of Uz, and his name [was] Job" (1:1). Even in English translation, the word orders of these two introductions are unmistakably similar, giving both characters a legendary, "once upon a time" quality.

The Midrash Esther Rabbah draws on different biblical parallels in order to offer yet another interpretation of this abrupt introduction of Mordecai into the story, regarding it not as a new beginning so much as a response to verse 4: "Who was the appropriate person for this task [i.e., the task pleasing the king and becoming queen instead of Vashti]? 'There was a Jew in Susa the capital, and his name was Mordecai, son of Jair, son of Shimei, son of Kish, a Benjaminite'" (XXXV:i). That is, Mordecai (and Esther, whose introduction follows?) is the appropriate person. The Midrash looks to an interesting series of biblical narrative parallels to support this interpretation of the relation between verses 4 and 5, each involving a similar apparently abrupt shift to introduction of a new character. In each case the new character ends up being the appropriate person for the task mentioned in the previous verse. For example, after God heard the groaning of the Israelites and took notice of them in Exod 2:25, the next verse turns abruptly to Moses ("Moses was keeping the flock . . ." [3:1]). The Midrash mentions similarly abrupt introductions of the "appropriate person" in 1 Sam 17:12 (David), Judg 4:4 (Deborah), and Judg 11:1 (Jephthah).

Most to the point as a parallel with Esth 2:5, the Midrash notes that after Samuel (following God's cranky recommendation) agrees reluctantly to appoint a king over Israel and sends the people of Israel home in 1 Sam 8:22, the next verse turns abruptly to an introduction of the father of the one who will become king, namely Kish, father of Saul: "There was a man [*ʾîš hāyâ*] of Benjamin whose name was Kish . . ." (1 Sam 9:1). This is a particularly appropriate parallel. Not only is it a clear example of an abrupt introduction following a decision to seek out the "appropriate person" (in this case a king rather than a queen), but it involves the introduction of the *father* of the appropriate person rather than the appropriate person himself, who has yet to be introduced (Saul). The same is true of Esth 2:5, in which Mordecai is the *adoptive father* (and also cousin) of the appropriate person, namely Esther, who will not be introduced until verse 7. Beyond that, the introductions of Mordecai and Kish identify them both with the tribe of Benjamin. Mordecai is identified as a "son of Kish." Both Saul and Mordecai are sons of Kish. Of course, Mordecai and Saul are not brothers, and so either this is a different Kish or Mordecai is being identified here with a very remote ancestor. Paton, following several ancient rabbinic sources, regards the names Shimei and Kish (though not Jair) as remote ancestors to Mordecai rather than as his actual grandfather and great-grandfather.[2] This may be the case, although one must then wonder why they would occur in a list along with his actual father (Jair). The question seems less important, however, if one considers these names to be fictional—whether fictionally remote or fictionally immediate. What is important in this series of ancestral identifications is the intertextual affiliations which these names add to Mordecai's identity in the story, especially with regard to his identity as Jewish and his conflict with Haman (on which see below). Mordecai and Saul are not brothers, but this parallel does indeed identify them with one another intertextually.

This intertextual identification of Mordecai with Saul does not stop, moreover, with the Benjamin and Kish connections. As we shall see in the discussion of chapter 3, Mordecai's identification with Saul will be set over against the story's antihero Haman, "enemy [or 'hater'] of the Jews," who is identified with King Agag, Saul's ancient Amalekite opponent in 1 Samuel 15 (see the commentary on Esther 3). Saul's fated failure to follow Samuel's orders in that conflict led to Samuel's (and God's) condemnation Saul's kingship. On the one hand, then, Mordecai's identification with Saul could suggest his own ill-fate; on the other hand, it may turn out to be an opportunity to redeem the Benjaminite royal line.

The word order in this introductory verse, which begins with "a Jewish [or Judean] man" also emphasizes Mordecai's identity as Jewish—and yet not without ambiguity. The word *yĕhûdî*, which the NRSV translates together with *ʾîš*, "man," as "a Jew," more literally means "Judean" or "Judahite," referring (like the earlier use of "Benjaminite") to affiliation with the tribe of Judah and/or the southern kingdom of Judah (with Jerusalem as its capital). David was Judahite, whereas Saul was Benjaminite. Mordecai is *yĕhûdî* like David and Benjaminite

---

[2] Paton, *Esther*, 167.

like the ousted King Saul whom David replaced. This tension between
the Benjaminite identity and the Judahite/ Judean/Jewish identity is
hightened, moreover, by Mordecai's further association with the name
Shimei. In 2 Samuel 16, precisely as David is going into exile, his house
crumbling all around him, he encounters opposition from a Benjaminite named Shimei (2 Sam 16:5-14), a voice from Saul's former regime.
In that narrative, the location of Shimei and the tribe of Benjamin in relation to David and the centralized Judahite monarchy is both marginal and subversive. David encounters him on the margins of his
kingdom at a point when his own reign is less than secure. On his way
into exile, Shimei meets him, hurling stones and curses. Indeed, he in-
trojects the harshest criticisms of David to appear anywhere in the
books of Samuel. David never forgets Shimei's curses, and at the end
of his life he charges Solomon to "bring his gray head down with
blood to Sheol" (2 Kgs 2:9), even though he had promised to spare his
life earlier on. Benjamin, moreover, is a sort of in-between tribe in biblical literature, located between Judah and Ephraim. After the Davidic
kingdom is divided, is it Judahite (the name of the southern kingdom)
or Israelite (northern kingdom)? It is assumed to be northern, but after
the division of the northern kingdom (Israel) and the southern kingdom (Judah, the tribe name which becomes the kingdom's name), it is
identified with the southern kingdom of Judah ("Judah, and the tribe
of Benjamin," in 1 Kings 12). Does Judean (Judahite) identity ultimately, after the fall of both kingdoms, subsume Benjaminite identity?
Does it become synonymous with Jewish identity? Does "Judean"
equal "Jewish"? If so, what is a "Benjaminite"? There emerges, then, a
certain incoherence concerning Mordecai's identification as both "Judahite" *(yěhûdî)* and "Benjaminite" *(yěmînî)*.

  This problem did not escape traditional Jewish commentators.
Rashi suggests that the reason he is called *ʾîš yěhûdî* ("a Jewish [or
Judean] man"; NRSV "a Jew") may be found in the next verse, 2:6, that
is, in Mordecai's association with those who were "carried away from
Jerusalem along the captives carried away with King Jeconiah of
Judah" (which took place in 597 B.C.E.).[3] That is, he is *yěhûdî* "because

---

[3] Levenson, *Esther,* 23, sees this introduction of Mordecai as a glaring example
of "grave chronological problems" in the book of Esther, insofar as he reads the
"who" in 2:6 ("who was carried away from Jerusalem . . . with King Jeconiah,"
which refers to the calamity of 597; cf. 2 Kgs 24:8-17) as referring to Mordecai, not
Kish (so also Paton and Moore, among others). The NRSV adds "Kish" to the beginning of this verse, erasing all ambiguity in this regard. Although I consider this insertion by the NRSV to be inappropriate (as the ambiguous gaps in this narrative are,
I believe, part of its craft), and although I have no interest in arguing for the historicity of this narrative, I contend that there are no chronological problems with

he went into exile with the Judean exile. All those who went into exile with the kings of Judah [*yĕhûdâ*] were called Judeans [*yĕhûdîm*] among the nations, even if they were from another tribe." In this sense, Jewish/Judean identity is an ethnic identity that is constructed from the outside, by other nations, who lumped all those tribal differences into one group identity—namely, those exiled from Judea. Thus, from the outside, distinctions between identities such as Benjaminite and Judean are erased. Yet, as we have seen, this introduction to Mordecai works against such an erasure of difference by including details that open up tensions within the Judean/Jewish identity that is being presented.

Rashi's explanation gains additional support from the emphasis on exile in verse 6: "who [NRSV 'Kish'] had been carried away from Jerusalem among the captives carried away with King Jeconiah of Judah, whom King Nebuchadnezzar of Babylon had carried away." Although it will not be mentioned again throughout the rest of the book, exile (*gālah*, "carried away," in noun or verb form) is explicitly mentioned four times in this verse: Kish was "*carried away* from Jerusalem among the *captives* who were *carried away* with Jeconiah king of Judah, whom Nebuchadnezzar king of Babylon had *carried away*." As Rashi rightly notes, the traumatic dislocation and dispersal of the Babylonian Exile is, ironically, formative for Jewish identity in the book of Esther.

As something of an adjunct to the introduction to Mordecai, the young woman Esther enters the picture: "Mordecai had brought up Hadassah, that is Esther, his cousin, for she had neither father nor mother; the girl was fair and beautiful, and when her father and her mother died, Mordecai adopted her as his own daughter" (2:7). Indeed, Esther is introduced first in terms of her relation to Mordecai, as an aspect of Mordecai's identity. This verse is structured such that it begins and ends with Mordecai acting on Esther (his cousin) in a way that locates her under his oversight: first, at the opening of the verse, she is the object of his "fostering" (or "bringing up," *ʾmn*);[4] and then, at the close of the verse, she is the object of his "taking" (*lqḥ*) "as daughter." Between these two actions of paternal fostering and taking, the text offers two important details: first, both her mother and father have

---

this particular verse. It is no stretch to read the relative *ʾăšer* ("who") at the beginning of verse 6 in reference to Mordecai's great-grandfather Kish, whose name immediately precedes it. To do so, of course, one cannot identify this Kish as Saul's father (1 Sam 9:1).

4 "Fostering" connotes Mordecai's legal role as foster parent as well as his rearing or "nursing" of her (cf. Num 11:12 [Moses as "nurse" to Israel]; Ruth 4:16; 2 Sam 4:4).

died; and second, she is "beautiful in form" (*yĕpat – tōʾar;* NRSV "fair")
and "pleasing to look at" (*ṭôbat marʾeh;* NRSV "beautiful"). The descriptive language here carries strong sexual connotations. The first phrase,
translated as "fair" in the NRSV, clearly refers to her figure (cf. Gen
29:17; 1 Sam 25:3), and the second phrase, translated as "beautiful" in
the NRSV, is the same phrase that was used to describe Vashti in 1:11.
Note, moreover, that this descriptive information is patterned in such
a way that her beautiful figure and good looks are couched between
two mentions of her lack of parents (that is, between "she had neither
father nor mother" and "when her father and mother died"). This peculiar mix of sexual attraction and lack of family raises questions with
regard to Mordecai's motivations for "taking her." Indeed, Esther
would have been a permitted marriage for Mordecai. The text appears
as if it is leaning in that direction: she had no family; she was sexually
attractive; and when her parents died, he took her for himself . . . "as
daughter." The reader might well expect "as wife" at this point. Indeed, the Talmud and many subsequent interpreters (including Rashi)
have read *lĕbat,* "as daughter," as a shortened form of *lĕbayit,* "as
house," in the sense of marrying her.

As we saw in the introduction to Mordecai (2:5), names can be very
significant in this story. Esther, interestingly, is given one name which
is immediately replaced with another: "Hadassah, that is Esther" (2:7).
Hadassah (*hădassâ*), which is given here and nowhere else in the story,
probably comes from the late Hebrew word "myrtle" (*hădas;* cf. Isa
41:19; 55:13; Zech 1:8, 10, 11), and reflects a common practice of naming girls after flowers and plants. In this name, as in the language used
to describe her later in the verse, the emphasis is on attractiveness. Yet
as soon as this name has been revealed it is withdrawn and will not be
mentioned again. It is replaced with Esther, *ʾestēr,* a name carrying very
different possible meanings.[5] It may be related to the Persian word
stâra, or "star," although most scholars identify it with the name Ishtar,
the principal goddess of the ancient Near East (closely related to the
Western Semitic goddess named Astarte).[6] This goddess is associated
primarily with love, eroticism, and sexual power. In this light, Esther's
name may be interpreted with a connotation of goddess-like sexual
power.[7] Finally, as discussed in the introduction, one may follow the

---

[5] See also Abraham S. Yehuda, "The Meaning of the Name Esther," *Journal of the
Royal Asiatic Society* (1946) 174–8; repr. Carey A. Moore, ed., *Studies in the Book of Esther* (New York: Ktav, 1982) 269–72.

[6] See William J. Fulco, "Ishtar," *Anchor Bible Dictionary* III (1992) 521–2.

[7] Note further that Mordecai's name is somewhat close to the name Marduk (cf.
the Persian *mardûka*).

Talmud and read her name to mean "I will hide" or "I am hiding"; that is, if read without the vowel pointing, *ʾstr* can be translated as a first-person imperfect form of the verb "to hide" (compare the Greek name Kalypso, which also can be translated "I hide"). This sense is intriguing in relation to her first name, Hadassah—a name which is hidden, or covered over, as quickly as it is disclosed. The Talmud offers two different ways of interpreting her name in relation to hiding. First, in Talmud Hullin 139b, we read, "where is Esther indicated in the Torah? 'And I will surely hide *[hastēr ʾastîr].*'" Here, the rabbis relate her name to Deut 31:18, in which God promises judgment against Israel for going after other gods: "I will surely hide my face from them." In this sense, then, Esther's name is interpreted as a reference to *God* hiding. This could be interpreted hopefully, suggesting that the book affirms God's subtle, hidden presence "behind the scenes" in the story. Yet, as discussed in the introduction, given the strong judgment theme in Deut 31:18, this could be interpreted as an indicator that the Jews in this story are very much on their own: they are living in the wake of exile and God, dreadfully, has hidden God's face (or presence) from them. In this sense, the name would suggest that the storied world of Esther is a godless world indeed. In support of reading her name as a reference to divine hiding as punishment, see also Gen 4:14, in which Cain declares, in terror, "I will be hidden [Niphal form of *ʾstr*] from your face." In this passage, moreover, the unpointed Hebrew verb is exactly the same as Esther's name.

Yet another Talmud reference suggests a less theological meaning to Esther's name: in Megilla 13a, R. Judah says that, although Hadassah was her original name, she was called Esther because she "hid facts about herself." This sort of hiding, as we shall see, will prove to be most significant as the story progresses.

One should not feel compelled to reduce these many connotations in Esther's name to one, for a name is always in some sense irreducible. The particularity of the name resists reduction according to larger categories of identity.

In relation to the preceding context (esp. 1:9-22 and 2:1-4), furthermore, verse 7 establishes Esther's identification *with* and *over against* Vashti. Vashti is the only other character described in the story as "pleasing to look at" (*ṭôbat marʾeh*, 1:11; cf. 2:2-3). But unlike Vashti, Esther has no status other than that of object as of yet: thus far she has been looked upon and acted upon only, and has shown no sign of refusing. Thus she is positioned in the narrative to fill the blank space left by Vashti while resolving the royal male crisis brought on by Vashti's refusal of status as object. In a way similar to the introduction of Mordecai in verses 5-6, then, the selective details offered in verse 7 about Esther are significant. On the one hand, these details indicate Esther's vulnerable status as orphaned, exiled woman within an outlandishly patriarchal social order (see chapter 1). On the other hand, they highlight her potential status as pleasing object of exchange between men. As 2:1-4 makes clear, this is to be her function for the king: to reflect well on him, as Vashti refused to do. Thus she finds herself, to borrow again from Luce Irigaray, "signed up" in a comical yet deadly serious game of male domination "without having begun to play."[8] Nevertheless, even here, as she is introduced, we must wonder whether there is more to Esther than meets the eye.

Immediately following this introduction of Mordecai and Esther in 2:5-7, the text returns to the king's pageant search for Vashti's replacement: "So when the king's order and his edict were proclaimed, and when many young women were gathered in the citadel of Susa in custody of Hegai, Esther also was taken into the king's palace and put in custody of Hegai, who had charge of the women" (2:8). Given the earlier call for "good looking" young virgins, and given the fact that Esther has just been described in precisely this way (and then some), it is no surprise that she is one of the enlistees. In this movement from one man's house to another's, moreover, Esther is an object of transfer: she goes from being "taken" *(lqḥ)* by Mordecai (2:7) to being "taken" (once again *lqḥ*), along with the other young women, into the king's house, into the hand of Hegai, who is literally described as "keeper of the women" (NRSV "who had charge of the women"). In the space of two verses, then, we read of a double-conscription for Esther. She has already been "taken" into two houses, from one man's house to another.

So far, as noted earlier, Esther appears in the story only as the object of verbs (with males and eunuchs as the subjects of those verbs). She is beautiful to look at (by men), she is "taken" (by Mordecai and by Hegai), and she is gathered and kept along with other women (by Hegai and other royal servants). Once in this new royal pageant realm, however, Esther becomes the subject of verbs: she "pleases" Hegai and she "wins his favor" *(ḥesed,* which can also mean "loyalty"), so that he hastens her preparations, giving her "seven chosen maids [or young women]" to serve her, and switches her up to "the best place in the harem" (more literally, the "best of the house of the women"; 2:9). In this series of passive constructions of Esther, what is the significance of the active verbal constructions involving her "pleasing" and "winning favor"? There are certainly other ways in Hebrew to phrase this in order to focus the action on Hegai's perception of Esther rather than her own construal of that perception. The effect here is, paradoxically,

---

[8] Irigaray, *Speculum*, 22.

to give the one being *objectified* a certain subjectivity. To "win his favor," or more literally to "*lift [nś³]* loyalty in his eyes," is essentially to "cause him to look loyally." This action is, in this sense, a play of appearances by the object. In one sense, of course, there is nothing surprising in this construction, for this is just the kind of female subjectivity that would be allowed in such an insecurely patriarchal world. After all, what is so subversive about pleasing him and winning his favor? Yet, given the connotations in her name (esp. the association with Ishtar/sexual power and with hiding/playing with appearances), this might also be an early, very subtle suggestion that Esther possesses a kind of agency in relation to male subjects that could hit them quite by surprise.

Verses 10-11 comprise a parenthetical aside (and remember that the contents of parentheses are often extremely significant) on the issue of Esther's identity as Jewish cousin and daughter to Mordecai. This aside complicates the transference of Esther narrated in the previous verses, insofar as it suggests that the new, royal context of Esther's identity does not mean that the old context, in Mordecai's house, has been erased. She is now being held accountable (is "signed up") to the households of two men.

"Esther did not reveal her people or kindred,[9] for Mordecai had charged her not to tell" (2:10). Mentioned almost as an aside here, this non-revelation of her people will eventually become an extremely important tool for undoing a plot (by Haman and the king) that would have been the end of all Persian Jews—or at least those whose Jewish identity had in some way been revealed. Note, in this regard, that Esther *does not actively hide* her people; rather, it is hidden simply by *not revealing* (the more basic meaning of the verb *ngd*, which the NRSV translates here as "tell," is "reveal" or "disclose"). Already, then, only five verses after the first Jewish character has been introduced (2:5), there is indication that the book of Esther does not assume that Jewish identity is in any sense self-evident or readily apparent; Jewish identity does not necessarily have anything to do with particular behaviors or appearances (either physicial features or dress).

In addition to providing the vital information that Esther does not at this point reveal her people, verse 10 also gives further indication of her subordination to Mordecai, insofar as she does exactly as he commands, even when she is no longer in his house. In this sense, her hiding

---

[9] The NRSV is somewhat misleading here, insofar as the phrase "her people or kindred" would appear to be a translation of two words, one for "people" and one for "kindred." In fact, there is only one Hebrew word, *ʿammāh*, most literally "her people," behind this phrase in the NRSV.

at this point does not appear to be part of any strategy *she* has in mind. It is simply another aspect of her being conscripted according the orders and regulations of men. It is an act of obedience to Mordecai.

On the other hand, neither does the text does give any clear indication why Mordecai commands or "charges" (*ṣwh*) her not to reveal her identification with her Jewish people. It is simply indicated that Mordecai ordered her not to reveal it. Is there some risk in revealing Jewish identity in this story world? We have no reason to believe so at *this* point, anyway. Is this identity hidden because it would discourage her rise, or even endanger her in the Persian court, as Ibn Ezra and many other commentators have suggested? There is no indication that this is so, either from within the book thus far or from what can be known about Persian history generally. For that matter, perhaps it is wrong to presume at this point in the narrative that "her people" (*ʿammāh*) necessarily refers to her Jewish identity. Might "her people" refer more particularly to her family? Is "her people" not revealed because Mordecai does not want anyone to know Esther's affiliation with *him*? Would (public) identification with Mordecai be (politically) disadvantageous, even dangerous? Perhaps, although again there is no indication as of yet that this is so. Very soon (in chapter 3) there will be strong indication that both reasons may be valid, as the conflict between Haman and Mordecai comes to the fore in tandem with Haman's plan to annihilate all Jews. Nonetheless, at this point the text leaves such questions hanging.

In verse 11, the parenthetical aside continues but turns attention briefly back to Mordecai: "Every day Mordecai would walk around in front of the court of the harem, to learn how Esther was and how she fared [lit. 'what was being done with her']." This notice makes clear Mordecai's continued interest, or *investment*, in Esther. That is, it indicates his concern for her personal welfare, as well as his investment in her for his own self-interest. These two kinds of investment will remain ambiguously entangled throughout the story. Here again, moreover, the focus is on "what was being done with her" (the last part of the verse, which the NRSV translates "how she fared"). This more literal translation makes clear that here she remains, literally, an *object of concern*. She is an object that has been exchanged between and circulated among the men and, as such, she is Mordecai's link with the central Persian politics. In this regard, Mordecai's investment in Esther suggests his own vulnerable dependence on her, especially at this point in the narrative, as she moves out from under his direct control and into a new royal sphere (the inner circle) to which he has little or no access without her. He can only watch from the sidelines to see what is happening to or with her, to see "what is being done with her" by others.

MAKEUP AND A ROYAL PARTY (2:12-18)

Following the brief parenthetical aside in 2:10-11, the narrative attention returns, in verses 12-18, to the internal affairs of the royal household. At 2:15, the narrative will shift once again from the general to the particular, that is, from "the turn for each young woman" (2:13) to "when the turn came for Esther" (2:15). Therefore 2:12-18 can be subdivided into two parts: (a) 2:12-14, which provides general background on the royal pageant procedure as it applies to all the young women; and (b) 2:15-18, which describes the procedure as it applies to Esther specifically.

> The turn came for each girl to go in to King Ahasuerus, after being twelve months under the regulations for the women, since this was the regular period of their cosmetic treatment, six months with oil of myrrh and six months with perfumes and cosmetics for women. When the girl went in to the king she was given whatever she asked for to take with her from the harem to the king's palace. In the evening she went in; then in the morning she came back to the second harem in custody of Shaashgaz, the king's eunuch, who was in charge of the concubines; she did not go in to the king again, unless the king delighted in her and she was summoned by name. (2:12-14)

Verses 12-14 describe in great detail the extravagent excesses of Persian bureaucracy in the year-long "cosmetic treatment" (six months with oil of myrrh and six months with perfumes) and the subsequent trafficking of each woman from the first royal "house of women" (or "harem") to the king's house and then back to a second house, where the concubines are kept. That is, after the twelve months of make-over, each young woman in turn would pass over at evening from this preparatory "house of women" to the "house of the king" for a royal inspection (2:13). The next morning she would go to the "second house of women," into the hand of another eunuch, Shaashgaz, "keeper of the concubines." Thus, as she is passed through the king's house, her identity changes: from "young woman," kept by Hegai, to "concubine," kept by Shaashgaz. She would not return to the king unless "he delighted in her and she was summoned by name" (v. 14b). The fact that the king will "summon by name" the one he "delights in," along with the ritualized, almost sacrificial sense of the procedure for making up and passing the women across, suggests that Ahasuerus functions as a sort of deity in this passage—albeit the ridiculous, farcical deity of an excessively ornate and labor intensive rite.

Note too that in these crossovers and exchanges of women, the eunuchs (Hegai and Shaashgaz) again serve as mediators between the sexes. The seven eunuchs in Esther 1 functioned similarly in the king's interchange with Vashti (1:10, 12, 15). In both cases the women are handled "by" or put "into the hand of" eunuchs (*bĕyad* or *ʾel – yad;* 1:12, 15; 2:3, 8, 14).

In all this procedure, moreover, there is an emphasis on everything being done "according to law" (2:12)—a concern which was likewise operative in the rules for drinking in 1:8 as well as in the exaggerated bureaucratic reaction to Vashti in 1:15 ("What, according to the law, ought to be done with Vashti?"). Once again, moreover, as with the legal action taken against Vashti, a primary concern of the king's bureaucracy appears to be sexual politics. Although not directly speaking to the book of Esther, Judith Butler's description of gender construction as a repetitive and constant marking of the body is particularly suggestive in relation to this beautification process: "Gender is the repeated stylization of the body, a set of repeated acts within a highly rigid regulatory frame that congeal over time to produce the appearance of substance."[10] Verses 12-14 detail the final touches of this royal engendering procedure. Indeed, this procedure is a most literal example of the law being written onto women's bodies.

These legal procedures for cosmetically engendering a queen in verses 12-14 are, in fact, a *continuation* of the legal procedure drafted in reaction to Vashti in chapter 1, insofar as this new legal pageant-procedure, like that earlier law, aims primarily to undo Vashti's traumatic refusal to be a pleasing object for the king. That is, the *objective* of the regulatory procedure described in verses 12-14 is to prepare these women to be pleasing objects for the king, so that the most pleasing one may replace Vashti, who slipped out of that object status. The farcical character of that earlier overblown legal reaction to Vashti might then suggest that this procedure be taken as further indication of the ridiculous character of the royal order being presented in the story.

Verses 15-18 then turn narrative attention onto Esther specifically. Of course, since verse 7, where Esther is described as the perfect candidate for the king's pageant ("good looking" [*ṭôbat marʾeh;* cf. 2:2-3), the expectation has been that Esther will be the chosen one.

> When the turn came for Esther daughter of Abihail the uncle of Mordecai, who had adopted her as his own daughter, to go in to the king, she asked for nothing except what Hegai the king's eunuch, who had charge of the women, advised. Now Esther was admired by all who saw her.

[10] Judith Butler, *Gender Trouble: Feminism and the Subversion of Identity* (New York: Routledge, 1990) 33.

When Esther was taken to King Ahasuerus in his royal palace in the tenth month, which is the month of Tebeth, in the seventh year of his reign, the king loved Esther more than all the other women; of all the virgins she won his favor and devotion, so that he set the royal crown on her head and made her queen instead of Vashti. Then the king gave a great banquet to all his officials and ministers—"Esther's banquet." He also granted a holiday to the provinces, and gave gifts with royal liberality. (2:15-18)

Verse 15 opens, peculiarly, with further family information on Esther: this time she is introduced as "Esther, daughter of Abihail, uncle of Mordecai who took [again *lqḥ*; NRSV 'adopted'] her."[11] She will be called "Esther, daughter of Abihail" again in 9:29. The name is used for both women and men elsewhere in the Bible, although here it must refer to a man, since he is also identified as Mordecai's uncle.[12] Beyond the slim ancestral record it provides (we have no other references in the Bible to this Abihail), it is significant that the name translates literally as "my father is might" or "strength" (cf. "army" in Esth 1:3). Given that the Abihail mentioned here is dead (2:7), the name may suggest that the true father of the orphaned Esther is strength. In this name, we may find a subtle foreshadowing of Esther's own power, which is yet to be revealed in the political arena.

Her ostensible deference is maintained at this point, however, as verse 15 continues: "she sought [*biqšâ*; NRSV 'asked for'] nothing except what Hegai the king's eunuch, who had charge of the women, advised." At this point, she "seeks" or "asks for" nothing but follows Hegai's advice. Indeed, there is a great deal of political "seeking" (*bqš*) in this story: the king *seeks* young women who might replace Vashti

---

[11] Esther is the only woman in this episode, and in the book of Esther as a whole, who is literally "taken" (the object of *lqḥ*, "take") by men. In fact, in the course of 2:5-18, she is "taken" three times: first by Mordecai into his house ("as daughter"; vv. 7 and 15), and then into the king's house (v. 16, in a passive construction of the same verb). It appears that the object-position for this verb is reserved for Esther. This serves rhetorically in the early passages about Esther to mark her as the privileged object of male taking. As we shall see, this rhetorical emphasis will add to the contrast between the Esther being taken and pleasingly ogled by men here and the Esther calling the shots for the men (Mordecai, the king, and Haman) in subsequent narrative action.

[12] In 2 Chr 11:18, Abihail (spelled with the variant *hey* rather than *ḥet*) daughter of Eliab is "taken" by Rehoboam as a wife; in 1 Chr 2:29 Abihail (also spelled with a *hey*) is mentioned in a list as the wife of Abishur; in 1 Chr 5:14, on the other hand, Abihail is a Gadite man; in Num 3:35 it is not entirely clear whether Abihail is a man or a woman (Zuriel is listed as the son of Abihail), although the pattern of ancestral lists in Numbers would suggest that it is a man there as well.

(2:2); later, the eunuchs will *seek* to assassinate the king (2:21); and Haman will *seek* to destroy all Jewish people in Persia (3:6). In every case the verb used is a form of *bqš*. As we shall see, Esther will have further opportunity to tell the king what she seeks (using the same verb; 7:2, 3)[13]; and it will be something more than softer rolls and an extra pillow (Esther 7-8).

The verse concludes with another notice anticipating her success with the king: "Now Esther was admired by all who saw her." The Hebrew phrase translated here as "was admired by all who saw her" can be translated more literally as "won [or 'lifted'; *nś*] favor [*hēn*] in the eyes of all who looked at her [*rōʾêhā*]." When translated thus, a clear connection can be seen between this note in verse 15 and earlier references to "winning [or lifting] favor" (*hesed*; 1:9) and the king's desire for a woman who is "pleasing to look at" (*tôbat marʾeh*), which uses the same verb (1:11; 2:2, 3, 7). Once again, the text is making clear that she fits the royal bill.

In the tenth month (Tebet—December/January), in the seventh year of Ahasuerus's reign (four years since the point at which the story began [1:3]), Esther is "taken" (again *lqh*) to the king (2:16), presumably according to the protocol described earlier in verses 12-14. Recall that Queen Vashti was supposed to be brought in to be looked at on the seventh day of the king's seven day party (1:10). Now Esther is taken to the king in the seventh year of his reign to be considered as a replacement for Vashti (and her "good looks" will obviously be a key factor in his consideration). By evening, the "the king loved Esther more than all the other women; of all the virgins she won [again *nś*] his favor [*hēn*] and devotion [*hesed*], so that he set the royal crown on her head and made her queen *instead of* Vashti" (2:17; cf. 1:19). This verse makes clear that, as far as the king is concerned, Esther's selection as queen is the undoing of the "gender trouble" brought on by Vashti's displeasing refusal. After *being taken* to his house in the seventh year (Vashti had refused to be brought by the eunuchs on the seventh day of his party; 1:10, 12), Esther gains love, favor, and devotion "in his presence" (*lěpānāyw*; Vashti had refused to be brought "into his presence"; 1:11)[14] above all other women, and therefore he crowns

---

[13] The NRSV often translates this verb, in reference to Esther's seeking, as "request" or "ask" (e.g., 7:2, 3). This translation, unfortunately, loses the parallel between Esther's political interests and those of Haman (3:6) and the king's would-be assassins (2:21). In reference to Haman in 3:6, a form of the verb is translated as "plotted," and in reference to the assassins in 2:21, it is translated as "conspired."

[14] Translation of *lěpānāyw* is omitted from the NRSV of verse 17, thereby erasing this important textual connection to the Vashti story.

her as queen *"instead of Vashti"* (as was recommended twice: by Memucan in 1:19 and by the attendants in 2:4).

This undoing of Vashti, and the return to what *appears* to be a secure patriarchy, is finalized by another drinking party—the "Esther drinking party"—as well as a holiday, including the giving of royal gifts (2:18). As with the parties in chapter 1, this royal extravagance involves all the chiefs and civil servants and touches "all the provinces," so that every realm of the kingdom that would have been disturbed (according to Memucan) by the Vashti catastrophe is re-secured—through drinking, of course! It has been four years since the king's seven-day party for the people of Susa was brought low by Vashti's refusal to come and be ogled. This new party appears to set things right again, to successfully fill the space left by the erasure of Vashti. Yet traces of Vashti remain throughout the rest of the narrative, reminding readers of the patriarchal dependencies and insecurities she introduced.

Chapter 4

COUP

Esther 2:19-23

Immediately following Esther's selection and coronation as a replacement for Vashti, the text makes an abrupt turn to a new potential political crisis for the king, namely an assassination plot by a couple of angry eunuchs. This new crisis will be resolved not by Esther exactly, but by Mordecai *through* Esther and by Esther *through* Mordecai. In the process, new spaces of betweenness emerge on the political map—threshold spaces that threaten the center.

This brief story within the story moves back and forth between Esther in the royal center and Mordecai on the margin: from the virgins being gathered in verse 19a (center), to Mordecai sitting at the king's gate in verse 19b (margin), to Esther not revealing her people in verse 20 (center), to Mordecai sitting at the gate while the eunuchs are enraged and seek to kill the king in verses 21-22a (margin), to Mordecai revealing the plot to Esther and, through her, to the king in verses 22b-23 (center), after which point the eunuchs are brought in from the margins to central justice through public execution and the writing of an official record. The marginal subversion is finally reined into the center.

The opening phrase of verse 19, "when the virgins were being gathered together," is more ambiguous in the Hebrew text than the NRSV translation admits, for it includes the qualifier "a second time" *(šēnît)*. As the many inconclusive scholarly arguments make clear,[1] the meaning is difficult to interpret, leading several to suggest that the text is

---

[1] For summaries of the various interpretive and text-critical proposals, see Bush, *Ruth, Esther*, 371–2; and Paton, *Esther*, 186–7.

corrupt at this point. If taken without textual emendation, it may suggest that the gathering described here takes place at a time later than that described in 2:8, perhaps after Esther has become queen (in order to increase the harem further, or to bring them to the "banquet of Esther," or for some other reason). Or it may be another stage of the same gathering described in 2:8, in which case this opening phrase ties the narrative action in this passage back to the time of the initial gathering of young women described in 2:8-11. Following the lead of the LXX, the NRSV and most other translations omit the word, relegating this ambiguous reference to a second gathering to a textual note.

Whether or not this second gathering takes place around the same time as the gathering described in 2:8, this passage is presented as a parenthetical aside that is parallel to the aside in 2:10-11 (which took place at the time of the first gathering), insofar as it turns attention away from Esther in the palace and toward Mordecai on the margins. In 2:11, we found Mordecai on the outside looking in, wandering around in front of the harem in order to learn what was being done with his niece/daughter Esther. In this passage, it becomes clear that Mordecai has been learning about other matters as well. As this window onto Mordecai opens, he is not wandering outside the harem, but is seated at yet another marginal location, "sitting at the king's gate" (2:19), literally on the threshold of royal quarters.

Just as the narrative attention turns to Mordecai, yet another parenthetical aside—a parenthesis within a parenthesis—is given in verse 20: "Now Esther had not revealed her kindred or her people, as Mordecai had charged her; for Esther obeyed Mordecai just as when she was brought up by him." This is a reiteration of the comment in 2:10 that Esther had not revealed her people (or kindred), "as Mordecai charged her." Although she is now beyond his reach, Esther continues to obey Mordecai, "just as when she was brought up by him." As with the aside concerning Esther's obedience to Mordecai in 2:10, this note in 2:20 helps to maintain the link (through a relationship of command and obedience) between the two emerging protagonists, even as it indicates the tenuousness of that link as their socio-political locations rapidly diverge. She does not really need to obey Mordecai now that she is queen, and the note that she does still obey him highlights this new circumstance. It also foreshadows the fact that soon enough *Mordecai* will be obeying *Esther's* commands, just as she used to obey him (4:17).

After this brief aside on Esther's obedience, the text of verse 21 immediately loops back, through repetition of part of verse 19 ("in those days, *while Mordecai was sitting at the king's gate*"), to Mordecai on the margins. And who should he get to know at this threshold location but two eunuchs, Bigthan and Teresh, "who guarded the threshold." Most literally, these eunuchs are "keepers of the threshold" *(miššōmrê has-sap)*, just as Hegai was "keeper *[šōmēr]* of the women" and Shaashgaz was "keeper *[šōmēr]* of the concubines." Here again, royal eunuchs are functioning as "keepers" or "guardians" of the threshold spaces between key political locations.[2]

As Memucan shares this threshold space with the eunuchs, the two eunuchs become angry and, most literally, "sought to lay hands on [NRSV 'conspired to assassinate'] King Ahasuerus." Significantly, the verb used to describe their rage here *(qṣp)* is the same verb that was used to describe the *king's* rage at Vashti's refusal of his command "by the hand of the eunuchs" in 1:12. Once again, this ostensibly straight-forward narrative suggests, through simple lexical connections and narrative parallels, more subtle and riddling associations, in this case between the king's royal rage and the eunuchs's anti-royal rage.

The next verse then reveals Mordecai's part as reconnaissance agent between the subversive margins and the royal center, indicating that he is not fully identified with either location: "But the matter came to the knowledge of Mordecai, and he told it to Queen Esther, and Esther told the king in the name of Mordecai" (2:22). Indeed, this verse serves as a sort of bridge that moves the affair (along with Mordecai's name) from the margins to the center. First, "the matter came to the knowledge of Mordecai." How? Why was he privy to such subversive information? Did the eunuchs simply talk too loudly about their plans to assassinate the king, or did they assume Mordecai could be trusted with such information? Second, "he told ['revealed to'; *ngd*] Queen Esther." How did he reach Esther in order to tell her? Are they still in contact with one another? Up to this point one would assume not. How is Mordecai privy to the royal goings-on inside the palace, where Esther now resides? How do words travel in this story when they do not ride on royal steeds? None of these questions are answered, and yet nothing about Mordecai's identification with and access to either realm is self-evident.

After hearing of the assassination plot from Mordecai, "Esther told the king in the name of Mordecai." Once the matter is "investigated" *(yĕbuqqaš*, literally "sought"—the same verb translated as "conspired" in relation to the eunuch plot in 2:21, and as "asked" in relation to Esther in 2:15), the two would-be assassins are "hanged on the gallows" (NRSV), or "impaled on the stake" (2:22)[3]—literally pinned in the center.

[2] See the earlier commentary on the eunuchs in 1:10-11.

[3] Although the NRSV and most other English translations (except Tanakh) have "hanged on the gallows," the text more literally reads "impaled on the stake" (i.e., "the wood [stake]"). As Moore, *Esther*, 31, notes, Herodotus indicates that Xerxes

Thanks to Mordecai, located precariously between those on the subversive margins and those in the center of political power, this particular coup fails. The subversion is subverted because the king has outsiders on the inside (or vice-versa?).

As a last word on the failed coup, this brief story within the story is concluded by being fixed in writing: "it was recorded in the book of the annals in the presence of the king" (v. 23b). Yet its fixation in writing *within the book of Esther itself* may be less conclusive, for it is not entirely clear what "it" is that is being recorded in the king's presence. What details were written down? Was it the execution that was recorded? Was it the names of those executed? Was *Mordecai's* name recorded? Esther, after all, "told the king *in the name of* Mordecai." Was it noted that Mordecai is Jewish, or that he was sitting at the king's gate? Indeed, later on, after re-reading this record, the king calls him *"the Jew* Mordecai who sits at the king's gate" (6:10). The reader is left to imagine what was important enough—let alone what details were known—to make the official record.[4] This fixation in writing appears, then, to fix a certain ambiguity and uncertainly into the relations between Esther, the king, and Mordecai.

---

carried out executions by impalement. Although crucifixion was also practiced (note that the LXX has them crucified), a gallows-type hanging is less likely. As Bush, *Ruth, Esther,* 373, points out, hanging was used in the ancient world as a means of exposing the body of someone *already* executed. In this regard, see also the commentary on 9:14, where Haman's already dead sons are "hanged" or "impaled."

[4] Levenson, *Esther,* 64, argues that Esther's revelation of the plot in Mordecai's name "surely should have given away the very information that her foster father had enjoined her not to divulge," namely "her people" (2:10, 20; cf. Fox, *Character,* 40, who reads this as a narrative "slip"). Yet it is not clear why this revelation in Mordecai's name would "surely" give away her people or her Jewish identity. The text does not indicate how she referred to his name. Did she call him "my uncle" or "foster father" (cf. 8:1)? Did she necessarily say that he was Jewish? Note, in this regard, that Mordecai's Jewish identity is not self-evident to Haman in the confrontation in the next chapter; on the contrary, he does not know that Mordecai is Jewish until it is "revealed" to him by the other servants (3:4, 6). On the other hand, note that after re-reading the annals, the king calls him "the Jew Mordecai," which would suggest that his Jewish identity was either included in the written record or was previously known by the king. In any case, Esther's revelation of the plot in Mordecai's name would not necessarily reveal her kinship with him.

Chapter 5

POLITICS OF AN ANTI-JEW

Esther 3:1-15

Thus far the narrative has been dominated by the king's (and the patriarchy's) crisis concerning Vashti. The action has been focused on matters of sexual politics, that is, finding a way to undo and forget the crisis in royal masculinity introduced by this "other woman." At this point, a new conflict is introduced which focuses on matters of ethnic politics, that is, projecting Jews as the nation's singular other, the one divergent threat within an otherwise unified and stable national identity, and marking them for annihilation. As was the case in chapters 1–2, this conflict begins on a personal level—between Mordecai and Haman—but quickly moves to a most universal decree. As we shall see, moreover, the narrative pattern and details of the conflict between Haman and the "other Jew" Mordecai in chapter 3 are strikingly parallel to those of the conflict between the king and the "other woman" Vashti, suggesting parallels between the dynamics of sexism and anti-Judaism.

Esther 3 can be divided into three parts, or scenes, each of which is introduced with a specific reference to time: (a) 3:1-6, the promotion of Haman, Mordecai's refusal to bow, and Haman's ensuing rage (introduced by "after these things . . ."); (b) 3:7-11, Haman's proposal to annihilate all Jews, and the king's approval (introduced by "in first month, which is the month of Nisan, in the twelfth year . . ."); and (c) 3:12-15, the authoring of the anti-Jewish decree, presumably quelling Haman's rage, and the return to drinking ("on the thirteenth day of the first month . . .").

Will Mordecai's Stand Stand? (3:1-6)

This episode begins rather abruptly, focusing on a new character and what appears to be a markedly different situation having little to do with Esther's new queendom or the eunuch coup: "After these things King Ahasuerus promoted Haman son of Hammedatha the Agagite, and advanced him and set his seat above all the officials who were with him" (3:1).

The opening phrase in 3:1, "after these things" (*ʾaḥar haddĕbārîm hāʾēlleh*) is identical to the opening phrase in 2:1. There in 2:1, as elsewhere in Hebrew narrative, this phrase served to link what was to follow in chapter 2 with what preceded (i.e., the story of Vashti), while simultaneously marking an indefinite distance from the previous action in time. Chapter 1 had been about Vashti, her refusal to be objectified, and the subsequent legal response to her refusal and the crisis it introduced for the king. As the action in chapter 2 began, some time had passed and yet the king still "remembered Vashti," and the pageant search planned and implemented in chapter 2 was a continuation of the royal response to the problem of Vashti. Thus one might expect something similar here in chapter 3. Immediately preceding this chapter was the subversion of the eunuch assassination attempt, which Mordecai apparently got credit for exposing (since Esther revealed to plan to the king "in the name of Mordecai"; 2:22). So, as we begin this narrative with "after these things," we might well imagine that the king will do something in response to that good deed. And so we read on: "after these things King Ahasuerus promoted . . ." Mordecai? No! Instead, we are abruptly introduced to a new character, "Haman, son of Hammedatha the Agagite" (3:1). The official position (or "seat," translated as "throne" in 1:2) of this new character is set over all the other officials who were with him. What precisely this "seat" would be in the Persian royal order is left unclear to the reader. Perhaps an ancient audience would have known exactly what his new position was. Or perhaps they would have been familiar with Haman himself as a Persian court official. Or perhaps the precise details of his official status were unimportant to an ancient audience just as they are inaccessible now. At any rate he is made a top official.

Although it frustrates certain narrative expectations, the advancement of Haman is not necessarily as inappropriate as it first seems. If we read this promotion as a matter of restructuring the Persian government in the wake of an attempted coup (perhaps the king is no longer certain that he can trust the current premier), then this action might be interpreted as directly related to the preceding story. If Haman is promoted above all other officials, someone else must have been bumped down in rank. In this light Haman's promotion could be seen as the replacement of a premier just as chapter 2 was about the replacement of a queen.

Yet the text offers another detail concerning Haman that anticipates the forthcoming conflict between him and our protagonists: he is an Agagite. Although this ethnic designation may refer to an otherwise unknown Persian lineage, within the book of Esther, it most clearly affiliates him with King Agag of the Amalekites, who appears elsewhere in Scripture in 1 Samuel 15 and Numbers 24. An oracle of Balaam son of Beor in Num 24:3-9 predicts that an Israelite king will "be higher than Agag, and his kingdom shall be exalted" (v. 7). This oracle is fulfilled in 1 Samuel 15—but not quite according to the divine plan: despite God's command that Saul utterly destroy the Amalekites "and all that they have" (15:3), Saul and the Israelites spare King Agag and the choice livestock for sacrifice to God (15:8-9, 15). This well-meant omission seals Saul's rejection by God as king over Israel (15:22-29).[1]

As noted earlier, moreover, Mordecai was introduced as a Benjamite (2:5), and this was Saul's tribal affiliation as well. Within the intertextual field of the Bible, then, Haman and Mordecai are identified with Agag (king of the Amalekites) and Saul respectively, and the forthcoming conflict between them is identified with the conflict in 1 Samuel 15, after which Saul's kingdom began its fated and rapid decline. Here, then, is an opportunity for Mordecai to redeem the Saulide/Benjamite record with Agag and the Amalekites.[2] Yet this intertextual connection not only further compounds the forthcoming conflict between Mordecai and Haman; it also threatens the possibility of a fate for Mordecai that is like that of Saul. Moreover, just as it was not Saul but Samuel who ultimately destroyed Agag (hewing him into pieces; 1 Sam 15:33), it may turn out that someone other than Mordecai (Esther, perhaps?) will ultimately defeat Haman. This set of intertextual relationships does not serve as an interpretive key to the book of Esther;

---

[1] For more details on the relation between the book of Esther and 1 Samuel 15, see William McKane, "A Note on Esther IX and I Samuel XV," *Journal of Theological Studies* 12 (1961) 260–1; and Jonathan Magonet, "The Liberal and the Lady: Esther Revisited," *Judaism* 29 (1980) 167–76.

[2] Note in this regard that when the Jews finally defeat Haman and their enemies, the text reiterates several times that they did not plunder them (9:10, 15). Note also that in a summary of Saul's victories in 1 Samuel 14, it is stated that Saul struck down the Amalekites "and rescued Israel out of the hands of those who *plundered* them" (14:48). This notice, along with the narrative of King Agag in the next chapter, is significant in relation to Esther because the original edict authored by Haman and Ahasuerus calls for the plundering of their Jewish victims (see the discussion below).

on the contrary, it compounds tensions and ambiguities while frustrating any clear anticipation of a tidy narrative resolution.

Verse 2 then moves attention from the scene of the promotion back to the king's gate, where all the servants are "bowing down and doing obeisance to Haman; for the king had so commanded concerning him. But Mordecai did not bow down or do obeisance." The honoring of Haman as new premier is by command of the king.[3] And yet Mordecai does not do it. Why? There is no obvious answer, although there are many interesting possibilities. Perhaps he is indignant that he did not get a promotion after revealing (via Esther) the assassination plot of the eunuchs in the previous episode. In this light he may be angry at the king (thus refusing the king's command) or indignant towards Haman (thus refusing to honor him) or both. Or perhaps he knows that Haman is an Agagite, and his own heritage stirs him to refuse to bow. Relatedly, perhaps there is a religious significance to Mordecai's refusal to bow; that is, he is refusing to practice idolatry. In support of this possible motivation, the two verbs used to describe the honor being given to Haman by the servants, kr^c ("bow down") and $šḥh$ (in a Hitpalel stem, "do obeisance"), can be used to describe homage to a deity. Against this as a motivation for Mordecai's refusal, however, is the absolute lack of explicity religious or theological references in the book of Esther, as well as the fact that such obeisance is done for kings in other biblical narratives (e.g., 1 Sam 24:9 [Eng. 24:8], where David bows and "does obeisance" *[šḥh]* to Saul). Thus, once again, the text leaves open the *possibility* of religious or theological significance without any confirmation whatsoever. As with Vashti's refusal of the king's command in 1:12, the motivation to go against the king's command is left entirely uncertain.

Another question that emerges for the first time in this verse concerns the status of Mordecai vis-à-vis the Persian government. In 2:19, Mordecai was found at the king's gate, and so it is not surprising that he is there once again. In that earlier episode, as was noted, he was privy to insider information on a coup being planned by eunuchs of the king, and this raised questions as to how he would have had access to such information. Although it is not at all clear, his location at the king's gate here suggests that Mordecai is in fact a "servant of the king" along with those around him. After all, the logic of the sentence suggests that it is the servants (and not necessarily other civilians,

---

[3] Compare the order of the king concerning drinking in 1:8. The phrase used there, "for thus the king had given orders to all the officials," is quite close in Hebrew to the one used in 3:2 (except that ṣwh, "commanded" is used instead of ysd, "ordered").

since none are mentioned) who are commanded to bow and do obeisance before Haman. Moreover, the other servants are the ones, in verse 3, who confront Mordecai: "Then the king's servants who were at the king's gate said to Mordecai, 'Why do you disobey [ʿōbēr, 'transgress'] the king's command?'"

Indeed, the servants ask the question for the reader! But like us they are refused an answer. The question posed to Mordecai by the servants makes clear, furthermore, that his refusal reflects poorly not only on Haman—who is as yet unaware that Mordecai is not bowing before him—but also on the king, who gave the command.

"Day after day," Mordecai refuses to bow before Haman at the king's command. The servants talk with him day after day, but he will not listen (šmʿ, which can mean "hear," "heed," or "obey" as well) to them (3:4a). So they tell (or better, "reveal," from ngd) this matter to Haman, "in order to see whether Mordecai's words [or 'things'] would avail; for he had told [or 'revealed to,' again from ngd] them that he was a Jew" (3:4b). The word translated as "avail" in this verse is ʿmd, which is normally translated "stand." The use of this verb here plays on the fact that "Mordecai's words" or "things" refers to his refusal to bow bown before Haman—that is, his insistence on standing. Will Mordecai's refusal to bow down *stand?* Will Mordecai's stand against Haman stand?

A crucial question is raised in this revelation (to Haman by the servants concerning Mordecai's refusal to bow) following a revelation (to the servants by Mordecai concerning his Jewish/Judean identity). Was Haman anti-Jewish before this incident or not? If not, then this is an instance of rage toward an individual—coincidentally Jewish—being generalized into destructive hatred toward a whole people; in other words it is an exaggerated reaction to an individual conflict, with Haman wanting to kill a whole people because his opponent happens to represent that people. If Haman was anti-Jewish *before* this incident, however, then this is an instance of the individual opponent's Jewish identity *intensifying* the particular conflict; that is, if Mordecai had not been Jewish, his refusal to bow would not have been so aggravating. I propose that the latter is the case with regard to Haman. The interest of the servants in seeing whether or not Mordecai's transgression will stand—"for [kî] he had revealed to them that he was a Jew/Judean"—suggests that they think that the Jewish identity of the one refusing to bow will make Haman's rage at being dishonored all the more intense.

Note also that this story suggests, once again, that Jewish identity in the story world of Esther is anything but self-evident. Just as Esther can hide her Jewish identity simply by not revealing it, so here Mordecai must reveal that he is Jewish for anyone to know.

As soon as Haman sees that Mordecai is not bowing down before him (apparently he had not seen this dishonoring behavior before the servants revealed it to him), he is "infuriated," or more literally "filled with rage [ḥēmâ]" (3:5)—the same rage (ḥēmâ) that burned hot in Ahasuerus at the news of Vashti's dishonoring refusal of his command (1:12). Whereas Vashti's refusal did not reflect well on the king's royal (male) status, Mordecai's refusal here, once it is brought to light, does not reflect well on Haman's new official (national) status. In both cases, the response is rage. Note, moreover, that in the case of Mordecai's refusal, as in the case of Vashti's refusal, the servants (or eunuchs) play a central part as mediators of the transgression. In both cases, it is possible that without their reports, there would have been no enragement.

Verse 6, which narrates the beginning of Haman's plot to annihilate all Jews, is somewhat ambiguous with regard to his thought process. As translated in the NRSV, the sense is that because he considered it "beneath him" to lay hands on Mordecai himself, and because Mordecai's people had been revealed to him, he would (instead of killing Mordecai himself) simply have all Jews killed throughout the entire Persian empire. This is accomplished in the NRSV by (a) translating the initial verb phrase (*wayyibez* [from *bzh*] *bĕʿênāyw*) as "but he thought it beneath him," and (b) translating the crucial phrase *kî – higgîdû lô* as the beginning of a new sentence, "So, having been told. . . ." Although the initial verb phrase can legitimately be translated as such, the NRSV translation of *kî – higgîdû lô* is more of a stretch.[4] A more literal translation of the first phrase would be "[and] he regarded with contempt" or "despised with his eyes." Translated in this way, the sense of contempt is not so clearly a matter of political or class hierarchy. This leads to the second phrase, which would be better translated not as a new sentence, but as indicating the reason for Haman's contempt, thus: "he regarded it with contempt to lay hands on Mordecai himself, for they had revealed to him Mordecai's people." The reason he despised the idea of laying a hand on Mordecai himself was because he knew Mordecai was Jewish. The verse then continues, "and Haman sought [*bqš*; cf. 2:15, 21] to destroy all the Jews, Mordecai's people, throughout the whole kingdom of Ahasuerus." In this light, Haman had been anti-Jewish before this incident ever took place.

---

[4] Note, furthermore, that this phrase is parallel with the phrase in verse 4, "for he revealed to them" (*kî – higgîd lāhem*). Compare also 8:1, "for Esther revealed [*kî – higgîdâ*] what he was to her."

Projection of the Other Jew (3:7-11)

"In the first month, which is the month of Nisan, in the twelfth year of King Ahasuerus, they cast Pur—which means "the lot"—before Haman for the day and for the month, and the lot fell on the thirteenth day of the twelfth month, which is the month of Adar" (3:7).

Although 3:7-11 is obviously directly related to 3:1-6, it is marked off as a new scene by the indication of the time: the first month (Nisan, that is, March/April) in the twelfth year of the king's reign—four years and two months since Esther was made queen. Since the time of Haman's promotion is indefinite ("after these things," 3:1), it is impossible to know whether this scene takes place days or years after he became enraged by Mordecai.

The fact that this woeful episode in the story takes place in Nisan is perhaps more important to the narrative than precisely how many years have passed, for Nisan is also the month in which Passover is celebrated (although there is no indication of it being celebrated by Jews in the story of Esther). This subtle linkage to Passover and the Exodus story highlights the tension between Mordecai and Haman by adding another layer of narrative background: now we may read between the lines not only Saul versus Agag, but also Moses versus Pharaoh. Recall, moreover, that it was Moses's *betweenness*—identified with both Hebrew slaves and Egyptian royalty (Exod 2:1-22)—that made him particularly well suited for leading the Exodus liberation. In this regard, the leadership role of Esther—another profoundly in-between character, as we have seen—may be anticipated. Finally, of course, this association with Passover highlights a radical difference between the conflict in the book of Esther and that of the Exodus narrative with regard to the question of divine presence. For Exodus 1-15 and the Passover liturgy insists repeatedly that Pharaoh's primary opponent is not Moses but God. No such insistence will be found in Esther, however, and one is left instead with unresolved, unresolvable questions as to the presence or absence of God in this fray.

Indeed, accident and chance appear once again to play a key part in the narrative, in this case in the advancement of Haman's plot. For in this month "they cast *pûr*—which means 'the lot'—before Haman for the day and the month" (3:7).[5] Some have argued that all of verse 7

---

[5] Literally, "from day to day and from month to month." However, as noted by David J.A. Clines, *Ezra, Nehemiah, Esther,* 295, this cannot mean that lots were cast every day throughout the year. The casting of lots in the first month, Nisan, for each day throughout the entire year makes somewhat more sense, since Babylonian tradition saw the first month of the year as the month of destinies.

is a later editorial insertion into the narrative, since it partially interrupts the narrative progression from 3:6 to 3:8.[6] Yet, as Abraham Cohen has pointed out, this verse, in particular the phrase *"pûr*—which means 'the lot,'" is crucial to the narrative as a whole, because it highlights the question of divine providence versus accident. Cohen argues that Esther, here and elsewhere, is describing a world of lottery and luck of the draw "in order to *parody* it." He continues:

> It portrays a course of causality, only to *invert* it. . . . The very name of the holiday, Purim, indicates the centrality of this inversion and, so, is entirely understandable to us. Purim which, to the nemesis of the Jew and to an alien system of thought, affirmed the operation of chance and fate in the universe, becomes, for the Jew, the anti-chance symbol, the symbol of that which God so readily controls to *His* ends. . . . *Purim is the appellation of a problem*; a problem both ancient and vitally contemporary. Do chance and determinism rule supreme in the universe, or does God?"[7]

The casting of the lots at this crucial point in the narrative certainly raises issues concerning the relation between accident and providence in the book of Esther. "Pur—that is 'the lot'" is certainly the "appellation of a problem," as Cohen has so eloquently put it. This problem is compounded in verse 7, moreover, by the wording used to describe the casting of the lots: most literally, "King Ahasuerus *caused to fall* [*pl* in Hiphil] pur—which is 'the lot.'" The verb "to fall" *(pl)* will be used in 6:13, in a different form, to describe Haman's predicted ill fate in relation to Mordecai: his advisors and wife Zeresh say to him, "if Mordecai, before whom you have already begun *to fall*, is of Jewish seed, you will not prevail against him but will *surely fall* before him." There, the sense is of certain doom, a fate that cannot be altered; there is no chance for Haman's survival (see the commentary on that verse).

[6] Such a view of this verse as a secondary insertion has also found support in the fact that something appears to be lost from the second date given in the Hebrew text, which reads most literally "from day to day and from month to month twelfth." We might read this as meaning something like "from the first month to the twelfth month [i.e., 'month twelve']," that is, throughout the year. Given that the plan Haman proposes is ultimately set for the thirteenth day of the twelfth month (3:13), however, most translators follow the AT and insert "on the thirteenth day of" before "the twelfth, which is Adar" (cf. 8:12; 9:1, 17; note that the LXX and Old Latin have "on the fourteenth day" rather than the thirteenth).

[7] Abraham D. Cohen, "'Hu Ha-goral': The Religious Significance of Esther," *Judaism* 23 (1974) 94.

Thus, even in the use of the verb "to fall" in this narrative, tensions are raised between the random falling of lots and the absolutely determined falling of the enemy.

Indeed, the Esther narrative as a whole is subtly preoccupied with this problem throughout. But we can go further than Cohen's rather affirmative answer to those questions. For the book of Esther does not allow any easy resolutions to this problem. It affirms the *problem itself* over all its possible solutions—from the most godlessly cynical to the most theologically hopeful. Recall the Hebrew phrase from the Talmud, which is also the name of a major Purim festival in Tel Aviv, *ʿad dĕloʾ yādaʿ*—"until one cannot know" or "determine."

It is this random casting of the lots, with all the ambiguity it entails, that gives Haman the floor. We already know, from verse 6, that he seeks to annihilate the Jews. Here is his opportunity to construct "the Jewish problem" and its "final solution"—all the more chilling for those of us whose reading is haunted by the Holocaust. Haman is often considered Hitler's (not to mention, centuries earlier, Luther's) precursor, and not without reason.

The lots cast, Haman is given the floor.

> Then Haman said to King Ahasuerus, "There is a certain people scattered and separated among the peoples in all the provinces of your kingdom; their laws are different from those of every other people, and they do not keep the king's laws, so that it is not appropriate for the king to tolerate them. If it pleases the king, let a decree be issued for their destruction, and I will pay ten thousand talents of silver into the hands of those who have charge of the king's business, so that they may put it into the king's treasuries." (3:8-9)

Haman's rhetoric of projection is a remarkable double-projection, much like that of Memucan in chapter 1. First he constructs the problem: there is "one people" (*ʿam – ʾeḥād*; NRSV "a certain people"), scattered and divided through all the Persian population; amid what is an otherwise homogeneous national identity, he claims, this one people diverges, following other laws than those of the king. Simultaneously "one" yet "scattered and separated," the Jews are projected as those who are singularly different and yet, paradoxically, difficult to locate, identify, and distinguish from the larger population of Persia. Despite their plurality and diffusion, they are projected as the single *other* over against all other peoples within the Persian empire. Thus, in this rhetoric, not only is the Jew constructed as the privileged other, but all other Persians are constructed as homogeneous and uniform. As is always the case with racist, sexist, and ethnocentric projections of otherness, the "them" here is constructed for the sake of establishing a stable, united "us."[8]

And yet, as Jonathan Magonet has made particularly clear, Haman himself is also an outsider, so that the dynamic of "othering" involves Haman's projection of the otherness that is part of his *own* Persian identity. Magonet writes,

> We forget that the information that he is an Agagite tells us not only that he comes from the line of Israel's enemies, but also that he, too, is an outsider in the Persian court. When he speaks of the people scattered throughout the land whose laws are different from those of every other people (3:8), he is also describing, in a projection, some aspect of his own outsider status. For Haman, too, is insecure, part of a minority group, relying on his wealth or other keys to power to maintain his position, ready to invent a scapegoat to insure the continuance of his power. Haman is nothing more than the alternative face of Mordecai, a distorted reflection of the same character. . . . and perhaps it is that deeper relationship that Rava is pointing towards when he says that a man is obliged to drink so much wine on Purim that he becomes incapable of knowing whether he is cursing Haman or blessing Mordecai.[9]

In this light, Haman's projection of Mordecai and all Jews over against Persian identity masks Haman's own identity ambivalence, as an outsider like Mordecai. Mordecai is Haman's own negative image. It is not Mordecai's or the Jewish people's *distinctiveness* over against a unified Persian "us" that brings on hatred. Indeed, up until this point Jewish identity has been anything but conspicuous within Persian culture(s); it is known only when it is revealed (2:10, 20; 3:5-6; cf. 7:3-6; 8:17). Rather than the conspicuous otherness of Jews, it is Haman's uneasy *identification with* Mordecai that leads to his projection of his own sense of otherness onto Mordecai and the Jews.

If one follows Magonet in this interpretation, the dynamic of self-projection in Haman's description of the "Jewish problem" is strikingly similar to dynamics of anti-Jewish and anti-Semitic projections which we have witnessed throughout Western history and especially this century.[10] Within this dynamic, the Jew-hater pushes all otherness (national, cultural, religious) onto the Jews and calls for their annihila-

---

[8] Note further that the two phrases, "there is not their doing the law" and "there is not for the king tolerating them," link back to Mordecai's earlier refusal to bow in 3:2: "there was no bowing down and no doing obeisance."

[9] Magonet, "Liberal and the Lady," 175.

[10] Although obviously related to the long and shameful legacy of anti-Judaism, the term "anti-Semitism" is reserved for the modern racist movement in the nine-

tion as a final, self-purifying solution. As Theodor Adorno and Max Horkheimer write in their classic analysis of Fascist anti-Semitism during World War II,

> The Jews . . . are branded as absolute evil by those who are absolutely evil, and are now in fact the chosen race. Whereas there is no longer any need for economic domination, the Jews are marked out as the absolute object of domination pure and simple. . . . The portrait of the Jews that the nationalists offer to the world is in fact their own self-portrait.[11]

Following his projection of the "Jewish problem" in verse 8, Haman makes his recommendation (3:9), again paralleling the rhetorical pattern of Memucan in 1:16-20. "If it pleases the king," he begins, "let a decree be issued for their destruction" (3:9a). In case the problem is not compelling enough to evoke the king's intolerance of this people, Haman concludes with a huge bribe (more accurately, a *bakshish*; v. 9b).[12] The amount of this bribe, as scholars since Paton have noted, is astronomical—as much as two-thirds of Persia's total annual income. On the one hand, this exorbitant amount, like the year-long drinking party in chapter 1 and the year-long cosmetic treatments in chapter 2, farces the king and his advisors as ridiculously excessive. On the other hand, one must wonder whether Haman could actually come up with this large sum. It might come from plundering the Jewish victims, but that is unlikely (see verse 13, in which the attackers themselves are allowed to plunder the Jews).

The king accepts Haman's proposal; indeed, he never has and never will reject a proposal. He removes his signet ring from his hand and gives it to Haman, now given the epithet "enemy [or hater] of the Jews" (3:10),[13] and offers him full support: "The money is given to you, and the people as well, to do with them as it seems good to you [lit. 'as

---

teenth and twentieth centuries which has sought to identify a "Jewish" or "Semitic race." On this phenomenon, see esp. Sander Gilman, *The Jew's Body* (London and New York: Routledge, 1991).

[11] Theodor Adorno and Max Horkheimer, *Dialectic of Enlightenment*, trans. John Cummings (New York: Continuum, 1991) 168.

[12] On the ancient and honorable business transaction system of the *bakshish*, see Max Vogelstein, "Bakshish for Bagoas?," *Jewish Quarterly Review* 33 (1942–43) 89–92. The fact that this kind of transaction does not normally carry dishonorable overtones (as does a bribe today) does not mean, however, that Haman's offer here to pay the king so that an entire people can be annihilated is any more honorable.

[13] This title, which is used here for the first time, will be used in reference to Haman three more times (8:1; 9:10, 24; cf. Esther's closely related description of him in 7:6).

is pleasing in your eyes']" (3:11). The king puts both the money and "the people" (he does not appear to know, yet, that the "certain people" described by Haman are the Jews) into his hands to do as he pleases. Not only does he accept Haman's proposal for genocide without question, but he refuses the money that Haman had attached to it.[14] By not accepting the money, he may be refusing to take as much responsibility for the planned genocide. This would be to his advantage later, in chapter 7, when he distances himself from Haman and his plan. On the other hand, his refusal may also suggest his own zeal—apart from financial motivations—for Haman's plan; that is, his desire to have this ethnic otherness eradicated from Persia has nothing to do with money.

PUBLISHING, DRINKING, AND TURMOIL (3:12-15)

> Then the king's secretaries were summoned on the thirteenth day of the first month, and an edict, according to all that Haman commanded, was written to the king's satraps and to the governors over all the provinces and to the officials of all the peoples, to every province in its own script and every people in its own language; it was written in the name of King Ahasuerus and sealed with the king's ring. Letters were sent by couriers to all the king's provinces, giving orders to destroy, to kill, and to annihilate all Jews, young and old, women and children, in one day, the thirteenth day of the twelfth month, which is the month of Adar, and to plunder their goods. A copy of the document was to be issued as a decree in every province by proclamation, calling on all the peoples to be ready for that day. The couriers went quickly by order of the king, and the decree was issued in the citadel of Susa. The king and Haman sat down to drink; but the city of Susa was thrown into confusion. (3:12-15)

As soon as the king approves Haman's plan, the scribes are called in to "write according to all that Haman commanded" (3:12). This royal order, along with the giving of the signet ring in verse 10, makes clear that king has put all power into Haman's hands. It does not, how-

---

[14] Many modern scholars (e.g., Bush, Levenson, Moore, and Clines) do not take this statement by the king as an actual refusal of the money, but rather as a polite initial response (e.g., "a courtly form of accepting the money" [Clines, *Esther*, 297]). In support of this reading scholars cite later statements by Mordecai (4:7, indicating the amount offered by Haman) and Esther (7:4, "we have been sold, I and my people"), as well as a somewhat shaky parallel with the negotiations between Abraham and Ephron in Genesis 23. Given that Mordecai only indicates Haman's *offer* in 4:7, and given that Esther's reference to being sold in 7:4 can be read figuratively, I take this statement at face value as a refusal of the money.

ever, indicate that the king is in any sense "off the hook" with regard to responsibility. On the contrary, the king is vesting his power in Haman (foreshadowing a later vesting of Mordecai, much to Haman's chagrin, in chapter 6).

As with the law drafted at the end of chapter 1, which served to erase Vashti while reinscribing patriarchal domination, so this new written law is "sent out" (3:13; cf. 1:22) to "every province in its own script and every people in its own language" (3:12; cf. 1:22), aiming to erase all Jews and thereby to reinscribe a certain fantasy of national identity and stability. If the king did not know that the Jews were the target of Haman's plan earlier, he certainly knows by now. Indeed, the text appears to be emphasizing his implicatedness in the plan: the law is written by the king's scribes, in the king's presence, in the king's name, and then is sealed with his ring and publicly announced everywhere.

This law is, most literally, a horrific plan for "ethnic cleansing." Yet all other Persians besides the Jews certainly were not of one *ethnos*. The ancient Persian empire was in fact very diverse, as Haman's own genocidal law indicates ("every people in its own language"). Rather, with regard to Haman's (and the king's, insofar as he accepts it) identity politics, all divergence and opposition to "us" and "our law" is *projected* here onto the other Jew and then marked for erasure. To remove Jews, in this fantasy, is to remove all otherness and to establish unity and wholeness.

The parallels between Haman's recommendation and its implementation in this chapter and Memucan's recommendation and implementation in 1:16-22 are striking. As a means of calming the king's rage toward Vashti—and the patriarchal crisis that Vashti's refusal introduced—Memucan recommended a universal law that would serve to erase Vashti and her transgression while establishing women's subordination to men "as lords" in every household, from greatest to least. There, national politics and sexual politics were explicitly linked. Here the dynamic is remarkably similar, except that Haman himself makes a proposal to the king for legal action that will (a) calm *his own* rage and (b) establish a more stable and homogeneous national identity by eradicating supposed ethnic (rather than sexual) otherness. The rhetorical structure of Haman's recommendation, moreover, is very similar to that of Memucan, in that it begins by presenting the problem in terms of national identity politics (this certain people is a threat to national stability and homeostasis just as Vashti's refusal was), and then turns to an extreme, nationwide legal recommendation, introduced by "if it pleases the king" (cf. 1:19). All this suggests an identification of Haman with Memucan—an identification that the Targums of Esther make explicit. It also suggests a parallel in the story between ethnic identity politics and sexual identity politics, as well as a narrative identification (and even solidarity) between the woman-as-other (or the "other woman") and the Jew-as-other (or the "other Jew").[15]

This episode concludes, as one might expect by now, with drinking: "the king and Haman sat down to drink" (3:15a). As we have seen in earlier episodes, drinking together in the book of Esther signifies a resting point, a settling down of rage, resolution of crisis, return of pleasure and security. It also signifies identification: to drink together is to identify with one another as insiders, as a unified, unthreatened "us." At the end of chapter 3, as the couriers speed throughout the kingdom with the new royal law to annihilate all Jews, the fact that "the king and Haman sat down to drink" (3:15) signifies their identification with one another (over against their newly projected ethnic other) as well as the settling of Haman's rage, which dissolves, along with the face of the other Jew, into the reflection in his wine glass.

But as Haman and the king curl up together with their drinks, "the city of Susa was thrown into confusion" (3:15b). The last verse in this episode creates a stark contrast between the authors of the law and their addressees, between the law's source and its destination, between inside and outside. As the narrative turns attention away from the king's and Haman's cozy spot within the castle walls and onto the city beyond those walls, an image of the palace bobbing in a sea of tumult emerges. The Hebrew verb translated as "thrown into confusion" is a Niphal (passive) form of *bwk*, a fairly uncommon verb meaning "stir up" or "confuse." It carries the connotation of chaos or wandering in confusion—an apt image for this scene.[16] This narrative window onto the scene outside the palace alerts readers to the fact that here, as elsewhere, what appears to be settled, stabilized, and resolved, often turns out to be quite the opposite.

[15] This parallel has been identified and considered at length in Beal, *Hiding*, esp. 54–9 and 112–5.

[16] Perhaps the best parallel to this use of the verb is found in Exod 14:3, where the Israelites are thrown into turmoil under the attack of Pharaoh's armies. See also Joel 1:18.

Chapter 6

ANOTHER QUARTER

Esther 4:1-17

The following episode, 4:1-17, marks a crucial turning point in Esther's relation to Mordecai within the narrative as a whole. Up to this point, the distance between them, as well as the distance between Esther and her (former?) people, the Jews, appears to be growing. As she rises within the Persian political order, Mordecai and the Jews find themselves in deeper and deeper trouble within that order. At the same time, up to this point the text has stressed that Esther has continued to be obedient to Mordecai, "just as when she was brought up by him" (2:20; see also 2:10). In this episode, as the distance between them is narrowed (but nonetheless continues to require mediation), the chain of command-obedience is reversed, so that by the end of this episode we find Esther in charge and Mordecai doing "everything as Esther had ordered [or 'commanded'] him" (4:17).

This episode can be outlined as a series of mediated interchanges between Esther inside the palace and Mordecai outside the palace, at the king's gate.

First Interchange (4:1-4)
    Mordecai approaches the king's gate in sackcloth and ashes;
        Jews are lamenting in a similar fashion throughout Persia
        (vv. 1-3)
    Esther hears about Mordecai, is distressed, and sends clothes
        to wear instead of sackcloth and ashes (v. 4a)
    Mordecai refuses her offer of clothing (v. 4b)

Second Interchange (4:5-9)

Esther sends Hathach to learn what is happening and why (vv. 5-6)

Mordecai reports everything to Hathach and sends back a copy of the decree, in order to charge Esther to go to the king (vv. 7-9)

Third Interchange (4:10-14)

Esther sends Hathach to tell Mordecai that she cannot go to the king without risk of the death penalty (vv. 10-12)

Mordecai sends back to Esther: "Do not think that you will escape . . ." (vv.13-14)

Fourth Interchange (4:15-17)

Esther sends reply to Mordecai, issuing him commands ("go, gather . . . fast") and indicating her intention to act on behalf of the Jews (v. 15-16)

Mordecai departs and does everything Esther commands (v. 17)

As this outline makes clear, the *words* between Mordecai and Esther are sandwiched between the *actions* of Mordecai. At the beginning, in 4:1-3, he boldly approaches "as far as the gate of the king" in sackcloth and ashes (on the threshold of breaking the king's law and also of disclosing his identification with Esther). These first actions incite Esther into the first interchange with him (she is distressed and sends clothing to him). At the conclusion of the episode (4:17), Mordecai departs, obeying Esther's orders. Whereas his first actions in verses 1-3 provoke Esther's initial exchange with him, then, his final actions in this episode are in response to Esther's last words (vv. 15-16).

The series of mediated interchanges which take place between Mordecai's coming and going are crucial to the narrative for at least two reasons. First, through them Esther learns of the genocidal decree and begins to make plans to subvert it (although neither Mordecai nor we have a clear sense of her plan!). Second, as these interchanges progress, the dynamic of relationship between Mordecai and Esther changes significantly. Before this chapter, Esther has been represented as almost entirely deferential to all men. As noted earlier, she has thus far been presented as the ideal female object in this patriarchal world, always reflecting well on the male (and eunuch) subjects. In relation to Mordecai, the text has reiterated her continued obedience to him, "just as when she was raised by him" (2:20; 2:10). Ironically, her obedience to Mordecai has been linked, up until this point, to *not* revealing her identification with the Jewish people (1:10, 20). By the end of this episode, in which Mordecai seeks to convince her to reveal her Jewish identity, the tables are turned, so that we find Esther delivering commands to Mordecai (4:16) and Mordecai doing everything just as she orders (4:17 and following).

THE FIRST INTERCHANGE (4:1-4)

The first interchange between Esther is instigated by Mordecai's actions of intense mourning and wearing sackcloth and ashes.[1] His mourning and dress are, in turn, reactions to "all that had been done" (4:1) in the previous episode, namely the legal decree to annihilate all Jews (3:7-15). Mordecai's actions are, moreover, in solidarity with many other Jews throughout the kingdom. Sackcloth and/or ashes and loud cries can signify a fairly wide range of reactions to catastrophe or news of forthcoming catastrophe in the Hebrew Bible, from mourning to repentance to protest. These actions do not necessarily carry religious connotations, however (see, e.g., 1 Kgs 20:31-32). In Esther 4, the text once again *leaves open the possibility* of interpreting these actions of mourning and protest (obviously not repentance) as entreaties to their God without in any way confirming that intepretation (cf. 4:16, below). Here again, then, one may recognize a subtly crafted agnosticism in the book of Esther ("until one cannot know").

As noted, Mordecai's actions of mourning in sackcloth and ashes identify him with the many other Jews throughout the kingdom who are mourning, fasting, and weeping in similar fashion.[2] This collective identity is formed, then, by common actions and dress (recall that Jewish identity can be hidden simply by non-disclosure [1:10, 20; 3:4, 6]). Over against this collective identity stands Esther—inside the palace rather than out in public with the other Jews, and wearing *anything but* sackcloth and ashes, "for no one might enter the king's gate clothed with sackcloth" (4:2). This prohibition of sackcloth not only means that no overt mourning or protest is allowed in the presence of the king—

---

[1] It is not clear when this narrative takes place relative to the overall time line of the story. If this interchange takes place immediately after the publishing of the anti-Jewish decree in chapter 3, and if the writing of the next decree by Mordecai (in 8:9-14) takes place immediately after Haman is killed, then there is clearly a chronological error in the narrative. See the discussion in the introduction to the commentary on 8:1-17.

[2] Note in this regard that in addition to the common attire, the Jews' lamenting, like Mordecai's, is called "great" (*gādôl*). However, the verbs describing their actions ("fasting and weeping and lamenting") differ from the one describing Mordecai's wailing (*zᵉq*).

an odd enough rule in and of itself—but also that with the turn of events in chapter 3, Esther's new identity as royalty marks her distance from identification with the Jews. She is in the realm of no sackcloth when sackcloth is the fashion of the day for the Jews of Persia.

Mordecai's wailing is particularly intense (lit., "he cried a cry, great and bitter"), which further intensifies the distance between himself and Esther. He approaches as far as (*ad lipnê*, "up to the face of") the king's gate, threateningly close to transgressing the king's law.

When Esther's eunuchs and servants tell her (what exactly do they tell her? the text does not say), she is "deeply distressed" (4:4;). Another translation of this phrase might be "writhed greatly" *(tithalhal . . . měʾōd)*. The verb translated here as "distressed" is a Hitpael (iterative) form of *ḥwl*, the basic Qal meaning of which is "whirl" or "writhe" (compare its use as a Hitpolel meaning "writhe" in Job 15:20). Contrary to those who argue for a more figurative meaning in this passage,[3] the sense of strong *physical* reaction is appropriate, establishing a parallel between Esther's reaction to Mordecai and Mordecai's intensely physical and emotional reaction to the decree in 4:1-2.

Whereas Mordecai is reacting to the decree, however, Esther appears to be reacting to Mordecai (not to the decree, and not to the other Jews described in 4:3). This is made immediately clear by the fact that in her agitation she sends Mordecai clothing to replace his sackcloth. The message is to change clothes and shut up. But what, more precisely, is it about Mordecai's behavior that bothers her so? (Recall that the actions we read about in verses 1-3 are reported to Esther through her maids and eunuchs and we do not hear their report. Did Esther get a similar description?) Is she distressed because Mordecai is so upset? Or is she agitated by the threat of transgression implied by his approaching the king's gate in illegal attire? If that is so, is she worried for his well-being or is she concerned to maintain the law? On the other hand, might she be concerned that his actions could get *her* in trouble by possible association with him? Whatever the reason for her distress, Mordecai refuses the clothing and in so doing (a) refuses to cease mourning/protesting and (b) clearly identifies himself with those now marked for obliteration.

THE SECOND INTERCHANGE (4:5-9)

As we might expect by this point in the narrative, Esther then calls on one of the king's eunuchs assigned to her service to mediate a conversation with Mordecai (4:5a; the clothes were sent by unnamed ser-

---

[3] E.g., Bush, *Ruth, Esther*, 390, 394; Moore, *Esther*, 48; and the NRSV.

vants). This eunuch, Hathach, has not been mentioned up to this point in the narrative; as with the other eunuchs, moreover, this one has no speech of his own in the episode. Yet to consider him or any other eunuch as a mere functionary within the narrative would be a mistake. Without him, there would be no communication between Esther and Mordecai; indeed, the precise content of their communication is determined by him, for no words are passed between them without first passing through Hathach's lips.

The mediation accomplished by Hathach is not only a mediation of verbal content, moreover. It is also a mediation between the sexes, between status levels within the Persian socio-political order, between inside and outside. As discussed earlier, the fact that the mediator here, as elsewhere, is a eunuch is not incidental to this role, for as a royal eunuch he occupies positions of betweenness and liminality. First and most obviously, as a castrated person without a wife or household of his own, he is sexually ambiguous; this ambiguity is heightened by the fact that eunuchs consistently serve as the go-betweens in male-female interchanges in this narrative (they are sent to bring Vashti and they mediate her refusal in chapter 1; they are the keepers of the "house of women" and the "house of concubines," and they conduct each young virgin's passage from the one house through the king's house into the latter house in chapter 2; and now here in chapter 4 a eunuch is once again mediating between Esther and her adoptive father/cousin Mordecai). Second, as "guards of the threshold" in 2:21, they are represented in the story as keepers of physical regions of betweenness within the kingdom; relatedly, we find they are able (unlike others such as Esther and Mordecai) to move easily back and forth between inside and outside the palace walls, as is the case here in chapter 4, where Hathach moves between Esther inside and Mordecai outside (see also 7:9, where a eunuch informs the king inside the palace of the execution stake recently built outside the palace, at Haman's house). Finally, the eunuchs are between status levels within the Persian socio-political order: as officials of the king they are often privy to key royal conversations concerning political matters, and yet their status is that of a servant rather than an officer. In the book of Esther, as we are beginning to see, such locations of betweenness and ambiguity are crucial to bringing about political transformation. The eunuchs in this story are to be watched closely.

Esther sends him to Mordecai with orders (lit., "she *commanded* [from *šwh*] him") "to learn what was happening and why" (4:5b). Hathach finds Mordecai where we would expect him to be, in the open square in front of the king's gate (4:6), and there Mordecai reports "all that had happened to him, and the exact sum of money that Haman had promised to pay into the king's treasuries for the destruction of the Jews. Mordecai also gave him a copy of the written decree issued in Susa for their destruction" (4:7-8a). The content of Mordecai's report, given in summary, follows the order of the narrative in chapter 3, albeit somewhat selectively. First, "all that had happened to him" refers to the story in 3:1-6 of Mordecai's refusal to bow, the servants' report to Haman about that refusal, and Haman's subsequent rage (it may also refer to Haman's promotion and Mordecai's lack thereof). Second, "the exact sum of money that Haman had promised . . . for the destruction of the Jews" refers explicitly to Haman's proposal for genocide in 3:8-9 (using many of the same words that Haman himself used).[4] Mordecai's report, then, focuses on Haman's anti-Jewish genocidal intentions, the bribe, and leaves out his initial projection of the Jews as other in 3:8; this suggests that the king's acceptance of Haman's proposal is motivated strictly by the money incentive (contrary to 3:10, where the king says, "the money is given to you, and the people as well, to do with them as you please"). Third, Mordecai gives Hathach a copy of the decree published in Susa (the same one issued throughout the kingdom), which is detailed in 3:12-14.

The purpose of this report—and, presumably, his purpose in approaching the king's gate in sackcloth and ashes with bitter cries—is then made clear: "that he [Hathach] might show it to Esther, explain it to her, and charge her to go to the king to make supplication to him and entreat him for her people" (4:8). A series of three infinitive verbs are used here to explicate what Mordecai wants: (a) "to show [*lĕharʾôt*] Esther"; (b) "to reveal [*lĕhaggîd,* NRSV 'explain'] to her"; and (c) "to command [*lĕṣawwôt,* NRSV 'charge'] her." Each of these verbs has carried significance thus far in the larger narrative, especially concerning ethnic and gender identity issues. First, "to show" was the king's aim in chapter 1: he threw his parties as a means of "displaying" or "showing" his wealth, honor, and riches (1:4),[5] and as a climax of this display

---

[4] The word *pārāšat,* translated as "exact sum" in the NRSV, occurs in the Hebrew Bible only here and in Esth 10:2, where it refers to the "full account" of Mordecai's greatness. Based on the use of the term in 10:2 (where anything close to "exact sum" is senseless) and on postbiblical uses, Levenson, *Esther,* 77–8, argues convincingly for translating it as "story" here. Thus, "the story of the money that Haman had offered." I propose "account" as a third alternative to "exact sum" and "story," since "accounting" and "giving account" in English carry both fiscal and narrative senses. The word *pārāšat* appears to function similarly in 3:7 (i.e., an exact account of [the story of] the money).

[5] Note that the verb in 1:4 is a Hiphil infinitive, as in 1:11 and 4:8. In 1:4, however, it is constructed with a *bet* preposition ("while" or "by displaying his great wealth . . .").

he wanted "to show" *(lĕharʾôt)* Vashti to the others as the privileged object of an all-male ogle, meant to reflect well on his own patriarchal identity (see the commentary on chapter 1). Second, public knowledge of one's Jewish identity has pivoted around the dynamics of revealing and not revealing: in the face-off between Mordecai and Haman in chapter 3, no one would have known Mordecai was Jewish had he not "revealed" it to the other servants (3:4, 6), and the text has reiterated that Esther has "not revealed" her people just as Mordecai commanded her, so that the king and Haman do not know yet that she is Jewish. Third, and relatedly, the nature of the relationship between Mordecai and Esther thus far has been one of command and obedience, respectively; Mordecai has commanded her not to reveal her people and she has obeyed, "for Esther obeyed Mordecai just as when she was brought up by him" (2:20; cf 2:10, 22). Indeed, as discussed earlier, at this point Esther lives under the command of both the king and Mordecai. In this situation, she will not be able to obey both commands, for they are in conflict with one another (one commands her to go to the king, while the other prohibits going before the king without being summoned). This double bind reveals Esther's own identity conflict as Persian royalty on one hand and as adoptive orphaned daughter of a people marked for annihilation according to her own Persian law on the other. In the end, as we shall see, her actions imply nothing so simple as obedience to either the king's command or Mordecai's command. She will go before him unsummoned, and later will issue *him* orders; and while she will go before the king "to seek" deliverance for her people as Mordecai charges, her actions are far from simple obedience to cousin/father Mordecai. Indeed, she will take matters into her own hands, as is clear by the end of this episode, by which time she is doing the commanding and Mordecai is obeying her every word (4:16).[6]

Hathach returned to Esther and told her "what Mordecai had said" (4:9). We may presume that he also showed her the copy of the decree which Mordecai gave him, since Esther demonstrates familiarity with its details later on (see 7:4).

THE THIRD INTERCHANGE (4:10-14)

Without showing any further concern or distress over the news about the genocidal decree which has just been "revealed" (again *ngd*)

---

[6] Note that even before 4:16, where Mordecai obeys Esther's command, the text hints at her new subjective status as one who issues commands by the fact that she twice "commands" Hathach to go to Mordecai in this episode (4:5, 10).

to her by Mordecai via Hathach (4:9), Esther sends back word concerning the king's law, which prohibits her from doing what Mordecai charges her to do: "All the king's servants and the people of the king's provinces know that if any man or woman goes to the king inside the inner court without being called, there is but one law—all alike are to be put to death. Only if the king holds out the golden scepter to someone, may that person live. I myself have not been called to come in to the king for thirty days" (4:11). Mordecai may "know" about the latest happenings *outside* the palace walls (4:1), which she ought to have known, but Esther feels the need to inform him about what everyone ought to know about proceedings *inside* the palace. She cannot go to the king, as Mordecai commands her to do (via Hathach), without being summoned by him. The comment that "there is but one law . . . death" indicates that the law on this matter is in no way conflicted and is in fact completely unambiguous and without loophole. What immediately follows in her explication, however, undercuts that singular clarity, for if the king extends his scepter to a person who comes without being summoned, then that person will be spared (4:11). Nonetheless, Esther's aim in offering this explication of the law and her position under it (she has not been summoned for thirty days) is to make clear why she cannot go to the king on behalf of the Jews. It is a long way of saying no—and of continuing to do exactly what Mordecai has commanded up until this point, namely, "not revealing," or "keeping silence" (cf. v. 14).

The threatening overtones in Mordecai's response to Esther's words (this time revealed by "them" rather than by Hathach)[7] indicate that he is worried that she is close to refusing is command. His opening imperative, "do not think that in the king's palace you will escape any more than all the other Jews" (4:13), can be read at least two different ways, depending on how one translates the *min* preposition before "all the other Jews." The NRSV presents one of the possibilities, translating this preposition as "any more than." When translated in this way, the sense is that Esther should not think that she will be able to "pass" as

---

[7] Despite the fact that Esther sent her message via Hathach (4:10), the text has it delivered to Mordecai by a "them," which harkens back to 4:4, when the servants and eunuchs collectively report to Esther on Mordecai and the Jews. Some propose, following the LXX, an emendation of the verb *wayyaggîdû* ("and they revealed") to *waygēd* ("and he revealed"; or *wayyuggad*, "and it was revealed," depending on how the verb is pointed). There is no substantial textual support for this emendation, however. It is more likely a narrative confusion (rather than an error in scribal transmission) in which the text inadvertently goes back to the collective mode of reporting in 4:4, before Esther appointed Hathach as the privileged mediator.

non-Jewish and thereby escape the annihilation decreed by the king and Haman, *"any more than* all the Jews,"[8] even though she is Queen of Persia. The other possibility is to translate the preposition in its most common sense, as "from," thus "do not think that you will escape *from* all the Jews." When translated thus, the sense is that Esther will not escape with her life *from the Jews*—that is, when "relief and deliverance" arises "from another quarter," at which time "you and your family will perish" (4:14a). Indeed, this latter confidence on the part of Mordecai that deliverance will come for the Jewish people against their adversaries, with or without Esther's help, supports the second, more literal translation. If she refuses to help her people in the struggle, then she should not expect to be treated differently from their adversaries who have authored the royal decree against them. His assertion that "you *and your family* will perish," moreover, reminds her of the fact that it is Mordecai, as adoptive cousin, who has preserved Esther's family name thus far. Whichever way these words are translated, Mordecai's statement indicates his concern that Esther's words and actions are distancing her from the Jews and their plight under the new decree.[9]

The phrase "from another quarter" *(mimmāqôm ʾaḥēr)* has captured imaginations for millennia. Many have read within it a subtle allusion to God and *divine deliverance*.[10] This reading finds roots in Talmudic tradition, where *māqôm*, "place," is used as an epithet for God. Although the possibility of a theological reference in "another place" should not be ruled out entirely, the potential political-revolutionary connotations of such deliverance (whether involving divine intervention or not) should neither be overlooked. We have seen how socio-political *location* has played an important part in the formation of identities and power relations throughout the story. Might it be that Mordecai, who is always located on the margins and often identified with marginal characters—for example, the "keepers of the threshold" who threatened an earlier coup—knows of another place from whence a violent political deliverance might erupt?

---

[8] The "other" in the NRSV's "all other Jews" is added by the translator; the Hebrew word for "other" *(ʾaḥēr)* does not occur in this verse.

[9] By using the language of "escape" *(mlṭ)* and "deliverance" *(nṣl)*, moreover, the rhetoric casts Esther's doom in terms of a judgment day for the Jews. This language lends subtle support to the theological reading of "another place" (on which see below).

[10] E.g., Moore, *Esther*, 50, 52; Paton, *Esther*, 222; and Helmer Ringgren, "Das Buch Esther," *Das Hohe Lied, Klaglieder, Das Buch Esther*, with Artur Weiser (Göttingen: Vandenhoeck & Ruprecht, 1958) 131.

It should be remembered, moreover, that even if "another place" is taken as an allusion to God, that does not mean that this "other place" is ultimately responsible for deliverance in the story. For Mordecai says that if Esther does *not* help, deliverance will come from another quarter. As we shall see, she does indeed decide to help, and so Mordecai's potential "other" source of deliverance is never needed. If, then, "another quarter" is taken to refer to God, it is a God whose help is, according to the logic of this text, preempted by deliverance from Esther.

Mordecai concludes by making a wise rhetorical turn from threat to invitation: "Who knows? Perhaps you have come to royal dignity for just such a time as this" (4:14b). Here again, one could read this as an affirmation of divine providence or of chance and accident. Perhaps Esther has risen for a reason, that is, to fulfill God's plan for deliverance. Or perhaps the Jews are simply lucky to have her there.

As Levenson points out, the phrase "who knows?" *(mî yôdēaʿ)* may support the theological reading, since it is used elsewhere in the Hebrew Bible to "preface a guarded hope that penitential practice may induce God to relent from his harsh decree, granting deliverance where destruction had been expected (cf. 2 Sam. 12:22; Joel 2:14; and Jonah 3:9)."[11] In Esther, however, the decree comes from the anti-Jewish political projections of Haman and the king, rather than from God's judgment. Here again, we find the book of Esther leaving open the possibility of a theological interpretation while at the same time rendering such an interpretation at best ambiguous and at worst deeply problematic.

Either way, it is up to Esther to accept or reject the task.

THE FOURTH INTERCHANGE (4:15-17)

In the final interchange between Mordecai and Esther in this episode (4:15-17), Esther has the last word. Whereas the series of interchanges between them was initiated by Mordecai's actions and report, aimed at delivering new commands to Esther inside the palace walls, it concludes with Mordecai departing in unquestioned obedience to Esther. In fact, Mordecai will not have another word with Esther until her deliverance of the Jews has been successfully accomplished (at which time *she* will promote *him*; see 8:2).

In this final interchange, the eunuch Hathach is not mentioned explicitly as mediator (4:15). He is, however, still functioning as such, and the literary effect of skipping over his role is to pick up the pace

[11] Levenson, *Esther*, 81.

and the intensity of interchange; that is, it makes the interchange seem more immediate. This also gives the impression that the following words between Esther and Mordecai (which have to do with a plan for subverting the new decree) are passed in secret. Yet they are not. Hathach knows all. Indeed, it is safe to assume that her other servants and eunuchs do too (see 4:4).

The sense of immediacy and intensity in this last interchange between Esther and Mordecai is heightened further by the fact that Esther's last words open with a series of forceful imperatives: "go . . . gather . . . hold a fast" (4:16). Clearly Esther has understood Mordecai's threat and has taken it seriously. She will transgress the law which she has just stipulated (4:12). In so doing, moreover, she will identify not only with the Jews but also with Vashti (she will come when not called, whereas Vashti refused to come when called). Although in one sense her agreement to go to the king is a heeding of Mordecai's command (4:8), it is not a matter of simple obedience to his authority, for what is at stake is not only the survival of all Jews but also her own survival, as his words made absolutely clear (4:13-14a). Moreover, her reply itself is very forceful, beginning with a string of three imperatives directed to Mordecai and the other Jews while revealing no details with regard to her strategy.[12] Mordecai and the other Jews will remain in the dark until she has succeeded in subverting Haman's plan.

Esther makes clear, finally, that death is a real possibility no matter what she does. Mordecai has already said that she and her family "will surely perish" if she keeps silent. Her last lines to him make clear that she risks the same end by *not* keeping silent: after the three days of fasting, she will go before the king unsummoned, "and if I perish, I perish" (4:16). The verb for "perish" is *ʾbd*, which is the same verb used in Mordecai's threat on her father's house, as well as in the genocidal decree in 3:13 (there translated in the NRSV as "annihilate").

"Mordecai then went away and did everything as Esther had ordered him" (4:17). In immediate response to Esther's imperatives, and without a word back, Mordecai departs to follow her orders without question.[13] Significantly, this statement draws several elements from the language that was used in chapter 2 to describe *Esther's* obedience

---

[12] The imperatives from Esther also suggest that Mordecai possesses a status of authority among the Jews of Susa, insofar as she commands Mordecai to gather all of the Jews in Susa together and appoint a fast on her behalf.

[13] The verb used to describe Mordecai's departure is *ʿbr*—most literally "crosses over"—the same verb used elsewhere in the book of Esther for *transgressing* (lit. "going over" or "across") a law (1:19; 3:3) or custom (9:27-28).

to *Mordecai*. In 2:10, as has already been discussed, Esther did not "reveal" her Jewish identity "because Mordecai commanded her *[ṣiwwâ ʿālêhā]* not to reveal it." In 2:20, this statement in 2:10 is reiterated along with the comment that "Esther did *[ʿōśâ]* what Mordecai said just as when she was brought up by him." Here in 4:17, it is *Mordecai* who "does" (*yaʿaś*, the same verb in another form) everything that Esther "commands him" (*ṣiwwĕtâ ʿālāyw*). From here on, the fate of Mordecai and all Jews hangs in the balance as Esther becomes the key player.

Before Mordecai's report to Esther via Hathach, it appeared that Esther, in the palace and at the center of political power, was completely in the dark about the political goings-on throughout the kingdom, even in those matters that pertain directly to her people. This lack of political knowledge on her part adds to our growing sense that the palace and the king's domain is a locus of ignorance (compare 3:15). It also marks the distance between Esther's new royal (Gentile) identity inside the palace and her former identification with Mordecai and the Jewish people outside the palace. As the knowledge passes via Hathach from Mordecai outside to Esther inside, this distance is bridged, and the result is further identity conflict within Esther. This convergence of identities in Esther is socio-politically impossible within this story world, for it simultaneously associates her with royal Persian national identity and with the Jews who have been marked for annihilation as that national identity's quintessential other, or "not-us." She is simultaneously self and other, "us" and "them." This tensive convergence of identities, if revealed, would bring about a political explosion. Indeed, its revelation will be dynamite, and Esther will need to strategize carefully so that it blows up in Haman's face and not her own.

Chapter 7

FACE TO FACE

Esther 5:1-8

Following the series of mediated interchanges between Esther and Mordecai in 4:1-17, the narrative moves quickly forward to the final (third) day of the fast commanded by Esther in her last words to Mordecai. This episode can be divided into two parts: (a) 5:1-5, in which Esther initiates a face-to-face (and hand-to-scepter) encounter with the king, and invites him and Haman to a drinking party which she has already prepared; and (b) 5:6-8, the scene of the drinking party itself, at which time she invites the king and Haman to a second drinking party the next day. This episode is doubly suspenseful. First of all, Esther is risking her life by going before the king without being called (see 4:11, 16). Second, Esther twice defers the king's invitation to make her request (which he grants in advance) by way of counter-invitations. The episodes thus concludes inconclusively, with the king and readers wondering what she will ask—and what she will reveal—the next day.

FACE TO FACE, HAND TO SCEPTER (5:1-5)

The opening line, "on the third day," establishes continuity between this episode and the previous interchanges between Esther and Mordecai, where she commanded a fast for three days, after which she would go before the king (4:16). Given that this is the last day of the fast which Esther and her servants conducted along with Mordecai and the Jews of Susa, this line is also a subtle reminder of the solidarity between Esther and the Jews at this moment: as the fast concludes, she is going before the king *on behalf of the Jews* who have been fasting *on her behalf*.[1] At the same time, this episode also presents sharp contrasts between, on the one hand, Esther and the king inside the palace and, on the other, Mordecai and the Jews outside. Whereas all have been fasting for three days, moreover, this encounter will center around banqueting (in fact, by hosting a banquet on the third day she will break the-fast early). Whereas Mordecai and the others have been wearing sackcloth (4:1-3), Esther will be wearing "her royal robes" (5:1; more literally "her royalty"). Whereas Haman and the king have marked the Jews for annihilation as other, the quintessential "not-us" of Persia, Esther will be treated precisely as one of "us," an insider, a favorite drinking companion. All these contrasts highlight the difficult and highly risky situation in which Esther finds herself: between overt identification with the king and the law *over against* the Jews on the one hand, and under-cover *solidarity with* the Jews over against the law on the other.

"On the third day," as the fast concludes, "Esther put on her royal robes and stood in the inner court of the king's palace, opposite the king's hall. The king was sitting on his royal throne inside the palace opposite the entrance to the palace" (5:1). Although it is difficult to get an exact picture of the court and palace layout, and therefore of the setting, for this encounter, it is clear from what follows that Esther's location, standing "in the inner court . . . opposite the king's hall," is plainly visible to the king from his seat on the throne. Any further significance that these details of the setting might once have afforded are lost on today's reader.

Esther's explication of the law to Mordecai in 4:11 (cf. 4:16) made clear that she would be risking her life by going before the king in this manner. At this point, moreover, the text does not dwell on this potential for disaster, but immediately signals the king's enamored acceptance of her coming. Indeed, his acceptance of her is linked directly to his *seeing* her: "*As soon as the king saw [kirʾôt]* Queen Esther standing in the court, she won his favor" (5:2a). As in all previous encounters with men and eunuchs (2:9, 15, 17), Esther "wins" or "lifts" (*nśʾ*) the king's favor—more literally, as earlier, she "wins favor *in his eyes [bêʿênāyw]*," thus linking the looking to the favor more explicitly than the NRSV lets on. Once his eyes have been favorably won over, moreover the king "holds out," or "extends" (*yôšeṭ*, from *yšṭ*) the golden scepter in his

---

[1] In 4:8, Mordecai's charge is that Esther come before the king and entreat him "for her people" (*ʿal – ʿammāh*); likewise, in 4:16, Esther's charge that Mordecai and the Jews of Susa fast "for me" (*ʿālay*; NRSV "on my behalf").

hand.[2] Recall that this action is the means by which the king spares one's life from the "one law" of death for coming before him without being called (4:11). Nonetheless, given the emphasis on Esther's good looks here and elsewhere, and given the premium the king has put on good looks thus far, the double entendre in this extension of his scepter at the sight of the queen is undeniable. To carry the erotic undercurrent further, Esther "approached and touched the top [rō'ōš] of the scepter" (5:2b).

Thus obliged, the king asks what it is that she "seeks" (bqš; 5:3a). Recall that in 2:15 Esther "asked for" or "sought" (bqš) nothing except what Hegai advised (see the commentary on 2:5-18). Soon after, in 2:21, the two eunuchs Bigthan and Teresh "sought" (bqš) to kill the king. They failed. Soon after that, in 3:6, Haman "sought" (bqš) to destroy all the Jews of Persia; and his recommendation to the king in 3:8-9 had this as its objective. From here out, although he will not know it until it is too late, *Haman's success* in achieving that which he seeks will depend on *Esther's failure* to achieve that which she seeks. For she seeks to subvert him.

By adding that "it shall be given you, even to the half of my kingdom" (5:3b), moreover, the king is essentially giving Esther advance approval for whatever she might seek. It is surprising, then, that she postpones her request, by instead inviting him *and Haman* to a drinking party (or "banquet," mišteh) which she has already prepared for them (5:4).

The king is not type to turn down a request, a recommendation, or an opportunity to drink, and so he does not hesitate to accept Esther's invitation. (In fact, it is beginning to look as though accepting offers and fulfilling requests is what pleases the king most of all.) He calls for Haman to come in haste "so that we may do as Esther desires" (or "to do what Esther says"; 5:5).[3]

ESTHER'S FIRST PARTY FOR THREE (5:6-8)

As they drink wine together, the king cuts straight to the chase, reiterating his earlier question: "What is your petition? It shall be granted you. And what is your request [again bqš]? Even to the half of my kingdom, it shall be fulfilled" (5:7). As Esther begins speaking, it

[2] This verb occurs in the Hebrew Bible only in Esther (4:11; 5:2; 8:4). Related verbs in cognate languages carry the sense of extension and/or penetration.

[3] Compare the king "doing what Esther says" here with 1:15, in which the king is upset by Vashti's "not doing what the king said."

appears that she will actually make her request at this time: "This is my petition and request: If I have won the king's favor, and if it pleases the king to grant my petition and fulfill my request, . . ." (5:6b-7). One fully expects what follows to be the content of the her petition and request. But Esther then defers that expectation for yet another day, inviting the king and Haman to a second drinking party the next day (i.e., the day after the three-day fast has been completed; cf. 4:16 and 5:1). *Then* she will answer the king's question.

Why does Esther defer the king's offer to fulfill her request, even up to half his kingdom? It certainly appears that she could have her way immediately. Perhaps she does not take the king's extravagant offer as a reliable gauge of how he will respond to a more concrete political request. For that matter, exactly how much of one's kingdom would the subversion of the earlier decree amount to? Perhaps, as Rashi suggests, she is building suspense as well as tension, wanting the king to think that there is something amorous brewing between her and Haman (what irony!) so that the king would be more likely to kill him later on.[4] Perhaps she wishes first to get into good favor with Haman, too. Certainly he is taken by high social honors (3:1-2), as is the king. Perhaps, as Levenson writes, "by seeming to honor Haman, she fattens him for the kill."[5]

Perhaps Esther has all or none of these reasons in mind as she makes her invitation. The text, as usual, leaves her motivations and strategies to the imagination. All we are given, from beginning to end, are her actions and words. This is in contrast, of course, to Haman, whose inner intentions, plans, joys and fears have been revealed in the narrative from the very beginning (3:6; cf. 5:9-14; 6:4-13; 7:6-8). If the narrative's insights into Haman's psyche lend a sense of insecurity and ill-fate to his character, the lack of windows into Esther's inner thoughts lend a certain mystery and confidence to her character

---

[4] See also Talmud Megillah 15b, discussed in the commentary on the king's sleeplessness in chapter 6.

[5] Levenson, *Esther*, 90.

Chapter 8

FIFTY CUBITS FOR MORDECAI

Esther 5:9-14

The story of Haman's second face-to-face encounter with Mordecai, in 5:9-14 (the first is found in 3:1-6), is one of two episodes (5:9-14; and 6:1-14) that take place in the space of a single day, between Esther's first and second drinking parties with Haman and the king (5:6-8 and 7:1-10). Both of these episodes involve encounters between Haman and Mordecai, the first private and the second public.

As far as Haman is concerned, the movement from the first to the second of Esther's drinking parties will be a movement from the heights of honor and happiness as the king's premier (5:9) to the depths of dread and demise as the king's despised and criminal other (taking Mordecai's place; 7:7-10). These three episodes provide windows into Haman's growing frustration and insecurity, thereby anticipating his ill-fate, as the violent destruction he seeks is violently subverted by what Esther seeks.

The narrative pattern of this episode parallels the earlier stories of Vashti's dishonoring refusal of the king's command (chapter 1; cf. 2:1-4) and Mordecai's dishonoring refusal of the king's command to bow before Haman. That is, it moves from (a) Haman's honor and good spirits in 5:9a, to (b) Mordecai's refusal to honor or fear him in 5:9b, to (c) a recommendation to undo this dishonor by destroying Mordecai in 5:10-14a, to (d) the return of Haman's good pleasure in 5:14b.

Happy and in Good Spirits . . . (5:9a)

The episode begins where 5:8 left off, as Haman goes forth from Esther's first drinking party "happy and in good spirits" (5:9a). Once again, as in 3:6, the narrative is offering insight into Haman's psychological state. The effect of these insights, as discussed in 5:1-8, is to make him appear needy and unstable, vacillating between honor and rage, happiness and fear, and therefore more vulnerable to being undermined by both Mordecai and his more dangerous opponent, Esther (whom he will not recognize as an opponent until it is too late).

The phrase "happy and in good spirits" suggests, of course, his happiness at having been honored by an exclusive audience with the royal couple (with another one planned for the next day). It also suggests that he is drunk, insofar as he has just left the drinking party, and insofar as *ṭôb lēb*, "in good spirits," is precisely how the drunk and happy king was described in 1:10, just before summoning Vashti.

. . . BUT NOT FOR LONG (5:9b)

Given the intertextual connection (through *ṭôb lēb*) between Haman's present state of honored, happy drunkenness and that of the king in 1:10, the reader may expect that his good spirits are about to be spoiled. And so it goes.

In the encounter between the king and Esther in the previous episode, Esther gains the king's favor "when he saw [*kirʾōt*] her" (5:2). Here in 5:9, as Haman encounters Mordecai, the same verb in the same form is used: "When Haman saw [*kirʾōt*] Mordecai in the king's gate, ..." But whereas Esther gains the king's favor when he sees her, quite the opposite happens when Haman sees Mordecai, for Mordecai "neither rose nor trembled before him, [and] he was infuriated with Mordecai" (5:9b). Unlike the previous conflict between Mordecai and Haman, which was mediated by the servants who reported Mordecai's lack of bowing as well as his Jewish identity, this encounter is immediate: Haman sees him and is enraged (*ḥēmâ*, the same rage felt by the king toward Vashti in 1:12 and by Haman toward Mordecai in 3:5). Ironically, part of what enrages Haman this time around is that Mordecai *did not rise before him*, whereas what enraged him last time was that he remained standing and *did not bow*. This time, moreover, Haman is also enraged by the fact that Mordecai did not "tremble" or "quake" (*zwʿ*). Like "doing obeisance" in 3:2, this verb can refer to reverence before God, as in Dan 6:27 (Eng. 26). However, it may also refer to trembling before the enemy or some other calamity, as in Hab 2:7 and Eccl 12:3. Here again, then, one may or may not read Mordecai's behavior as having something to do with his Jewish religious identity. As before, the text allows such an interpretation of his motivations, but in no way confirms it.

The Recommendation (5:10-14a)

Given the narrative pattern established in earlier conflicts between the king and Vashti (chapter 1) and between Haman and Mordecai (3:1-15), it is about time for someone to make a recommendation. Indeed, just as the king never turns down a proposal, neither do Haman or the king ever act on their rage before a recommendation is made. And so Haman does not immediately act on his rage. He "restrains" himself at this point,[1] and continues home, where he calls for his friends and his wife, Zeresh (5:10).

Once in the company of his loved ones, he recounts "the splendor of his riches, the number [multitude] of his sons, all the promotions with which the king had honored him, and how he had advanced him above the officials and the ministers of the king" (5:11). "The splendor of his riches" *(kĕbôd ʿāšrô)* is particularly significant, in that this is precisely what the king intended to exhibit in 1:4, "while he displayed the *great wealth [ʿōšer kĕbôd]* of his kingdom . . . ." Once again the narrative is identifying Haman's insecure desire for honor with that of the king. Likewise, the last indicator of greatness listed by Haman, "how [the king] had advanced him above the officials and ministers of the king," refers explicitly to the promotion in 3:1, just before his first enraging encounter with Mordecai. In this sense, Mordecai stands precisely for that which undermines Haman's identification with the king, and vice versa.

After recounting all his kingly honors and possessions, Haman adds that, on top of everything else, "Even Queen Esther let no one but myself come with the king to the banquet that she prepared. Tomorrow also I am invited by her, together with the king" (5:12). Whereas Haman sees Mordecai undermining his own high honor and identification with the king, he considers Esther's attention flattering, and a means by which he can further identify with the inner circle of royalty. The irony in this misperception is due not only to the fact that Esther is Mordecai's daughter/cousin (and a Jewish "enemy"; 3:10), but also to the fact that Mordecai will never be as much of a threat to Haman as is Esther. In fact, in this scene as in his next encounter with Haman, Mordecai only digs himself deeper into trouble, and without Esther's help he surely would be doomed.

Even with all these great and kingly honors (as he perceives them), Haman finds no pleasure, he says, "so long as I see the Jew Mordecai

---

[1] Rashi comments that he restrains himself, or "stands against his anger," at this point "because he was afraid to take revenge without permission" (i.e., from the king).

sitting at the king's gate" (5:13). Again, the emphasis here is placed on the frustration at *seeing* Mordecai, who does not reflect well on his premier subjective status. Whereas everyone, including the king, who *sees* Esther is pleased (she is literally "pleasing to look at [*ṭôbat marʾeh]*"), winning favor *in everyone's eyes* (2:7; cf. 2:9, 15; 5:2), whenever Haman sees Mordecai the opposite reaction takes place.

In response to this account of his troubles, "Zeresh and all his friends" collectively recommend that he order the construction of a gigantic gallows (more literally, "a wood" or "stake," for execution by impaling), "and in the morning tell the king to have Mordecai hanged on it; then go with the king to the banquet in good spirits [or 'happy']" (5:14a).[2] If Mordecai is the real source of displeasure for him, then he simply must be removed. The fact that the execution they recommend is on a huge stake or gallows would suggest, moreover, that the execution should be a great public spectacle: it must be easily seen by all. This in turn suggests that Mordecai's offense to Haman has been public as well (although there are no witnesses mentioned in 5:9, the servants were heavily involved in 3:1-6).

The time of the execution is also significant. Recall that this latest encounter with Mordecai has taken place on the third day of the fast on behalf of Esther (commanded by Esther in 4:16), on his way home from Esther's first drinking party. The proposed public execution of Mordecai would then be scheduled to take place on the morning after completion of the three-day fast.

HAPPY RETURNS (5:14b)

Not surprisingly, "this advice pleased Haman, and he had the gallows made" (5:14b). Can advice ever displease anyone in this story?

If Haman follows this advice, it is promised, he will be able to attend Esther's second drinking party happy (at which time, he knows, Esther will finally disclose what it is that she seeks). The great irony here is that he will face his greatest threat in Esther at the drinking party—with or without Mordecai impaled on the stake that morning.

---

[2] Although the NRSV has "in good spirits," the Hebrew here is *śāmēaḥ,* translated earlier as "happy." 5:14 does not include the phrase that was translated "in good spirits" in 5:9. Indeed, since that phrase connoted drunkenness as well as pleasure (see the comments on 5:9a; cf. 1:10), it would make no sense to say he would be going *to* the drinking party in such a state.

Chapter 9

SLEEP DESERTS

Esther 6:1-14

Esther 6:1-14 is the second of two episodes sandwiched between Esther's two drinking parties. Both involve face-to-face encounters between Haman and Mordecai. As discussed earlier, the first episode, 5:9-14, followed a well established narrative pattern in Esther: it began with Haman happy and in good spirits; his happiness turned to rage at the sight of Mordecai's dishonoring behavior; a recommendation was made to undo Mordecai's offense and thereby return Haman's good pleasure; Haman was pleased with the recommendation, carried it out (had the giant stake built), and his happiness returned.

Although 6:1-14 does not follow this same narrative pattern, it is closely linked to 5:9-14 in several ways: first, it takes place immediately following the previous episode ("that night," after Esther's first drinking party and after Haman had begun planning Mordecai's execution); second, it involves Haman coming before the king to request that Mordecai be hanged on the stake which he just had built; and third, it concludes with a major public event—although nothing like the public event *Haman* had in mind—and another conversation between Haman and his household companions. Between the public event that Haman had in mind (5:14; 6:4, 6-9) and the one that actually takes place (6:10-11), and between what Haman's companions say in response to the first encounter with Mordecai (5:14) and what they say in response to the second encounter (6:13), it appears that Haman's fortunes (recounted in 5:11-12) are taking a turn for the worse.

This episode can be divided into three parts, based on the characters involved and the location of the action: (a) the king, his servants, and Haman inside the palace (6:1-10); (b) Haman and Mordecai in the

open square of the city (6:11); and (b) Mordecai and Haman returning
to their respective homes, at which point Haman's friends predict his
doom (6:12-14). This episode is structured, moreover, so that it hooks
directly into the next episode, for as Haman's companions are talking
to him about his certain fall, the king's eunuchs arrive to escort him to
Esther's second drinking party (6:14).

THAT NIGHT (6:1-10)

The episode begins on "that night," that is, on the night after Esther's first drinking party with Haman and the king, the same night on
which Haman had the fifty-cubit stake built for Mordecai (5:14). The
next morning, Haman plans to have Mordecai publically executed by
royal order (5:14). His final task in accomplishing this plan is to get the
king's approval. Given that the king has yet to refuse a recommendation or request, this would seem an easy approval to get. But Haman
will never have the opportunity to present his request. On this night, a
bout with insomnia gets in the way not only of the king's good rest but
also of Haman's desire to put to rest his on-going troubles with the
other Jew.

"On that night the king could not sleep" (6:1a). The Hebrew behind
this translation is intriguing. Most literally it reads, "in that night, the
sleep of the king *fled*" or *"deserted"* (*ndd*).[1] This is a fascinating expression for the restlessness of insomnia: sleep resists capture, it escapes.[2]
It is this restlessness that opens the king to a revelation that radically
changes the status of Mordecai in relation to Haman. For this reason,
Rashi and others claim that the king's insomnia was a miracle. This is
not, of course, the only or even most obvious interpretation. Indeed,
the Talmud suggests that he cannot sleep because he is bothered by the
fact that Esther had invited Haman to the drinking parties. Perhaps,
the sages suggest, he wonders if she has eyes for Haman, and if the
two of them are planning to kill the king at the second party.

---

[1] The verb can also mean "wander" or "stray" (Isa 16:2; Hos 9:17; Jer 49:5). The
idea of sleep "wandering" or "straying" is likewise intriguing here, suggesting that
the king might have been experiencing strange dreams rather than insomnia. In
this regard, note that Rashi says that the reason Mordecai knew, in 4:1, about the
money Haman offered the king during their private meeting (3:9) was that "the
master of dreams told him" (Rashi 4:1).

[2] For a reading of this passage in relation to Emmanuel Levinas's idea of insomnia as a disturbance in identity, a situation in which the body is working
against its own desire for rest and stability, see "Insomnia and a Lost Dream of
Writing," in Beal, *Hiding*, 75–84.

> A thought occurred to him: What is the meaning of Esther inviting
> Haman? Perhaps they are conspiring against me to kill me? He thought
> again: If that is so, is there no man who is my friend and who would tell
> me? Then he thought again: Perhaps there is some man who has done
> me a good turn and I have not rewarded him; and therefore men refrain
> from informing me. Straightway, he commanded to bring the book of
> records of the chronicles. (Talmud Megillah 15b, Soncino trans.; see also
> Rashi 6:1)

On the other hand, maybe he had too much (or too little) to drink at
Esther's party. Here again, the text allows for a theological interpretation without either encouraging or discouraging it.

The king, unable to lay hold of sleep, reaches instead for something
much more readily accessible and less likely to slip away: "he gave
orders to bring the book of records, the annals [lit. 'memories of the
things/words of days'], and they were read to the king" (6:1b). Why
the annals, at this hour? Why have "memories of the things of days"
read during the night? These are not your typical bedtime stories.

One possible reason that the king calls for the annals is because
they serve to reflect well on his own royal subjectivity. This interpretation gains subtle support from the fact that the language of his order
(*wayyōmer lĕhābî' 'et . . . lipnê hammelek*, lit., "he said to bring . . . before the king") is identical to the order given to bring *Vashti* into his
presence in 1:10-11 (*'āmar lĕhābî' 'et . . . lipnê hammelek*, lit, "he said to
bring . . . before the king"). The contrast this parallel sets up—between his order for the annals in 6:1 and his earlier order to bring
Vashti, who reflects badly on the king when she refuses to be made
present as he wishes (see the commentary on ch. 1)—highlights the
fact that the annual records are readily accessible (they never refuse to
come or be seen) and are written precisely to reflect well on the king.
Thus they may save him from the restless insecurity of insomnia.

Perhaps, on the other hand, the king is restless because of the wake-
ful presence of a haunting, the apparition of a face which solicits his
obligation. Perhaps this face awakens a sense that something in the
order of things as it now stands is not right, not just, out of adjustment.
And so he goes to the annals to find a name to match the face and to
set the records straight.

Or perhaps there is a more concretely political reason for reading
the annals at this restless moment. Recall the rabbinic view that the
reason for the king's insomnia is that he is worried that Esther may
have eyes for Haman, and that Haman may be plotting to kill him (see
above). If that is his concern, perhaps he calls for the annals in order to
search for clues as to the trustworthiness of Haman and Esther. What
were the details of the last attempted coup, after which Haman was

promoted (2:19–3:1)? Did they not involve Esther? And when Esther revealed that coup by Bigthan and Teresh, did she not mention the name of another person as her informer?

As the servants read to the king, "It was found written how ['that which revealed how'; *ʾǎšer higgîd*] Mordecai had told about Bigthana and Teresh, two of the king's eunuchs, who guarded the threshold, and who had conspired to assassinate King Ahasuerus" (6:2). The passive construction "it was found," like the earlier description of the lot being cast in 3:7, once again leaves the question of providence versus accident intriguingly open.

This late night/early morning reading from the annals recalls Mordecai's unrewarded revelation of the eunuch coup, which he had reported to Esther and which Esther had reported to the king "in the name of Mordecai" (2:22). Recall that in 2:23 it was not clear which details from the incident had been recorded, thereby adding to the suspense as the annals are reopened at this point. As it turns out, Mordecai's name *had* been included in the written report.

Upon hearing his servants read this report, the king asks, "What honor or distinction has been bestowed on Mordecai for this?" (6:3a). As discussed in chapter 1, "honor" (*yěqār*) and "distinction" (*gědûlâ*, "greatness" or "promotion") carry great significance within the Esther narrative. The explicit aim of the king's extravagant drinking parties, for example, was to "display" them (1:4)[3]; and Vashti's refusal to come when he called (1:12) was a threat to that honor, as the aim of the law against her makes clear: "that all women will give honor [*yěqār*] to their husbands, high and low alike" (1:20). Later, after the failed coup, just when one might have expected the king to honor or otherwise distinguish Mordecai for his work as informer, "King Ahasuerus promoted"(*giddal*, a verbal form of *gědûlâ*) not Haman but Mordecai (3:1); and Mordecai's refusal to bow and do obeisance before Haman, like Vashti's refusal of the king's order, was interpreted as an undermining of that "promotion" or "distinction."

The servants (here, as in 2:2, they are *naʿǎrîm*, "young men") tell him that nothing has been done for him (6:3b). Like the eunuchs, these servants possess a great deal of knowledge/power as mediators of information. In the first encounter between Mordecai and Haman in chapter 3, what would have happened if the servants had not revealed to Haman that Mordecai was not bowing to him (3:4)? The logic of the narrative at that point suggests that Haman would never have known

---

[3] Esth 1:4 includes both words, although they are difficult to identify in the NRSV translation: "while he displayed the great wealth of his kingdom and the splendor [*yěqār*] and pomp of his majesty [*gědûlātô*]."

and so would never have been dishonored by Mordecai. Furthermore, what would have happened if they had not revealed to Haman that Mordecai was a Jew? The logic of the narrative at that point suggests that Haman would not have known that Mordecai was Jewish, and he might not have been so motivated to propose his plan for annihilation of all Jews.[4] Here in 6:3, too, everything depends on the servants as mediators. If they lie and say that something indeed had been done for Mordecai, the king would pass over this story from the annals and move on to the next without further comment. But the servants are very clear: "Nothing has been done for him" (or more literally "a thing has not been done with him"). This statement is ironic, since Haman is now seeking to do something radically *dishonorable* with him even as they speak. Yet Haman has done nothing with him either, as of yet.

The king then asks a second question, which is not obviously connected to his first question: "Who is in the court?" (6:4a). The narrative answers before the servants: "Now Haman had just entered the outer court of the king's palace to speak to the king about having [or 'to tell the king to have'] Mordecai hanged on the gallows that he had prepared for him" (6:4b). This is a continuation of the action in 5:9-14. Haman has completed the building of the stake, or gallows, and now is coming to the palace to "tell the king to have Mordecai hanged on it," just as Zeresh and his friends recommended (5:14). Following this fuller explanation by the narrator, the king's servants answer him, "Look [*hinnēh*], Haman is standing in the court" (6:5a).[5] The opening word in this brief statement, *hinnēh* ("behold" or "look"), is unusual in the context of this conversation, and lends a certain emphatic tone to their response. Moreover, although this particle is common throughout Hebrew biblical narrative and poetry, it is used only two other times in Esther, and in each other instance it draws attention to speech concerning the downfall of Haman and the corresponding rise of Esther and Mordecai: during Esther's second drinking party in 7:9, as the king burns with rage at Haman, the eunuch Harbona says, "Look [*hinnēh*], the very gallows that Haman has prepared for Mordecai . . .";[6] later,

---

[4] This depends on how one reads 3:6 (see the commentary on that verse). Was he already seeking to destroy the Jews, or does he begin seeking to destroy them after his troubles with Mordecai? If one goes with the latter line of interpretation, then Haman *definitely would not* have proposed his genocidal plan had Mordecai's Jewish identity not been revealed to him by the servants.

[5] The NRSV translates the opening *hinnēh* (usually "behold!" or "look!") as "there," thus "Haman is there," rather than "Look, Haman."

[6] Compare, moreover, the similarly terse and pointed orders given by the king in response to the revelations in 6:5 and 7:9: "let him come" (6:5) and "hang him on it" (7:9).

after Haman has been hanged on the stake he built for Mordecai, after the king gives Esther Haman's house, and after she gives the house in turn to Mordecai, the king summarizes the plot reversal in a speech to Esther, "See [*hinnēh*], I have given Esther the house of Haman, and they have hanged him on the gallows . . ." (8:7). The use of this particle here in 6:5, then, is the first of three uses which will ultimately mark the complete reversal of fortunes for Haman on the one hand and Esther, Mordecai, and the Jews on the other.

The servants' description of Haman "standing in the court," moreover, is precisely how Esther is described in 5:1, suggesting that he, like Esther, is at this point coming before the king in order to make his petition.

The king's response to the news of Haman's arrival is terse: "Let him come in"—in Hebrew, simply *yābô*ʾ, "let him come" or "he will come." Haman does so, and before he begins to tell him about his plan to execute Mordecai, the king asks him a question that sends his imagination in another vain direction. "What," the king asks, "shall be done for the man whom the king wishes [or 'delights'] to honor?" (6:6a).[7] This question looks superficially to be something like the offer made by the king to Esther when she stood before him in 5:1, and which he repeated again during Esther's first drinking party in 5:6. Whereas the narrative offered no insight into Esther's hidden desires or intentions on those occasions, here once again it opens a window onto Haman's soul: "Haman said to himself, 'Whom would the king wish to honor more than me?'" (6:6b). Everyone but Haman knows the right answer (it is his arch-enemy, Mordecai), and so this insight into his inner thoughts once again makes him appear vulnerable and in the dark.

At this royal offer, as he interprets it, Haman's self-aggrandizing fantasies run wild, and he imagines nothing less than masquerading as king in the most public way:

> For the man whom the king wishes to honor, let royal robes be brought, which the king has worn, and a horse that the king has ridden, with a royal crown on its head. Let the robes and the horse be handed over to one of the king's most noble officials; let him robe the man whom the king wishes to honor, and let him conduct the man on horseback through the open square of the city, proclaiming before him: "Thus shall it be done for the man whom the king wishes to honor." (6:7-9)

First, Haman focuses on the attire and mode of transportation: he will wear royal robes that have been worn by the king, and he will ride on

---

[7] On the use of "wish" or "delight" in this passage, see the discussion in the next section.

a horse that has been ridden by the king. Whether the crown is to be placed on the horse or whether it was placed on the king when he rode the horse during his coronation is somewhat ambiguous,[8] and there may indeed be some humor implied by this ambiguity. Either way, the image is extravagant, and emphasizes the fact that the man is to look most kingly (perhaps more kingly than the king himself).

Second, Haman gives procedural directions: one of the king's highest officials (who is higher than Haman? [3:1]) will robe the man and then will parade him through the public square of the Susa, proclaiming that this high public honor is granted according to the wishes of the king. A close biblical parallel to this kind of embodiment of another's royal status may be found in 1 Kgs 1:33-40, in which the aging King David orders that Solomon be made to ride on his royal mule while his priestly escorts publically proclaim him to be king over Israel, and that he then be placed on the royal throne in David's place.[9] Haman clearly imagines himself taking the king's place, and he may even be suggesting something like a coronation ceremony.

Although Haman's proposal is outrageous, and although granting it should be out of the question for any self-respecting royal, we fully expect that the king will approve it, and so he does. The king follows Haman's recommendation without qualification. The problem, of course, is that the king and Haman have not had the same honoree in mind. "Quickly, take the robes and the horse, as you have said, and do so *to the Jew Mordecai* who sits at the king's gate. Leave out nothing that you have mentioned" (6:9). The narrative does not need to register Haman's shock in order for the reader to imagine it.

Note, moreover, that the king refers to Mordecai as "the Jew" (or, as discussed earlier, "the Judean"). This rubs salt into Haman's new wound, emphasizing that the one he is about to honor in such royal fashion is not only his personal opponent but also his ethnic "other," one of the ones who he claims "do not keep the king's laws, so that it is not appropriate for the king to tolerate them" (3:8). Moreover, this makes clear that the king knows that Mordecai, whom he delights to

[8] The clause "with a royal crown on its head" is missing from LXX. Some suggest that it may refer to the horse which the king rode when he [the king] was crowned. The image reproduced in Moore (*Esther*, Plate 4) has often been cited as evidence for ancient Persian practice of decorating a horse in such manner. The adornment on that horse, however, is probably not a crown but a dressing of its mane. Moreover, as Clines, *Ezra, Nehemiah, Esther*, 308, makes clear, there is no strong evidence elsewhere in Assyrian inscriptions for the placement of royal insignia (i.e., anything that might be described as a "royal crown" [*keter malkût*]) on horses.

[9] See also 1 Sam 18:4, in which David puts on the robe and armor of Jonathan, King Saul's heir to Israel's throne.

honor now, is Jewish (he also knows where he "sits," at the king's gate). Perhaps that information was included in the annals, in which case Esther must have "revealed" Mordecai's people even while keeping secret her own affiliation with him and with the Jews. In that case, perhaps this ethnic identification did not register with him at the point of Esther's revelation, and so it did not register as a conflict when Haman and he drafted the decree for annihilation of the Jews (3:12-15). Whether or not this is the case, one must ask at this point whether or not the king is aware that the genocidal decree targets Mordecai and his people. Part of the craft of this narrative is that just as it is difficult to determine Esther's plans and intentions until they have been implemented, it is similarly impossible to know what the king knows and what he does not know at any given point in the narrative.

Since chapter 3, there have been two royal documents pertaining to Mordecai: the annals, which identify him as a friend and protector of the king and the royal order; and the genocidal decree, which identifies him and his people as the king's quintessential other and marks them for annihilation as such. At the beginning of chapter 3, at which point Haman began his rise, it had appeared that the record of Mordecai's honorable deed for the king had been lost in the files forever. But a royal bout with insomnia has reopened that text. Obviously the two writings concerning Mordecai—an honor roll and a death sentence— are perfectly incompatible with one another. Which one will ultimately stand and which will be undone?

Haman's Worst Nightmare (6:11)

Once again, then, Haman's desire for public honor is to be radically subverted by Mordecai. On the night in which sleep deserted the king, Haman's greatest fantasy has been transformed into his worst nightmare. "So Haman took the robes and the horse and robed Mordecai and led him riding through the open square of the city, proclaiming, 'Thus shall it be done for the man whom the king wishes to honor'" (6:11). Haman does for Mordecai just what he had expected to have done for himself. This is the first of several reversals of fate for these two opponents.

The phrase, "the man whom the king wishes [or 'delights'] to honor," which Haman repeats many times as he escorts Mordecai through the square, has been used four times prior to this (vv. 6 [twice], 7, 9 [twice]; cf. "wish to honor" in v. 6b). Its repetition is significant within this highly dramatic episode. As mentioned earlier, "honor" has been the desire of the king and Haman from their beginnings; indeed, Mordecai has been the primary obstacle to Haman's attainment of honor. Thus the revelation to Haman that "the man whom the king wishes to honor" is not him but Mordecai is his ultimate dishonor. The king's "delight" (*ḥpṣ;* NRSV "wish") in honoring anyone in such a manner, moreover, suggests that this parading of Mordecai through the city is a joke not only on Haman but also on the king. This is not only a moment of reversal involving Mordecai and Haman; it is also an even more outrageous moment of reversal involving Mordecai and *the king*. Like those standing in the public square during this parade, readers— like a congregation celebrating Purim—may also delight at this extravagant masquerade. Yet that delight is very different than the king's; indeed it is at his and Haman's expense.

BACK HOME (6:12-14)

As was the case with the previous episode involving Haman and Mordecai (5:9-14), this episode concludes with a scene at Haman's house. But whereas his last trip home brought him comfort and a sense of direction in the face of Mordecai, this one will bring him a forecast of doom.

After the parade, "Mordecai returned to the king's gate, but Haman hurried to his house, mourning and with his head covered" (6:12). Mordecai's public honor is thus contrasted against Haman's corresponding public shame.[10] This contrast is sharpened by the fact that Haman "hurries" home whereas Mordecai simply "returns." Note, moreover, the contrast between their respective destinations: the king's gate for Mordecai and a house for Haman. In fact, the narrative never mentions Mordecai's actual home (unless the king's gate is actually it). As with Esther, the narrative gives away very little as to the private life or inner psyche of Mordecai. Contrast this lack of insight into their characters with the many windows into Haman's heart and home. Unlike the typical villain of modern narrative, who is represented as having neither heart nor home, Esther's villain is perpetually exposed. Here, moreover, we have a window not only onto Haman's home life but also onto what he shares with his companions in private there.

Haman once again tells his companions everything that has happened to him (6:12a). The night before, they had been able to make a recommendation that promised to undo his rage and frustration in relation to Mordecai. Certainly he is hoping for a similar recommenda-

---

[10] The act of covering one's head is obviously a public act, but so is mourning; cf. the Jews mourning in sackcloth in 4:3.

tion to undo his sense of shame now. He gets no such help, however. Instead, they (again collectively) give him a bad omen: "If Mordecai, before whom your downfall has begun, is of the Jewish people, you will not prevail against him, but will surely fall before him" (6:13b). Clearly they interpret the previous parade scene (which he has just described to them) in the same way we do: Haman has already begun to fall before Mordecai. It is likewise clear from their statement that Haman had not told them before now that Mordecai is Jewish—or, to be more precise, "from the seed of the Jews" or "of Jewish seed" (*mizzera* *hayyĕhûdîm*). How these two factors (that Haman has already begun to fall before Mordecai, and that Mordecai is "of Jewish seed") are related to their most certain prediction of his ultimate fall before him is less clear.[11] It is easy to read this statement as the narrator speaking through them, that is, as a meta-narrative affirmation of ethnic pride. That is, this statement can be read as utterly reliable and true: there is no chance that Haman will ultimately prevail, and there never was; "Jewish seed" must survive (whether by God's providence or by Jewish political savvy is another question), and anyone who opposes the survival of the Jews will fall. In this case, of course, Esther's future plans are really inconsequential, for the game is already over. On the other hand, why should we be so quick to rely on the words of these characters? For that matter, what special powers does the narrative attribute to "Jewish seed" before or after this scene? In fact, the only one who has claimed any special significance to the Jews has been Haman, who saw them as dangerously other. Might his friend's attribution of special powers to a person "of Jewish seed" be interpreted as a further *projection* of the other Jew's dangerous otherness?

The narrative does not linger over their words, however, but concludes this episode with a hook into the next: "While they were still talking with him, the king's eunuchs arrived and hurried Haman off to the banquet that Esther had prepared" (6:14). Just as he had hurried home in shame earlier (6:12), so now he is hurried away from home, this time to face ultimate humiliation. According to Haman's plan (5:14), by this point Mordecai should be hanging on a fifty-foot stake in ultimate shame, and he should be happily on his way to Esther's second drinking party. Instead his mind is filled with echoes of the dooming words of his wife and friends, and with a dreadful vision of Mordecai looking more like the king than the king himself does.

---

[11] The sense of certainty in their prediction is connoted especially in the use of the infinitive absolute construction, "you will surely fall," or "falling, you will fall" (*nāpôl tippôl*).

Chapter 10

COMING OUT PARTY

Esther 7:1-10

Esther 7:1-10 is the story of Esther's second drinking party, her "coming out party," which takes place on the day after the three day fast which Esther commanded for the Jews and for herself in 4:16 (but recall that Esther broke the fast on the third day; 5:1-8).[1]

This episode is organized around *dialogue* involving Esther and the king (as well as Harbona) and *action* involving the king and Haman (the king storms in and out of the garden; Haman throws himself on

---

[1] As noted earlier, the drinking party *(mišteh)* in Esther signifies for its participants a sense of security, well-being, and victory. Fasting, by contrast, is done by those in crisis, whose political situations are unstable and whose survival is uncertain. Thus the king parties with his officials, with Haman, and with Esther when he is feeling secure on his throne, and the Jews will likewise party once Haman and their enemies have been vanquished (Esther 9). Thus, too, the Jews fast in response to news of the decree to annihilate them, and Esther commands Mordecai and the other Jews to fast for three days, along with her, as she begins to implement her life-endangering plan to subvert that decree (Esther 4). Feasting connotes security and victory, whereas fasting connotes threat and uncertainty. Yet Esther clearly breaks this pattern, insofar as she feasts with Haman and the king *while still in peril, before victory has been secured.* On the one hand, this may be subtle indication of her confidence (and the reader's or hearer's confidence) that she (or she and God) will overcome. On the other hand, it may indicate her own distance from the other Jews who continue to fast, even while our awareness of her intention to subvert Haman, and thus her identification with the Jews, indicates her own otherness within the scene of the two feasts she hosts (on which see the discussion below). I am grateful to Eric Gadol for his insight on this matter.

Esther's bed to beg his life); that is, Esther and the king talk (esp. 7:1-8a), and Haman and the king act (esp. 7:8b-10). By the end of the episode, the combination of Esther's words and Haman's actions, as interpreted by the king, ironically place Haman in his loftiest public position yet: impaled on a stake fifty cubits high.

This episode picks up exactly where Esther's last drinking party left off (5:8). At that point Esther had promised the king that she would make her petition known at a drinking party that she would host the next day. During the day, between her first party and this one, moreover, Haman has encountered some serious setbacks in his quest for honor and also in his desire to overcome the Jew Mordecai (5:9-14; 6:1-14). Yet these setbacks are nothing when compared with what he is about to face. Indeed, although these frustrating encounters with Mordecai foreshadow Haman's doom, they do nothing to bring it about. The real turning point in the narrative takes place here with Esther at her second drinking party.

Disclosing the Impossible (7:1-6a)

As soon as the king and Haman arrive (7:1),[2] the king repeats his offer, almost word for word, for the third time: "What is your petition, Queen Esther? It shall be granted ['given'] you. And what is your request ['your seeking'; again *bqš*]?[3] Even to the half of my kingdom, it shall be fulfilled ['done']" (7:2). As mentioned before, it appears from this offer that the king expects that Esther seeks some*thing*, that is, some property of value rather than a political objective. Yet the offer is ambiguous, for "up to half my kingdom" could also refer to royal power and control. The latter, of course, is closer to what Esther has in mind. Yet in the end she will have both: the king will be waiting on her orders (9:12) and she will be given Haman's household (8:2).

At this third invitation from the king, Esther finally makes known that which she seeks (7:3-4). Her words are rhetorically masterful, matching—even subverting—the best work of both Memucan on the

---

[2] The text reads, most literally, "and the king came, and Haman, to drink with Queen Esther," again emphasizing that drinking is specifically the focus of the party. This focus is further emphasized in the new phrase, "the drinking party of wine" or "drinking of wine" *(mišteh hayyayin)*, which is used throughout the episode. Paton, *Esther*, 257, suggests that this phrase indicates that the episode takes place during the latter part of the feast, after the food has been served. Although this may be the case, the narrative emphasis is nonetheless placed on drinking.

[3] See the earlier discussion of "seeking" *(bqš)* in the commentary on 2:15 and 5:3.

other woman (1:16-20) and Haman on the other Jew (3:8-9). It begins
with two conditional clauses, "if I have won favor in your eyes" and
"if it pleases the king." The first condition is certainly true: when he
first met her in 2:17 she "won favor" with him; and in 5:3, just before
he makes his initial offer to her, the text indicates once again that she
"won favor in his eyes"; indeed, she wins favor in the eyes of all who
see her (2:9, 15).[4] The second condition, "if it pleases the king," is of
course the preface to all requests made to King Ahasuerus. As discussed earlier, he never has and never will turn down such a request.
Yet the dynamics here are somewhat different from the dynamics of
earlier requests. Whereas earlier requests or recommendations have
been made in order to solve a problem (often to quell the king's rage),
this request, once it is unpacked, will not initially please the king, but
will bring on rage, not toward Esther but Haman.

Esther then presents the content of her request. This content is presented in such as way as to tie rhetorically into the king's own offer.
The king had made his offer in parallel structure: (a) "What is *your petition* ['asking'; *šĕʾēlātēk*], Queen Esther? It *will be given* to you"; (b)
"And what is *your request* ['seeking'; *baqqāšātēk,* from *bqš*]? Even up to
half my kingdom, it *will be done*" (7:2). Esther's words match this structure: (a) "let my life *be given* as *my petition* ['asking']"; (b) "and ['let be
given'] my people as *my request* ['seeking']." Just as the king's offer
moves from personal address in the first line (addressing Queen Esther
directly) to a reference to the larger political order in the second line
("my kingdom"), so Esther's "petition" in the first line is personal (i.e.,
her own life) whereas her "request" in the second line is more broadly
political (i.e., her people).

By inserting "the lives of" before "my people" in this verse, the
NRSV translation makes the text of Esther's request appear to have
more of an *internal* parallel structure (paralleling her "petition" with
her "request") than it actually has. The second part of Esther's request
in Hebrew reads, most literally, "and my people as my request [or
'what I seek']." Given the ambiguities of Jewish identity in this narrative, and given Esther's own ambiguous (even tensive) identification
with the Jewish people up to this point, the language here is intriguing: "my people as what I seek."

---

[4] The text in 2:15 reads, "she won favor in the eyes of all looking at her." Although the language of "winning favor in the eyes of . . ." is the same in 2:15 as it
is in 2:9, 5:3, and 7:3, the NRSV translation misses this Hebrew narrative parallel by
translating 2:15 as "now Esther was admired by all who saw her." This translation
also plays down the emphasis in the text on Esther as good-looking (cf. 2:7). For a
possible interpretation of this dynamic of translation, see "The Bible as Moral Literature" in Beal, *Hiding*, 40–9.

At this point, of course, neither the king nor Haman have the foggiest idea who Esther's people are, let alone why her life might be in peril. The next sentence makes this identity clear, however, by quoting directly from the genocidal decree drafted by Haman and sealed by the king in chapter 3.

> For we have been sold, I and my people, to be destroyed, to be killed, and to be annihilated. If we had been sold merely as slaves, men and women, I would have held my peace; but no enemy can compensate for this damage to the king. (7:4)

The string of infinitives, "to be destroyed, to be killed, and to be annihilated," is taken directly from the decree in 3:13, a copy of which had been delivered to her by Mordecai in 4:8. The money involved in the original deal is also indicated by the phrase "we have been sold" (recall that Mordecai had reported "the exact sum" or "full account" of Haman's proposal to the king in 4:7).

The last part of Esther's speech in verse 4 (beginning "but no enemy" in the NRSV) is difficult to translate. Most literally, the second half of this verse reads "for there is not [or 'would not be'] the enemy worth injuring [or 'annoying'] the king." The basic sense, then, is that if her people were being sold into slavery rather than for annihilation, she would not ask the king to annul the sale and lose the money that this "enemy" had offered.[5]

Note, moreover, that although Esther apparently thinks that the king stands to gain financially from the decree to annihilate the Jews, this may not be the case. Recall that in the original agreement between Haman and the king to annihilate the Jews, when Haman had offered an exorbitant sum of money to the king's treasury, the king *appeared*, at

---

[5] Following Paul Haupt, "Critical Notes on Esther," *American Journal of Semitic Languages and Literatures* 24 (1907/8) 146, one might understand the trouble to the king not as financial loss but simply as annoyance, thus "for the enemy would not be worth the annoyance to the king." See also Bush, *Ruth, Esther*, 427–28, who translates ṣar not as "enemy" but "trouble," thus "for the trouble would not be commensurate with the annoyance to the king." As Levenson, *Esther*, 100, rightly points out, however, the king's subsequent question ("Who is he . . .?") suggests that she was referring to a specific adversary, and Esther's answer in 7:6 identifies Haman as ṣar, "enemy" (cf. the closely related verbal noun ṣōrēr, "enemy," in 3:10; 8:1; 9:10, 24). Thus the context strongly indicates "enemy" as the best translation.

Rashi offers yet another interpretation of this text. Esther's point, Rashi suggests, is that Haman is not interested in the king's welfare, for if he was, he would have recommended that they be sold as slaves rather than killed (which is a waste of potential labor force).

least, to turn the money down: "The money is given to you, and the people as well, to do with them as it seems good to you" (3:11). As discussed earlier, this may simply have been a polite way of accepting the money, but not necessarily so. Indeed, the king's ostensible rejection of the money may be interpreted as an indication that the king was fully convinced by Haman's presentation of the "Jewish problem," and that he supported Haman's "final solution" whole-heartedly. Whether or not the king accepted the money from Haman, Esther thinks that he did, for Mordecai had included the account of Haman's bribe in 4:7.

However one understands the original agreement between Haman and the king in chapter 3, it is clear that both men were responsible for the decree against the Jews. Even if the king did take the money, he undersigned the decree without reservation; indeed, Haman had presented it as an urgent matter of national security, not personal revenge or ethnic hatred. In this sense, both Haman and the king are enemies of the Jews. Thus Esther is in an extremely difficult political situation: she must distance the king from any public responsibility for the decree and place all the blame on Haman. Otherwise, aside from revolution or assassination, she and the Jews (with whom she is now clearly identified) are doomed.

The king's next question gives her a perfect opportunity to distance him from Haman with regard to the decree. He asks, "Who is *he* [singular], and where is he, who has presumed to do this?" (7:5). Esther's answer is brief and forceful: "Foe and enemy, this wicked Haman!" (7:6a). Just as Haman had secured his identity with the king by projecting the Jew as their mutual enemy—Persia's privileged other—so here Esther's verbal marking of Haman as "foe," "enemy," and "evil" serves to identify the king with herself *over against* Haman, thereby erasing the king's own former identification with Haman over against the Jews. In verses 3-4, Esther had disclosed the convergence of her identity as Persian royalty with her identity as Jew, marked for oblivion by Persian royal decree. This convergence is politically impossible, that is, it cannot be maintained within the present political order, because it means that she embodies both the same and the other simultaneously. With her declaration here in verse 6, she identifies the anti-Jewish decree with Haman and dissociates it from the king. Thus the Jews are presented as Haman's other but not necessarily as the king's or the nation's other. At this moment, with this pronouncement, Haman's identification with the law and the king is radically destabilized.

The position of the king, too, is radically destabilized: his right hand man is now being presented as his enemy by his queen, who also turns out to be one of those marked for annihilation as the nation's intolerable other. With a few choice words of disclosure, Esther has engendered a great deal of ambiguity and tension in the dynamics of relationship within this drinking party, as well as within the larger political scene.

BEGGING, FALLING, HANGING (7:6b-10)

So far the episode has been dominated by dialogue between Esther and the king, with Haman's voice noticeably absent. At this point, narrative attention turns from speech to action, namely the actions of Haman and the king, with Esther's movements noticeably absent. But whereas Esther's words have worked in her favor with the king, Haman's actions will work against himself.

"Haman was terrified before the king and the queen" (7:6b). The verb translated here as "terrified," *bʿt*, carries the sense of being startled or disturbed to the point of terror. Interestingly, the word occurs primarily in Job, and usually describes Job's oppression by God (e.g., 3:5; 7:14; 9:34; 13:11, 21; 15:24; 18:11; and 33:7). In Dan 8:17 and 1 Sam 16:15, it refers to the terror experienced by Saul after God sends an evil spirit on him, dooming him and his reign. Significantly, this follows immediately after the passage in 1 Samuel 15, discussed earlier, in which the Benjamite Saul is criticized for keeping booty after defeating Agag. Likewise here, for the reader, Haman's terror marks not only his shock but also his certain doom.

As was the case when the flow of the king's earlier drinking party was interrupted by Vashti's refusal to come and be ogled (1:12), so here the king flies into a "rage" (*ḥēmâ*), storming out of the drinking party and into the garden (7:7). Given his patterns of reaction and decision thus far in the narrative, we assume that he has no idea what to do.

Alone with Esther, Haman approaches her to "seek [again *bqš*] his life"—just as she has sought "her people" from the king (7:4)—"for he saw that the king had determined to destroy him" (lit., "that evil was destined for him from the king"; 7:7).[6]

---

[6] The verb translated as "was destined" (*kāltâ*) is a Qal perfect third-person feminine singular form of *klh*. Although in its Qal stem it is normally translated as a non-transitive verb ("to be complete," "to be destined"), it is interesting to consider the possibility of reading Esther as its subject and "evil" as its object, in which case the phrase would be translated as "that Esther had destined evil for him," thus emphasizing Esther's agency in bringing about Haman's fall. Compare Exod 5:13-14, in which the object of this verb (in Piel) does not take the marker of the direct object (*ʾet*). Note, moreover, that *min*, "from," in the phrase "from the king" might carry the sense of "through" or "by way of" in this text, thus further adding to Esther's agency; that is, Esther has determined evil for Haman *through* the king, using

As Haman is begging his life from Esther, the king returns from the garden to find Haman "had thrown himself on the couch where Esther was reclining" (7:8a). Note that the Hebrew verb translated by the NRSV as "had thrown himself" is a participle form of *npl*, which almost always means "fall." No doubt the NRSV is trying to capture the sense of him approaching Esther to beg for his life (7:6b). But this translation misses an important dynamic within the narrative, insofar as Haman's "falling" here is a literal recollection of the prediction of his friends in 6:13, which uses the same verb three times: "if Mordecai, before whom you have begun to fall *[linpōl]*, is of Jewish people, you will not prevail against him, but will surely fall *[nāpôl tippôl]* before him." To Haman's surprise, however, he is not falling before the other Jew Mordecai but before the other Jew—now become other woman as well—Esther.[7]

The king's question, "Will he even assault *[likbôš, from kbš]* the queen in my presence, in my own house?" (7:8b), clearly indicates that he thinks that Haman is trying to rape Esther. Indeed, the description of his "falling" before her leaves that possibility open, for the text reads, most literally, "and Haman was falling upon the bed, which was Esther *[ʾăšer ʾestēr]*, upon Esther." In order to make the relative pronoun construction ("which was Esther") clearly indicate possession ("which was Esther's") there ought to be a *lamed* preposition before Esther's name, as in 1:9, "which was King Ahasuerus's" *(ʾăšer lammelek ʾăḥašwērôš)*. While it is not incorrect to read the clause as "which was Esther's" rather than the more literal "which was Esther," it should be recognized that the text is ambiguous, thereby adding to the sense of ambiguity and the play of appearances. The addition of "upon Esther" at the end of the description adds further to this ambiguity. Is Haman falling over the bed or Esther or both?

At any rate, Haman's falling is taken by the king to be an assault on his wife. Indeed, his question indicates that what is most offensive is not that Haman might be assaulting Esther but that he would assault *the king's* wife in *his* presence and in *his* house. That is, the king interprets Haman's actions as offensive to *him*, as patriarch, more than to Esther! From here on it is not clear what decisively seals Haman's doom in relation to the king. Is Haman's fate sealed by his intended assault on Esther as Jew (through the decree) or his assault on her as the king's wife (through falling on/assaulting her?). For that matter, is there *ever* a decisive moment?

---

that royal power against Haman. I am thankful to Krista Becwar and Erik Hiltunen for these insights.

[7] Compare also the subsequent uses of the verb *npl*, "fall," in 8:17; 9:2, 3, all of which relate to the dreadful fate of those opposed to the Jews.

The shaming force of the king's question/accusation for Haman is powerfully and poetically conveyed at the end of verse 8: "As the words left the mouth of the king, they covered Haman's face."[8] Here words are physical: they leave one's mouth, they travel to their addressee, and they cover him. The king's words leave Haman speechless, buried under words.

Esther's revelation has left Haman in a panic and the king in a rage, with Haman's panicked actions contributing to the king's rage, and vice-versa. Given the narrative pattern of instigation—rage—recommendation—implementation—return of pleasure, by now well established (cf. 1:13-22; 2:2-4; 3:5-15), it is about time for someone to make a recommendation. Enter Harbona, another "one of the eunuchs of the king," who says, "Look, the very gallows that Haman has prepared for Mordecai, whose word saved the king, stands at Haman's house, fifty cubits high" (7:9a). Harbona indicates the means of abating the king's rage. Beyond that, he further compounds that rage by indicating Haman's violent opposition to Mordecai, whom the king had only just remembered to honor, to Haman's shame, in the previous chapter (6:1-11).

In earlier episodes involving recommendations to the king, the advice given has been explicit with regard to the details of procedure (1:16-20; 2:2-4; 6:8-9). This time, however, the king does not need to have things spelled out for him. He immediately tells Harbona to "hang him on that." This royal order is carried out at once, and the narrative concludes with the now familiar report that "the rage [again ḥēmâ] of the king abated" (7:10; cf. 2:1).

In the previous episode (6:1-11), Mordecai had taken the place Haman had imagined for himself, promenading in honor through the town center, as a king. In this episode, Haman winds up taking the place he had imagined for Mordecai once again, hanging shamefully from a giant stake, as a criminal (cf. Bigthan and Teresh in 2:23). He has, then, in a sense "surely fallen before" Mordecai, as his friends predicted (6:13). Yet he does not owe his fall to any strategic efforts on the part of his imagined opponent Mordecai; rather, he owes his fall to the work of Esther, whom he did not imagine to be his opponent until it was too late. He falls, then, on account of the ambiguities inherent in his own constructions and projections of otherness.

[8] The sense of this covering is that of shame. Compare the similar image of Haman covering his head as he returned home after honoring Mordecai in 6:12.

Chapter 11

OVERWRITING

Esther 8:1-17

Although Haman has been executed, the decree he and the king authored, calling for the annihilation of all Jews on the thirteenth day of Adar (the twelfth month), has not disappeared with him. The undoing, or rather the overwriting, of this edict is the focus on the next episode (8:1-17).

All the events in 8:1-17 apparently take place in the course of single day, and the opening phrase, "on that day," indicates that this is the same day as Esther's second drinking party, which concluded with Haman's execution. Later, in 8:9, this day is given as the twenty-third day of Sivan, the third month (8:9). Thus these events take place two months and ten days after the king and Haman had authored and published the decree for annihilation of the Jews. As Clines astutely notes, this seventy-day interval would not only connote a sense of perfect completion in the reversal of fortune about to take place, but also "would have struck a chord with every attentive post-exilic reader of the book," insofar as it would stand symbolically for the seventy years of Judean exile.[1]

Yet there is some difficulty in making this date, the twenty-third of Sivan, jibe with the time-frame of the narrative. As mentioned earlier, Haman's decree was written on the thirteenth of Nisan (the first month; 3:12). *If* the events of chapter 4, when Mordecai comes to Esther for help after hearing of the decree, take place immediately following the publication of the decree, and *if* Mordecai has the second

[1] Clines, *Ezra, Nehemiah, Esther,* 316.

decree written on the same day as the preceding events in chapter 8 (which take place on the day after the three-day fast commanded by Esther in chapter 4), then Mordecai's decree must have been written less than a week after Haman's. There are two points in the narrative at which one might insert the missing sixty-five or so days. The first point is at 4:1, "when Mordecai learned all that had been done." Perhaps Mordecai did not hear the news (or "all" the details) until some time after the decree against the Jews had been issued; or perhaps the "when" here does not mean that he approached the king's gate in sackcloth and ashes immediately after hearing news of the decree. The second point at which one might insert the missing days is 8:9, in the phrase "at that time." This phrase does not necessarily mean that "that time" is the same day as the preceding events in chapter 8. Instead it may be read as a rhetorical means to draw attention to the date that the decree was written. Of course, it may simply be the case that the narrative contradicts itself with regard to dates. Given the emphasis the narrative places on dates and connections between events throughout the story, however, it would be strange that such a blatant error would slip by. Rather, following Clines, it seems most likely that the narrative is trying to hold together two largely incompatible intentions: to present the series of events since chapter 3 as happening in rapid succession; and to relate this interval of uncertainty between the first decree and the second decree to the seventy years of Judean exile.[2]

8:1-17 can be divided into three main parts: (a) the king's gift to Esther of Haman's household, and Esther's promotion of Mordecai over that household, in 8:1-2; (b) the king's approval of Esther's request to write a decree that would undo the decree against the Jews, and Mordecai's writing and publishing of that decree, in 8:2-14; and (c) Mordecai's emergence, in royal robes, as honored leader of the now powerful, even fearful Jews, in 8:15-17. As this outline makes clear, 8:1-17 not only narrates the undoing of the decree against the Jews; it also narrates a shift in power from Esther to Mordecai. The opening section (8:1-2) picks up where chapter 7 left off, with Queen Esther making the important political decisions and recommendations while Mordecai stands in the background. By the final section (8:15-17), however, we find Esther taking a back seat in the narrative while Mordecai rises to prominence, embodying a merger of royal Persian power and leadership over the now politically dominant Jews. The turning point is found in the center section, focused on the new decree: Esther alone makes the request to the king; the king authorizes Esther and Mordecai ("you" in the plural) to write a new decree, against the earlier de-

---

[2] Clines, *Ezra, Nehemiah, Esther*, 316.

cree, in the king's name (8:8); and when it comes time to write the decree it is Mordecai alone, not Esther, who serves as its author (8:9). The movement is from Esther alone, to Esther and Mordecai together, to Mordecai alone. Esther and Mordecai are given the royal authority to write the decree, but Mordecai assumes that authority. From that moment on, Esther will fade to background as Mordecai takes the foreground.

ESTHER PLACES MORDECAI (8:1-2)

The episode opens with two gifts from the king. First, the king "gave to Queen Esther the house of Haman, the enemy of the Jews" (8:1a).[3] This gift would include all his property and likely all his servants and family members as well. Within the narrative, this gift signifies Esther's assumption of Haman's political status and authority.

Mordecai then presents himself before the king, "for Esther had *revealed* [*higgîdâ*, from *ngd*; NRSV 'told'] what he was to her" (8:1b). She had revealed "her people" as the Jews in the drinking party earlier that day (8:4; cf. 2:10, 20). Now she has revealed "her people" in the narrower, familial sense, as Mordecai. Once he is revealed as her kin, the king makes a second gift: he "took off his signet ring, which he had taken from Haman, and gave it to Mordecai," once again signifying an assumption of Haman's political status and authority. With these two gifts from the king, then, *both* Esther and Mordecai assume Haman's political position.

Esther then makes a remarkable move: she "set Mordecai over the house of Haman" (8:2b). Of course, one might argue that in this move, she is handing over her share of Haman's former status and authority to Mordecai, so that Mordecai takes Haman's place completely. Yet the text does not say that Esther *gives* Haman's household to Mordecai; rather, she "sets" (*śym*) him over it. She places him there, *over* Haman's household. This is a promotion through placement (and remember that Mordecai's place has not been easy to identify up to this point). Moreover, this action of promoting by "setting over" is precisely what the king had done for Haman earlier: "King Ahasuerus promoted [or

---

[3] As indicated by Clines, *Ezra, Nehemiah, Esther,* 314, a very formal air is given to these dispensations by adding titles to each of the personages: "King Ahasuerus," "Queen Esther," and "Haman, the enemy of the Jews." This title for Haman was also used in 3:10; cf. 7:6. As Esther and Mordecai rise over him in power, his former title ("son of Hammedatha the Agagite") is replaced by a title which identifies him as "enemy" or "hater."

'magnified'] Haman . . . and advanced [or 'set'] his seat above all the officials who were with him" (3:1). The verb translated in this verse as "advanced" *(śym)* is the same verb translated as "set" in 8:2. Queen Esther's action of setting Mordecai over Haman's household may thus be interpreted not as a means of self-subordination but as an exercise of royal power which is otherwise reserved exclusively for the king.

There is a bit of the macabre in this promotion of Mordecai over Haman's household: recall that the fifty-cubit stake (NRSV "gallows") which Haman had constructed for Mordecai's execution—on which Haman himself is now impaled—stands in front of this very house (as Harbona pointed out in 7:9). Thus, while Mordecai has now been "set over" Haman's house, Haman's own body hangs high above that same house.

WRITING OVER (8:3-14)

As far as the king is concerned, the matter has been put to rest with the execution of Haman and the gift of Haman's household to Esther. Perhaps he has forgotten the decree which he and Haman published a little over two months ago. Perhaps he does not care about it or those anonymous Jews marked for death by it. Or perhaps, since the annihilation it calls for is not scheduled to take place for another nine months, he assumes that with Haman now dead the decree will go unheeded. Clearly Esther would not agree. This earlier written decree must be overwritten by another.

Esther therefore approaches the king with yet another request, this time falling at his feet (reminiscent of Haman falling before/over Esther in 7:7-8), "weeping and pleading with him to avert the evil design of Haman the Agagite and the plot that he had devised against the Jews" (8:3). Interestingly, although the text gives a graphic description of the intensely emotional manner of Esther's plea, it does not provide the speech itself; rather, it offers a brief summary of its objective, namely, to "avert" (literally "to transgress" or "revoke")[4] the earlier decree against the Jews (here identified solely with Haman, although the reader knows that Haman had the king's full support at the time). The same mode of narration—detailing the emotional manner of speech while briefly summarizing the speech itself—is found in 4:1-8, the

---

[4] Note that the law against Vashti in 1:19 was described precisely as "irrevocable" or "not to be transgressed," using the same verb translated in this verse as "avert" (cf. 3:3). This suggests that Esther wants the law, which cannot be transgressed, to be transgressed.

opening exchanges between Mordecai and Esther. There the distraught behavior of Mordecai and the extreme agitation of Esther are described but their speech to one another is not quoted directly. In 8:3, as in 4:1-8, this mode of narration adds dramatic intensity to Esther's character even as it distracts attention from the objective content of her request.

The king's response, as in 5:2, is to extend his golden scepter (8:4). Esther rises from foot-level and stands before the king, as she had been standing before him when he extended his scepter to her for the first time in 5:1. The opening words of her quoted speech, in verses 5-6, likewise parallel the opening of her earlier requests: "If it pleases the king, and if I have won his favor, . . ." (compare 5:4, 8; 7:3). Of course by now she knows very well, as do we, that she pleases the king and wins favor in his eyes. Then she adds two more conditions: "and if the thing seems right [or 'advantageous'; *kāšēr*] before the king, and I am pleasing in his eyes, ..." The first of these conditions suggests that what she proposes should be done if it is the proper thing to do. Given that *kāšēr* can mean not only "proper" or "right" but also "advantageous" (what a perfect term for politicians to use!), Esther also may be suggesting that the thing she is about to propose will be to his own financial and/or political advantage. With her last condition, "if I am pleasing in his [the king's] eyes" (*ṭôbâ ʾănî bĕʿênāyw)*, Esther reverts to her typical rhetorical pattern of request, thereby sandwiching the new condition ("if the thing seems right") between stock conditions that she knows will be affirmed.

The NRSV translates this last condition as "if I have his approval." This is a very loose translation, apparently aiming to make it parallel the official tone of the third condition. It is, however, more of a stretch than the text can bare. Moreover, it misses the connection between this text and similar Hebrew phrases which are used throughout the book of Esther to convey the fact that Esther is "pleasing in the eyes of the king" and all others who *see* her (see the commentaries on 2:4, 9, 15; 5:2, 8; and 7:3).

Following this series of conditions, the content of Esther's request is given, and it appears to be the specifics of that which she was pleading for at his feet moments before: "let an order be written [or 'let it be written'] to revoke the letters devised by Haman son of Hammedatha the Agagite, which he wrote giving orders to destroy the Jews who are in all the provinces of the king. For how can I bear to see the calamity [or 'evil'] that is coming on my people? Or how can I bear to see the destruction of my kindred?" (8:5b-6). The verb phrase "let it be written to revoke" (*yikkātēb lĕhāšîb)* closely parallels Haman's earlier request, in 3:9, to "let it be written to destroy them" (*yikkātēb lĕʾabbĕdām)*. In both cases the request is constructed as a Niphal (passive) imperfect, third-person singular form of *ktb*, "to write," plus an infinitive construct ("let it be written to . . ."; cf. 3:13). This close parallel makes the purpose of this newly proposed decree absolutely clear: to overwrite the former writing completely. As we will soon see, this reversal of the earlier writing, by overwriting, amounts to *reversing the destruction* intended by it.

The two questions in verse 6 are in poetic parallel with one another: each one begins with "how can I bear" and then refers, using parallel terms, to the potential ill fate ("evil" in the first question and "destruction" in the second) of her people ("my people" in the first question and "my kindred" in the second). The rhetorical effect of this construction is to conclude the request in the form of a lament aimed at averting her people's annihilation. Note, in this regard, that the opening questions in Lam 1:1, 2:1, and 4:1 all begin with *ʾêkâ*, ("how?") which is obviously related to *ʾêkākâ* (also "how?"), with which Esther opens both questions in 8:5b-6.[5] The parallel structure also allows Esther to repeat the vital information that the people who have been marked for annihilation are *her* people ("my people . . . my kindred"), lest he has forgotten.

The king's response in verses 7-8 is addressed to *both* Queen Esther and Mordecai, and has two parts. First, in verse 7, he cites all he has done so far on their behalf: "See, I have given Esther the house of Haman, and they have impaled him on the stake [or 'hanged him on the gallows'],[6] because he plotted to lay hands on [or 'stretched forth his hand against'] the Jews." Second, in verse 8, he grants Esther's most recent request: "You [plural] may write as you please with regard to the Jews, in the name of the king, and seal it with the king's ring; for an edict written in the name of the king and sealed with the king's ring cannot be revoked" (8:7-8). Indeed, with this he goes beyond her request, authorizing them to write as they wish *in his name* and *with his signature*. The irony in the king's claim that "an edict written in the name of the king and sealed with the king's ring cannot be revoked" or "reversed" *(lĕhāšîb)* is striking, for the proposed edict, to be written in the name of the king and sealed with the king, is intended precisely to revoke Haman's edict, likewise written in the king's name and sealed with his ring (3:12; see also 8:3)!

Esther alone addressed the king with this request, and yet by using "you" *(ʾattem)* plus a plural imperative, the king appears to grant both

---

[5] Compare also Lam 1:14, "the Lord gave me over to those whom I cannot bear *[ʾûkal]*." This is the same verb used by Esther twice in this verse ("how can I bear *[ʾûkal]*").

[6] For the translation "stake" as opposed to "gallows," see the earlier commentary on 5:14.

Esther and Mordecai the authority to write the new decree. In this way the king's address anticipates—perhaps even precipitates—the fact that Esther will soon fade into the background as Mordecai comes to the fore. As discussed earlier, it is Mordecai alone who directs the writing of the edict in verses 9-14.

That the decree "was written according to all that Mordecai commanded" (8:9) parallels the authoring of this new decree with that of the earlier decree, in which "was written according to all that Haman commanded" (3:12). Except for the names, the Hebrew of these two passages is identical. Indeed, 8:9-14 closely parallels 3:12-15 from start to finish.[7] Yet it does not follow it exactly: the word and phrase order is often turned around, and several lines are added. Some additions emphasize the Jews as its primary addressees: "to the Jews" (v. 9); "and also to the Jews in their script and their language" (v. 9). Still others serve to emphasize that the action called for by this new decree is intended to counter the action against them which the former decree called for: "allowed the Jews who were in every city to assemble and defend their lives" (v. 11); and "to take revenge on their enemies" (v. 13).

In fact, the parallels between the description of this decree and the earlier anti-Jewish decree raise profound questions with regard to the action commanded, or allowed, by the decree. On the surface, these parallels emphasize the fact that this new decree intends a complete reversal of fortunes, on a national level, for the Jews and those who would have destroyed them—matching, of course, the reversal of fortunes, on a personal level, for Haman and Mordecai. By a radical reversal of fortune, the Jews, formerly marked as quintessential other, or "not-us," by decree of the king, have suddenly found themselves at the center of political power. Yet beyond the simple presentation of this reversal, might these parallels also be raising more profound questions concerning this reversal? Why does the text describe the slaughter to be done by the Jews in language so close to that of the earlier decree in chapter 3?[8] Certainly the text could have used more sharply contrastive

---

[7] For a helpful chart of these parallel texts in English, see Bush, *Ruth, Esther,* 442–3. Unfortunately, the NRSV loses some aspects of the close parallel by changing word order and varying translations of Hebrew words, presumably to smooth out the presentation in English. Compare the NRSV translations of 3:14a and 8:13a, which are identical in Hebrew: "a copy of the *document* was to be issued as a decree in every province *by proclamation, calling on* all peoples . . ." (3:14a); "a copy of the *writ* was to be issued as a decree in every province *and published to* all peoples . . ." (8:13a; italics mine).

[8] Most disturbing in this regard is the fact that it is quite possible to read the decree as empowering the Jews to kill the wives and children of their enemies *along*

language to distinguish the newly decreed action of the Jews from the actions planned by the Jew-haters. Fox rightly cautions against viewing the actions decreed here and carried out in the subsequent narrative as *identical* to the actions against them proposed earlier.[9] After all, Haman's decree for the total annihilation of all Persian Jews is already in place. Moreover, the success of this new decree, which is intended to overwrite the former one, is not at all certain. Their enemies could still destroy them. In this sense, this new decree calls for a defensive strike against "any people or province that might attack them" (8:11). But does this decree cross the line, from *defensive* to *preemptive* strike— calling for the slaughter of those that *might* attack them?[10] Of course, even if one reads the slaughter decreed here as preemptive rather than defensive, it is nonetheless to be distinguished from the slaughter based on greed and ethnic hatred that was decreed in chapter 3. Still, up to this point in the narrative, as we have seen, many questions have emerged concerning social dynamics involving the construction of a group identity over against a projected other, or "not-us." Might the parallels between these two decrees invite still more disturbing questions concerning the problematics of distinguishing clearly between us and them, self and other? These are important questions to ask with regard to any revolution, whether fictional or not, and no matter which side you are on.

GOING OUT PARTY (8:15-17)

After reporting that this new decree was published throughout all the provinces of Persia, the last sentence of verse 14 points out specif-

---

with their enemies, thereby further paralleling the original anti-Jewish decree in 3:13. This NRSV translation, "to annihilate any . . . that might attack them, with their children and women" (8:11), leaves the meaning of the decree sufficiently ambiguous in this regard. It could mean that the Jews are empowered to kill those attacking them and also to kill their attacker's families; or it could mean that the Jews are empowered to kill those attacking the Jewish men and their Jewish families (so Robert Gordis, "Studies in the Esther Narrative," *JBL* 95 [1976] 49–53, who proposes the translation, "attacking them [the Jews], their women, and their children"). The Tanakh translation, on the other hand, is not at all ambiguous: the Jews are empowered to "exterminate its armed force together with women and children" (likewise NEB; NAB).

[9] Fox, *Character and Ideology*, 220ff.

[10] In this regard, note that in the brief narrative concerning the slaughter of enemies in the capital city (9:6-15) there is no mention of the Jews themselves being attacked. The reader may assume that they are killing those who are trying to kill them, but that is not certain.

ically that "the decree was issued in the citadel of Susa." Here again, the text of 3:14 is identical. What follows, however, is radically different. In chapter 3, the issuing of the decree against the Jews in Susa leaves the city in a state of confusion and turmoil (3:15). Here, by contrast, the issuing of the new decree in Susa is followed by Mordecai himself, who "went out from the presence of the king, wearing royal robes of blue and white, with a great golden crown and a mantle of fine linen and purple, while the city of Susa shouted and rejoiced" (8:15). In both cases a decree is issued in the city and the entire city responds as one: it reels tumultuously in response to the first decree (3:15) and it shouts and rejoices in response to the second (8:15). This city's second response, moreover, is not simply a response to the decree, but also a response to its author Mordecai, who arrives along with the decree, dressed as a king once again (compare 6:10-11). Contrast Haman and the king in 3:15, who drink inside the palace walls, oblivious to their effect on the city.

The text now turns from the collective response of the city to the collective response of the Jews, for whom "there was light and rejoicing [NRSV 'gladness'],[11] joy and honor" (8:16). This fourfold language of rejoicing, "light and rejoicing, joy and honor," in response to the decree and to Mordecai's ascendency, reverses the fourfold language of mourning, "mourning . . . fasting and weeping and lamenting," in response to the earlier anti-Jewish decree (4:3), further emphasizing the dynamic of reversal taking place. The middle two terms, "rejoicing" (*śimḥâ*) and "joy" (*śāśōn* or *śāśôn*), which appear again in the next verse (8:17), are frequently used as a pair in Hebrew narrative and poetry to describe uplifted spirits (e.g., Pss 4:7 [Eng. 8]; 45:7, 15; 51:8-12 [Eng. 10-14]; Isa 22:13; 35:10; 51:3, 11; Jer 7:34; 15:16; 16:9; 25:10; 33:11; Zech 8:19), often in response to divine presence and/or deliverance.

The first and fourth terms, "light" (*'ôrâ*) and "honor" (*yĕqār*), on the other hand, are quite unusual in this context.[12] Clines points out that "light" (*'ôr*) can be a metaphor for prosperity (e.g., Job 22:28; Pss 27:1; 36:9; 97:11), although in most instances it could also mean something closer to its more common sense of "enlightenment," or even general well-being.[13] If taken in its most common sense, then "light" here simply connotes an experience radically opposed to the dark, lamentable situation that the Jews were facing before this reversal of fortune

---

[11] The word translated "gladness" (*śimḥâ*) here is a noun form of the verb that was translated "rejoiced" in the previous verse.

[12] Note, in this regard, that these two terms do not appear along with the pair "rejoicing" and "joy" in the next verse.

[13] Clines, *Ezra, Nehemiah, Esther*, 318.

began. If taken as a metaphor for prosperity, however, "light" stands in nice poetic parallel with the fourth term, "honor." As discussed earlier, "honor" in Esther is a means of consolidating political power. It was the king's objective in the opening drinking parties (1:4); it was what Vashti threatened and what Memucan and the king thought women ought to give to their husbands/lords (1:20); it was Haman's objective in relation to the king in chapter 6; and when Mordecai got it instead of Haman, Haman was visibly shamed (6:10-12). Clearly, then, "honor" is a political objective, bestowed and recognized publically. If "light" is taken in terms of prosperity, then the first and fourth terms in this description of the Jews may connote a public significance to their newfound well being (prosperity and honor, for them collectively as for Mordecai individually), whereas the two middle terms connote their inner emotional response.

After describing the city of Susa's response to the decree and to Mordecai, the text turns to the reaction of the Jews throughout Persia: "In every province and in every city, wherever the king's command and his edict came, there was gladness and joy among the Jews, a festival and a holiday" (8:17a). The term translated here as "festival" is *mišteh*, the same term used for the drinking parties (or "banquets") throughout the narrative.[14] The term translated "holiday" *(yôm ṭôb)* is literally a "day of pleasure" or "good." Given that drinking has been the focus of every *mišteh* in the book thus far, and given that *ṭôb* ("good" or "pleasing") has been used in the context of other drinking parties to suggest drunkenness (1:10; 5:9), this phrase might even suggest that the pleasure of that day has much to do with the flowing of the wine.

The episode closes with a fascinating statement: "Furthermore, many of the peoples of the country professed to be Jews, because the fear of the Jews had fallen upon them" (8:17b). The verb translated as "professed to be Jews" *(mityahădîm)* is the only instance in Hebrew Scripture of a verbal form (Hitpael participle) of the word for "Jew," "Jewish," "Judean" *(yěhûdî)*. Most literally it could be translated as "being Jewish," or even "Jewing."

Through a play on *yěhûdî* ("Jewish") and *yěhîdî* ("one," "singular," also "lonely"), the Midrash on Esther suggests that this verb is related to the religious character of Mordecai himself. That is, in his refusal to bow before Haman, he, like Abraham before him, insisted on the oneness of God's name.

> Even as our father Abraham allowed himself to be cast into the fiery
> furnace and converted his fellowmen and made them acknowledge the

---

[14] On this term and its emphasis on drinking, see the commentary on chapter 1.

greatness of the Holy One, blessed be He, as it says, And the souls which they had gotten in Haran (Gen. XII, 5), so in the days of Mordecai men acknowledged the greatness of the Holy One, blessed be He, as it says, And many from among the peoples of the land became Jews [*mityahădîm*] (Est. VIII, 17), and he proclaimed the unity of God's name and sanctified it. Therefore he was called YEHUDI, as it says, A JUDEAN MAN [Esth 2:5]; read not YEHUDI but *yĕḥîdî*. (Midrash Esther Rabbah VI:2; Soncino translation)[15]

On this midrashic interpretation, then, those who are "Jewing" in 8:17 are actually converting by proclaiming the oneness of God, as Mordecai had done by his refusal to bow before Haman. They are Jewing by one-ing.[16] Although lacking in such creative interpretive play, most modern scholars likewise read this text as meaning that many people were *converting* to Judaism.

But what precisely would these people be converting to? Where in the book of Esther is there a clear link between Jewish identity and religious practice? Moore and Fox rightly counter that this verb be understood as a reference to people *behaving* as Jews, that is, performing Jewish identity.[17] Of course, that still leaves one wondering what this behavior might look like. Indeed, perhaps being Jewish is less a matter of acting or appearing a certain way (since Jewish identity is not known unless it is "disclosed"; 2:10, 20; 3:4, 6; 7:3-6) and more a matter

---

[15] Insofar as *yĕḥîdî* also can mean "lonely" or "alone," the Midrash may also be playing on Mordecai's solitariness throughout most of the narrative.

[16] Rashi's interpretation is closely related. The LXX translates *mityahădîm* as *Ioudaizon*. The LXX and Old Latin both add that these people were circumcised, whereas the AT describes many Jews circumcising themselves without opposition from other people. One point of comparison might be the Greek apocryphal addition to Daniel, *Bel and the Dragon,* in which the Persian people express frustration that their king has "become a Jew" (*Ioudaios gegonen ho Basileus;* v. 28). This Greek text does not, however, use a verbal equivalent to "to Jew." Unlike Esther, moreover, the presence of God in *Bel and the Dragon* is beyond doubt, as is Daniel's devotion to Jewish worship practices, so that the sense of the king's "becoming a Jew" is that of religious conversion. In Esther, however, there has been little if anything religious to attribute to Jewish identity. Cf. also the Greek word *ioudaizein,* literally "to jew," in Galatians 2:14. Interestingly, this is the only verbal form of "Jew" (*ioudaios*) in the New Testament. (I thank Gary Phillips for drawing my attention to this text.) Luther's use of "Judaizing" as a negative, anti-Jewish term—opposed to living under grace by faith, according to spirit rather than flesh—is closely related to Galatians. Of course, the use of *mityahădîm* in Esth 8:17 is by no means negative or anti-Jewish, but rather indicates the subversion of Haman's earlier projection of the Jews as quintessentially other.

[17] Moore, *Esther,* 82; Fox, *Character and Ideology,* 105.

of *sounding* or *writing* a certain way, for the text has indicated that different peoples have different languages and different scripts (1:22; 3:12; 8:9).[18] Or perhaps "being Jewish" is simply a matter of calling oneself a Jew.

Whatever "being Jewish" might entail, Persians everywhere are doing it, "because the fear of the Jews had fallen upon them" (8:17b; cf. 9:2, and "fear of Mordecai" in 9:3). Earlier, to be identified as Jewish was to be marked for death; now *not* being Jewish may put one's life in jeopardy.[19]

Some commentators see in this reference to "fear" *(paḥad)* a subtle allusion to God's deliverance of the Jews.[20] That is, the text may be suggesting that their deliverance is by God and thus the people's fear of God's chosen people is, indirectly, a fear of God. And so they convert. The falling of fear here upon non-Jews, then, would be related to the earlier prediction against Haman: "if Mordecai is of Jewish seed . . . you will surely fall"; 6:13). Such an interpretation, however, detracts from the more obvious significance of the people's sudden fear of the Jew, who had until now been marked as other over against Persian law and Persian national identity. One might even argue that any allusion to God in this passage is self-subversive, accentuating precisely God's *absence* during this perilous time for the Jews, and therefore the absence of any divine guarantees for their well-being.

[18] To be more precise, 1:22 and 3:12 indicate every *province* has its own script and every *people* has its own language. At the end of 8:9, however, it is further indicated that the Jews (a people, but not a province) have their own script *and* their own language.

[19] See also the commentary on earlier references to "falling" in 6:13 and 7:8.

[20] E.g., Jacob Horschander, *The Book of Esther in Light of History* (Philadelphia: Dropsie College, 1923) 247; Helmer Ringgren, "Esther and Purim," *Svensk Exegetisk Årsbok* 20 (1956) 140; and Werner Dommershausen, *Die Estherrolle: Stil und Ziel einer alttestamentlichen Schrift* (Stuttgart: Katholisches Bibelwerk, 1968) 110.

Chapter 12

AFTERMATH

Esther 9:1–10:3

The last two chapters of the book of Esther jump ahead almost nine months, to the events of the thirteenth and fourteenth of Adar. Within the narrative as a whole, these chapters offer a three-fold explication of the "aftermath" of the decree issued in the previous chapter: first, they report the details involved in carrying out Mordecai's and the king's decree (called "the king's command and edict" in 9:1), which ends up taking two days rather than one; second, they make explicit the reversal of fortune for Mordecai and the Jews; and third, they link these events to the festival of Purim, including reasons for its celebration on different days (the thirteenth and the fourteenth) by different Jewish communities.

Even a cursory reading of chapters 9 and 10, especially 9:20–10:3, reveals significant differences in style, vocabulary, and (arguably) content from the narrative material in the previous chapters, as many commentators have noted.[1] Therefore many scholars consider all or part of chapters 9 and 10 to be later additions by another author.[2] Perhaps, as some have recently argued, certain scholars have overemphasized the

---

[1] E.g., Moore, *Esther*, 90–1; Charles C. Torrey, "The Older Book of Esther," *Harvard Theological Review* 37 (1944) 1–40; David J.A. Clines, *The Esther Scroll: The Story of the Story* (Sheffield: Sheffield Academic Press, 1984) 39–63; see also Clines, *Ezra, Nehemiah, Esther*, 320–32.

[2] The literary independence of 9:20–10:3 has been more obvious to scholars than that of 9:1-19. See esp. Paton's discussion (*Esther*, 57–60), which summarized scholarly arguments since J. D. Michaelis, *Deutsche Uebersetzung des A.T. mit Anmerkungen für Ungelehrte* (Göttingen: J. C. Dieterich, 1783). Some of the negative literary

differences in *content* between all or part of chapters 9–10 and the previous narrative. Although differences in style and vocabulary are undeniable, contradictions in content are not at all clear. Whether or not one believes that an earlier ("original"?) version of the story ended at 8:17, we can at least acknowledge that chapters 9 and 10 involve a strikingly different—even incongruous—mode of narration. Perhaps a different author or different authors were involved here; perhaps a new secretary was hired at this point; perhaps the same writer or writers wrote this part some time after, or before, writing the material in chapters 1–8; perhaps chapters 9 and 10 were heavily edited by later editors. More than likely, still other factors were involved which we cannot imagine. There are severe limits to our ability to determine details of authorship, editing, and transmission of ancient Jewish and other Near Eastern texts, especially a text such as Esther which is rooted in a context (the Jewish Diaspora in Persia) to which we have very little access. At any rate, we ought always to avoid the badly oversimplified notions of authorial origin that these discussions too often assume.

It is difficult to outline this narrative material in the manner we have outlined previous chapters. Bush argues that 9:1-5 can be read as an integral narrative unit, structured as an inclusio.[3] Whether or not one is convinced that these verses are intentionally structured in this way, Bush is correct to identify them as a general introduction to the content that follows, as well as an explicit linking of that content to the preceding content, especially the decree of Mordecai and the king (8:9-17). Following 9:1-5, however, we have a series of shorter units with unclear transitions between them.[4] The most obvious points of division

---

evaluations of this material, which focuses on the institution of the Jewish festival of Purim, may in fact be informed by anti-Jewish ideology which has dominated much of modern biblical criticism on Esther (on which see Beal, *Hiding*, 4–12); indeed, Luther's oft-quoted hostility toward Esther and 2 Maccabees as "Judaizing" is clearly related to the importance of these texts in particular Jewish festivals (Purim and Hanukkah, respectively).

The most forceful and clearly articulated arguments for reading 9:1-19 as an appendix to Esther 1–8 are found in Clines, *The Esther Scroll*, 39–49. For recent arguments to the contrary, see Bush, *Ruth, Esther*, 456–60, which draws on the earlier discussion by Michael V. Fox, *The Redaction of the Book of Esther: On Reading Composite Texts* (Atlanta: Scholars Press, 1991) 114–5. For arguments against the literary independence of 9:20–10:3, see Bruce William Jones, "The So-Called Appendix to the Book of Esther," *Semitics* (1978) 36–43.

[3] Bush, *Ruth, Esther*, 456–7.

[4] That it is difficult to determine the beginning of one unit and the end of another within chapters 9 and 10 (esp. 9:1-32) is clear from a comparison of the variety

within this material are at 9:20, which shifts attention from the killing in Susa and elsewhere to the formal institution of Purim, and at 10:1, which returns attention to the king. Yet 9:20-32 is not an integral unit (note the shift to a different mode of explanation vv. 24-28 [is this a summary of the letter's content?]), and several passages in 9:20-32 loop back to the preceding material for their sense. And 10:1-3 appears truncated—as Clines puts it, "an introduction to a narrative that is summarily truncated . . . a false start."[5] Indeed, one might say the same about much of the material in chapters 9 and 10: again and again, it cuts to a different focus or mode of narration just when things are about to get rolling. The overall sense is that of a hodgepodge of conclusions. It is less a continuation of the narrative flow from chapter 8 and more a narrative "aftermath." Therefore we will do well to avoid relying heavily on formal or structural divisions in our analysis of the material.

At the end of chapter 3, as Haman and the king sat drinking while the city reeled in turmoil, "that day" (i.e., the thirteenth of Adar) was determined by irrevocable decree to be a day for the total annihilation and plundering of the Jews. In chapter 9, "that day" finally arrives, but not as had been expected. As an opening to this chapter, 9:1 sumarizes this complete reversal of fortune in clear and succinct terms:

> In the twelfth month, which is the month of Adar, on the thirteenth day, when the king's word and decree were to be carried out—the very day that the enemies of the Jews had reserved to gain mastery over them—there was a reversal, by which the Jews themselves had mastery over those who hated them. (my translation)[6]

Up to this point the text has left it to readers to recognize the dynamics of reversal within the story, based on more subtle textual clues such

of divisions offered in recent scholarly commentaries (e.g., Moore, *Esther,* 90–91; Clines, *Ezra, Nehemiah, Esther,* 320–33; Bush, *Ruth, Esther,* 472–74; and the subdivisions of Levenson, *Esther,* 118–34).

[5] Clines, *The Esther Scroll,* 57.

[6] The NRSV translation of verse 1 is as follows: "Now in the twelfth month, which is the month of Adar, on the thirteenth day, when the king's command and edict [*dat;* elsewhere translated 'decree'] were about to be executed, on the very day when the enemies of the Jews hoped to gain power over them, but which had been changed to a day when the Jews would gain power over their foes, ..." By translating *wĕnahăpôk hû*ʾ (lit., "and/but the reverse happened" or "and/but it was reversed") as "but which had been changed to . . . ," the strong sense of reversal is deemphasized. Yet explicating this reversal is clearly the focus of the verse (and of 9:1-5 overall).

as word and phrase repetitions (e.g., in the language of the decrees) and inverted events (e.g., Haman on the stake intended for Mordecai and Mordecai receiving the honors Haman had intended for himself). Here, however, the reversal is spelled out as clearly and unambiguously as possible.

A new verb is introduced to describe the significance of this reversal: *šlṭ*, "have mastery" or "overpower." The reversal is a reversal of mastery, or political power, and not simply a reversal of violence. It also makes clear that the ethnic hatred (3:6) that fueled Haman and those who would carry out the decree against the Jews cannot be divorced from political motivations—any more than one can divorce ethnocentrism from politics in today's world.

The emphasis here is on the reversal of political power as much as it is on the reversal of intended slaughter. This is further indicated in 9:3 by the fact that "all the officials of the provinces, the satraps and the governors, and the royal officials *were aiding [mĕnaśśĕ'îm]* the Jews." This is a participle form of the same verb *(nś')* that has been used to describe Esther's "gaining" or "lifting" favor in the eyes of the king, Hegai, and all who see her (2:9, 15, 17; 5:2). Perhaps more significantly in the present context, this verb is also used, with the same stem as it takes in 9:3 (Piel), to describe the king's promotion of Haman over all his other officials (3:1; 5:11). It was immediately after that promotion, moreover, that Mordecai refused to bow before Haman (3:2-6). In 9:3, then, it is not simply a matter of the officials now helping the Jews; rather, they are *"promoting"* them, or their cause, in a way that affords them greater political power or "mastery." This "promotion" of the Jews parallels Esther's promotion of Mordecai when she "placed" him over Haman's house (8:2). As discussed earlier, the language of "placing" in that passage likewise draws from the language of Haman's promotion in 3:1 in order to indicate the reversal of status and power involving Mordecai and Haman. Thus both promotions, one individual (Mordecai) and one collective (the Jews), draw from the language of Haman's promotion in 3:1 in order to emphasize these advances as reversals of political status and power. Indeed, this parallel is confirmed by what immediately follows in 9:3b-4, which turns attention back onto the individual Mordecai: the Jews and their cause are being promoted by the officials "because the fear of Mordecai had fallen upon them. For Mordecai was powerful in the king's house, and his fame spread throughout all the provinces as the man Mordecai grew more and more powerful." Their political objectives are being advanced out of "fear of Mordecai" who now holds power over them. This "fear of Mordecai" is in turn linked to the general "fear of the Jews" mentioned in 9:2, and earlier in 8:17. Note, moreover, that the word used here to describe Mordecai's growing "power" (*gādôl*) is yet another of the words used to describe Haman's promotion 3:1. Their collective rise in power (over the collective "enemies of the Jews"; 9:1; cf. 8:13) is explicitly linked to Mordecai's individual rise (over Haman, the individual "enemy of the Jews"; 3:10; cf. 7:6). As an introduction to chapters 9 and 10, 9:1-4 indicates that what follows is not simply a matter of bloody vengeance but a matter of political mastery.

This is not to say that the text is unconcerned with the details of the slaughter, as verse 5 makes clear: "So the Jews struck down all their enemies with the sword, slaughtering and destroying them, and did as they pleased to those who hated them." Bush has shown how this verse is linked to 9:1, forming the opening and closing elements of an inclusio in 9:1-5.[7] This does not mean, however, that verses 1 and 5 are saying the same thing. Whereas the emphasis in verse 1 is on gaining political mastery over those who had intended to gain political mastery over them, here the emphasis is placed on the extreme violence in which this mastery issues forth. In this regard, note that whereas the language of the earlier verses alluded the political promotion of Haman by the king (3:1), thereby rendering the promotion of the Jews here as a reversal of political status and power, the language in verse 5 (esp. "slaughter" [*hrg,* 'kill'] and "destroy" [*ʾbd*]) alludes to the violence of Haman's decree against the Jews (3:13; cf. 8:11).[8]

In 9:6-10, interestingly, the parallel between individual reversals and collective reversals continues: in verse 6, the text reports that the Jews collectively "killed and destroyed" (the same verbs used in 3:13; 8:11; and 9:5) five hundred nameless people in Susa on the thirteenth day of Adar; in verses 7-10, the text returns to the more individual conflict against Haman, by reporting that the Jews killed (*hrg*) his ten carefully named sons.

Verse 10 concludes with an important qualification: "but they did not touch the plunder." This note appears somewhat peculiar and out of place until one considers it in relation to 1 Samuel 15. As discussed earlier, Haman is introduced as an Agagite, identifying him with Agag, king of the Amalekites; and Mordecai is identified with the tribe of Benjamin, identifying him with King Saul, who defeats King Agag in 1 Samuel 15. After defeating the Amalekites in that battle, Saul had displeased God and Samuel by saving livestock and other valuables, along with King Agag himself (God had said to "utterly destroy" everything). As a result, Saul was rejected as king over Israel. Here in

---

[7] Bush, *Ruth, Esther,* 457.

[8] The NRSV translates *ʾbd* as "annihilate" in 3:13 and 8:11, and as "destroy" in 9:5. It translates *hrg* as "kill" in 3:13 and 8:11, and as "slaughter" in 9:5.

Esther, where the conflict between Mordecai and Haman parallels the conflict between Saul and Agag, the text makes clear in 9:10, and again at 9:15 and 9:16, that the Jews do not take any of the enemy plunder. And this despite the fact that in Esther there is no God commanding them *not* to take the plunder. In fact, the decree authored by Mordecai in 8:11 calls for them to take it! As Magonet and others suggest, this insistence that they did not plunder the enemy appears to be an undoing of Saul's (and the Israelites') earlier mistake, and thereby a subtle redemption of the Saulide (Benjaminite) name.[9]

On the same day, the number killed in Susa is reported to the king (9:11). In 9:12, the king in turn reports to Esther, and asks her what she wants to have happen next: "In the citadel of Susa the Jews have killed five hundred people and also the ten sons of Haman. What have they done in the rest of the king's provinces? Now what is your petition? It shall be granted you. And what further is your request? It shall be fulfilled." With these words, the king submits himself and his position to Esther's will. His speech here draws from elements of his earlier speeches: in words almost identical to 5:3, 5:6, and 7:2, he asks for her "petition" (*šĕ᾽ēlātēk*, "your asking") and her "request" (*baqqāšātēk*, "your seeking"), promising that they will be "granted" and "fulfilled"; as in 8:7, moreover, this speech opens with his report of all that he has done to fulfill her requests thus far. Unlike any of these previous speeches, however, Esther does not come before the king to make her request (5:1; 8:3); rather, he comes before *her* for directions.

Esther calls for a second day of killing in Susa, and adds that the dead sons of Haman be impaled (9:13). Both of these requests would serve to increase the sense of "mastery" gained by the Jews over their enemies (9:1). Moreover, the public execution of Haman's already killed sons makes clear once again that this mastery is not simply a matter of killing one's enemies (and their family), but of publicly exhibiting that they have been killed. Execution is not so much concerned with death but with the publication of death, including a public claim of responsibility for that death. In this sense it is possible to publicly execute someone who has already been killed. The dead can be executed.

The king issues another decree in Susa to this effect, and has Haman's sons impaled like their father (9:14). The next day, the Jews in Susa muster forces once again and kill another three hundred people there (9:15), bringing the total killings in Susa to 810. This report on the second day of killing concludes, once again, by reiterating that the Jews did not touch the plunder.

[9] Magonet, "The Liberal and the Lady," 167–76.

In 9:12 the king had asked, "What have they done in the rest of the king's provinces?" The narrative now gives answer, as it reports on the killing throughout Persia: "Now the other Jews who were in the king's provinces also gathered to defend their lives, and gained relief from their enemies, and killed seventy-five thousand of those who hated them; but they laid no hands on the plunder" (9:16). As in previous reports, this report draws its language from that of the decree in 8:11, while yet again indicating that the Jews swerved from following that decree only insofar as they did not plunder their enemy for goods. Here ends the reports on the slaughter accomplished by the Jews, bringing the grand total to an outrageous 75,810.

By the end of chapter 8, there were two conflicting decrees—both of them irrevocable and not to be transgressed (8:8): the decree of Haman and the king calling for the annihilation of the Jews and the decree of Mordecai and the king calling for the annihilation of those who seek to annihilate the Jews. As Paton comments, "Lively times are to be anticipated."[10] That is, the narrative of chapters 3 and 8 have set up for an intense conflict between two parties, the Jews and their haters, who will battle to determine which decree and which party will overcome. Yet the text of 9:1-16 reports only on the number killed by the Jews, and gives no indication that the Jews met with any opposition whatsoever. The sense in these verses is that there was a slaughter, not a battle. Given that this day had been determined in chapter 3 to be a day for annihilating the Jews, the total victory reported in chapter 9 is excessive and entirely unbelievable. Indeed, it is excessive and unbelievable by design, for this is not historical reportage in the modern sense. Rather, as Craig makes clear, it is the outlandish, *carnal* culmination to a work of the "literary carnivalesque," a term he borrows from Mikhail Bakhtin.[11] Carnivals like Purim and carnivalized literature like Esther are expressions of festive outbreak against the structures and norms of moral, economic, ethnic, and sexual hierarchies which structure relationships between individuals and groups in a society. In carnival, those structures are radically undermined. Social and symbolic norms and privileges are thrown into a wild slide, identities within the normal order of things blur, and life and death cocontaminate—a time of "pregnant death," highlighting "the ambivalent nature of life itself: destruction and uncrowning are related to birth and renewal; death is linked to regeneration; . . . Symbols of change and

---

[10] Paton, *Esther,* 282.

[11] Kenneth Craig, *Reading Esther: A Case for the Literary Carnivalesque* (Louisville: Westminster/John Knox Press, 1995); Mikhail Bakhtin, *Rabelais and His World,* trans. Hélène Iswolsky (Bloomington: Indiana University Press, 1984).

renewal highlight the rejection of prevailing truths and authorities."[12] This is the carnivalized, radically unbelievable and morally disturbing world of reversal in Esther 9—a new beginning fraught with death.

In this light, it is not surprising to find these reports of the slaughter linked directly to festival in the narrative that follows: "a day for drinking parties [*mišteh;* NRSV 'feasting'] and gladness [*śimḥâ*]" (9:17 and 18); "a day of pleasure [*yôm ṭôb;* NRSV 'holiday']13 and sending gifts of food one to another" (9:19). Except for the gifts of food (most appropriate for a carnival!) in 9:19, the language used here to describe the festivities is the same as that used in 8:17 to describe the reactions of the Jews in every province upon receiving the decree of Mordecai and the king. The same language will be drawn from and expanded upon once again in the institution of Purim in 9:22.

Beside this focus on the festivities in 9:17-19, there are some calendar issues which also need to be clarified. The Jews outside Susa celebrated on the fourteenth of Adar, whereas those in Susa celebrated on the fifteenth, because they were still busy killing on the fourteenth. What we have in 9:17-19, then, is an odd mix of glad drinking parties and scheduling details, as the text explicates why there are two traditionally recognized days for celebrating Purim.[14]

Verses 17-19, which refer both to the days of killing and to the festivities that follow, serve as a transition into the institution of Purim as an annual festival to be observed forever (9:20-32). This material can be subdivided into three parts (9:20-23; 24-28; and 29-32). The focus throughout these verses is on summary and wrap-up. There is no direct speech, and the dominant actions involve the writing, sending, and receiving of the letter.

First, 9:20-23 summarizes Mordecai's letter enjoining all Persian Jews to observe these two days (the fourteenth and the fifteenth) every year, "as the days on which the Jews gained relief from their enemies, and as the month that had been turned for them from sorrow into gladness and from mourning into a holiday; that they should make them days of feasting and gladness, days for sending gifts of food to one another and presents to the poor" (9:22). That the emphasis of this

---

12 Craig, *Reading Esther,* 30.

13 See the commentary on the same word in 8:17.

14 Note that this verse does not simply acknowledge the different dates for observing Purim, but links those dates with what are assumed to be contemporary practices within different regions of the Persian empire. It appears that this note assumes a Persian-period audience, and thus provides support for dating the composition of this version of Esther to the Persian period rather than to the later Hellenistic period.

new annual festival is to be placed on Jewish *deliverance* rather than on *overpowering* their enemy is clear from the fact that they are enjoined to observe the *day after* their victory, that is, the day when they "gained relief from them" *(nāḥû bāhem)*. The verb translated here as "gain relief" *(nwḥ,* "rest") alludes back to Haman's original projection of the Jews as the nation's ethnic other in 3:8, at which point he said that "it is not appropriate for the king to tolerate them [or 'give rest to them,' *lĕhannîḥām].*"[15] Whereas Haman had recommended that the king not let this matter of the Jews rest (i.e., he should not tolerate them but should have them destroyed), now the Jews have found "rest" from that intolerance.

The language of holiday and feasting is the same as in 8:15-17 and 9:17-19 (on which see the earlier commentary), except that it adds that presents should be given to the poor (presumably not only poor Jews but all poor people). Like the celebration of Passover, and like the observance of the law given at Sinai, the festal response to deliverance in Esther is, by this injunction, linked to more general issues of economic justice. Such a practice also parallels other reversals of social status which have taken place within the narrative (i.e., those based on gender and ethnic identities). So long as this gifting of the poor is not reduced to a matter of piety, moreover, such a practice would also be consistent with the social phenomenon of carnival, discussed above.[16]

9:24-28 then provides a selective nutshell summary of the entire plot of the story. The relationship of this material to the preceding verses is not at all clear. Its placement immediately after the report on Mordecai's letter would suggest that it be understood as "these things" which Mordecai recorded (9:20), that is, as the content of Mordecai's letter, providing details and background for those Jews outside Susa who have up to this point only heard the content of the decrees themselves (including, by the way, the decree against Vashti and "other" women). The problem with reading verses 24-28 in this way is that this material is introduced by *kî,* "for," which would indicate that what follows is linked to the preceding verse (23) rather than to "these things" in verse 20.[17] That is, this nutshell narrative would be the *narrator's* (not the narrative character Mordecai's) explanation *to readers* (not to Mordecai's fellow Persian Jews) as to why the Jews adopted these festivities as an annual

[15] This is a Hiphil infinitive form of the same verb. The sense is that the king should not *let this matter of the Jews rest.* See also Levenson, *Esther,* 126.

[16] See also Craig, *Reading Esther,* 162–3; and Theodor H. Gaster, *Purim and Hanukkah in Custom and Tradition* (New York: Henry Schuman, 1950).

[17] The NRSV solves this problem by simply not translating the introductory *kî* at all.

custom. But there are also problems with reading these verses as the
narrator's own summary. As Clines has made most clear, the content of
this summary swerves from the story at important points and ignores
a number of key events and characters.[18] If this is a summary by the narrator, why would it swerve so far from the story just narrated? Why, for
example, would the narrator(s) responsible for chapters 1–8 "spin" that
narrative in such a way as to minimize Esther's role? Why, for that
matter, would the narrator minimize the king's earlier complicity with
Haman, and maximize his "sense of justice and goodwill towards the
Jews" as the cause of Jewish deliverance?[19] And why, in such a brief,
two-sentence summary, would the narrator include details of the royal
orders—including a written decree never mentioned before—to execute Haman *and his sons?* (Note, by the way, that in the narrative itself
the king's verbal order to impale Haman immediately [7:9] is separated
by nine months from his order to have the sons impaled [9:13].) Such
disjunctions are taken by most scholars to indicate that this material is
the work of another narrator—perhaps even a separate piece of literature or liturgy—which has been added to the book at some point in the
text's transmission as a way of linking the story explicitly to the observance of Purim (see the earlier discussion). Insofar as it drastically
minimizes the role of Esther, and excludes the entire story of Vashti in
chapter 1, one may also wonder whether this brief summary, along
with other materials in 9:1-10:3, serves to diminish potentially subversive sexual-political dynamics within the story.

Indeed, the narrative material throughout chapters 8–10 appears to
be in tension with itself with regard to Esther's part in the political
reversal which has taken place. As noted earlier, after Esther's promotion of Mordecai in 8:2, Mordecai begins moving into the foreground
while Esther gradually slips into the background. Thus Mordecai
alone commands the writing of the decree (8:9), even though Esther
alone had requested such a decree and even though the king had au-
thorized both Esther and him to do so (8:7-8); and Mordecai is dressed
in royal garb and celebrated as hero in 8:15, despite the fact that without Esther his next public appearance would have been at the top of a
fifty-cubit stake (cf. also "fear of Mordecai" [9:3], over against Haman's
ultimate "terror" in the face of Esther [7:6]). Thus, too, Mordecai alone
appears to write the letter in 9:20-23 on his own authority. Yet in 9:29-
32 we find that this letter relies for its authority on Queen Esther:

[18] Clines, *The Esther Scroll*, 52–4.
[19] Clines, *The Esther Scroll*, 53.

> *Queen Esther daughter of Abihail, along with the Jew Mordecai, gave full writ-*
> *ten authority, confirming this second letter about Purim.* Letters were sent
> wishing peace and security to all the Jews, to the one hundred twenty-
> seven provinces of the kingdom of Ahasuerus, and giving orders that
> these days of Purim should be observed at their appointed seasons, *as*
> *the Jew Mordecai and Queen Esther enjoined on the Jews,* just as they had laid
> down for themselves and for their descendants regulations concerning
> their fasts and their lamentations. *The command of Queen Esther fixed these*
> *practices* of Purim, and it was recorded in writing. (emphasis added)

It is not clear whether this passage is describing a second, alternative
account of the letter purported to have been written by Mordecai alone
in 9:20-23, or whether this passage is describing a follow-up letter by
Esther and Mordecai together. Either way, this passage suggests that
Mordecai continues to depend on Queen Esther for his authority. Note,
moreover, how their titles ("Queen Esther, daughter of Abihail" and
"the Jew Mordecai") mark a certain distance that continues to exist between them (contrast "Esther, daughter of Abihail the uncle of Mordecai, who had taken her as his own daughter" in 2:15). This distance
suggests that the reversal of fortune for Mordecai and the Jews has not
resulted in Esther's status being resubsumed under Mordecai's command. 9:29-32, then, stands out over against what immediately precedes
and follows it as an affirmation of Esther's continued prominence in
Persia, among the Jews and more generally.

This passage also makes an explicit connection between the newly
instituted festival of Purim and other Jewish holidays, insofar as
Esther and Mordecai enjoin the Jews to observe Purim "just as they
had laid down for themselves and for their descendants regulations
concerning their fasts and their lamentations" (9:31). Presumably these
other "fasts and lamentations" are those traditional Jewish holidays
instituted in the Torah.[20] Indeed, Gerleman and others have argued
that the story of deliverance and the festival established to commemo-
rate that deliverance in the book of Esther are presented in ways that
closely parallel the Exodus story, the initial institution of Passover, and
the giving of the law at Sinai in the book of Exodus.[21]

---

[20] In addition to linking Purim to other Jewish holidays, this passage also places
Esther and Mordecai in a position of Jewish religious authority, insofar as they are
presented here as the ones responsible for ordering and regulating all Jewish holidays.

[21] Gillis Gerleman, "Studien zu Esther: Stoff-Struktur-Stil-Sinn," *Biblische Studien*
48 (1966); *Esther,* BKAT 21 (Neukirchen-Vluyn: Neukirchener Verlag, 1982); supported and developed by Levenson, *Esther.*

Esther then disappears once again as the book finishes, in 10:1-3, with a sputtering and somewhat out of place "happily ever after" for the king and Mordecai. This material begins in verse 1, very oddly, with a general report that "King Ahasuerus laid tribute on the land and on the islands of the sea." This language bears little resemblance to any we have seen thus far in the narrative. Bush suggests that it may harken back to "both the extent of the Persian empire and the unrestricted power of Ahasuerus, its ruler" as depicted in 1:1-4.[22] As noted in the commentary on chapter 1, the king's objective in displaying that power and greatness at that point in the narrative was closely related to his objective in displaying his queen, Vashti; that is, his political power and greatness was linked to his subjective status as patriarch. It is interesting to note that here in 10:1-3, as his political power is finally reaffirmed, Queen Esther (who has, more than anyone but Vashti, exposed his rule as a farce) is noticeably absent.

The last two verses (10:2-3) heap equal portions of praise onto the king and Mordecai, his right hand man (literally: "second to king" [*mišneh lammelek*]). Insofar as this text bears some relation to Mordecai's promotion in 8:2, and insofar as 10:1 may harken back to 1:1-4, one might consider this a fitting conclusion. It would be too much, however, to call it a good fit.

To say that this conclusion is not a good fit, however, is not to say that there is no literary value to it as it stands. As we have seen, the material in 9:1-10:3 as a whole does not exactly flow, and lacks the sense of narrative coherence and interconnectedness that one finds in chapters 1–8. As a conclusion to this collection of "aftermath" material, the last three verses do not bring these different threads together. They do not wrap anything up. On the contrary, the narrative trails off once again into the grand affairs of the king, this time bringing Mordecai along with him. The narrative appears to be oblivious to the reader's or congregation's desire for a tidier sense of an ending. The effect of this is to leave readers and hearers somewhat disoriented, restless. Like Mordecai in chapter 2, we are left standing on the edge of this narrative world wondering what happened to. . . .

---

[22] Bush, *Ruth, Esther*, 496.

FOR FURTHER READING

This is by no means a comprehensive list of important Esther studies. Rather these are suggestions for finding one's way further into the field. Most of the works listed are in English. For fuller bibliographies, see Levenson, Fox, and especially Moore, *Studies*, all listed below.

COMMENTARIES

Bush, Frederic W. *Ruth, Esther.* Word Biblical Commentary. Dallas: Word Books, 1996.
Clines, David J. A. *Ezra, Nehemiah, Esther.* The New Century Bible Commentary. Grand Rapids: Eerdmans, 1984.
Gerleman, Gillis. *Esther.* BKAT. Neukirchen-Vluyn: Neukirchener Verlag, 1982.
Levenson, Jon D. *Esther: A Commentary.* Old Testament Library. Louisville: Westminster John Knox Press, 1997.
Moore, Carey A. *Esther.* Anchor Bible. Garden City: Doubleday, 1971.
_____. *Daniel, Esther, and Jeremiah: The Additions.* Anchor Bible. Garden City: Doubleday, 1977.
Paton, Lewis Bayles. *The Book of Esther.* International Critical Commentary XX. New York: Charles Scribner's Sons, 1908.

BOOK-LENGTH STUDIES AND EDITED VOLUMES

Beal, Timothy K. *The Book of Hiding: Gender, Ethnicity, Annihilation, and Esther.* Biblical Limits. New York and London: Routledge, 1997.
Berg, Sandra Beth. *The Book of Esther: Motifs, Themes, and Structure.* Missoula: Scholars Press, 1979.
Bickerman, Elias J. *Four Strange Books of the Bible: Jonah, Daniel, Koheleth, Esther.* New York: Schocken, 1967.

Brenner, Athalya, ed. *A Feminist Companion to Esther, Judith, and Susanna.* Sheffield: Sheffield Academic Press, 1995.

Clines, David J. A. *The Esther Scroll: The Story of the Story.* Sheffield: Sheffield Academic Press, 1984.

Craig, Kenneth. *Reading Esther: A Case for the Literary Carnivalesque.* Literary Currents in Biblical Interpretation. Louisville: Westminster/ John Knox, 1995.

Day, Linda. *Three Faces of a Queen: Characterization in the Books of Esther.* Journal for the Study of the Old Testament Supplement Series 186. Sheffield: Sheffield Academic Press, 1995.

Fox, Michael V. *Character and Ideology in the Book of Esther.* Columbia, S.C.: University of South Carolina Press, 1991.

_____. *The Redaction of the Book of Esther: On Reading Composite Texts.* Atlanta: Scholars Press, 1991.

Gaster, Theodor H. *Purim and Hanukkah in Custom and Tradition.* New York: Henry Schuman, 1950.

Gordis, Robert. *Megillat Esther: The Masoretic Hebrew Text with Introduction, New Translation and Commentary.* New York: Ktav, 1974.

Jobes, Karen. *The Alpha-Text of Esther: Its Character and Relationship to the Masoretic Text.* SBL Dissertation Series. Atlanta: Scholars Press, 1996.

Moore, Carey A., ed. *Studies in the Book of Esther.* New York: Ktav, 1982.

Niditch, Susan. *Underdogs and Tricksters.* San Francisco: Harper & Row, 1987.

Walfish, Barry. *Esther in Medieval Garb: Jewish Interpretation of the Book of Esther in the Middle Ages.* Albany: SUNY Press, 1993.

ARTICLES AND CHAPTERS

Bal, Mieke. "Lots of Writing." *Semeia* 54 (1992) 77–99.

Clines, David J. A. "Reading Esther from Left to Right: Contemporary Strategies for Reading a Biblical Text." *The Bible in Three Dimensions.* Ed. David J. A. Clines, Stephen E. Fowl, and Stanley E. Porter. Sheffield: Sheffield Academic Press, 1990.

Cohen, Abraham D. "'Hu Ha-goral': The Religious Significance of Esther." *Judaism* 23 (1974) 87–94.

Fuchs, Esther. "Who Is Hiding the Truth? Deceptive Women and Biblical Androcentrism." Feminist Perspectives on Biblical Scholarship. Ed. Adela Yarbro Collins. Chico: Scholars Press, 1985.

_____. "Status and Role of Female Heroines in the Biblical Narrative." *Mankind Quarterly* 23 (1982) 149–60.

Goldman, Stan. "Narrative and Ethical Ironies in Esther." *Journal for the Study of the Old Testament* 47 (1990) 15–31.

Humphreys, W. Lee. "A Life-style for Diaspora: A Study of the Tales of Esther and Daniel." *Journal of Biblical Literature* 92 (1973) 211–3.

Jacobs, Louis. "Purim." *Encyclopedia Judaica* 13:1390–5.

Magonet, Jonathan. "The Liberal and the Lady: Esther Revisited." *Judaism* 29 (1980) 167–76.

McKane, William. "A Note on Esther IX and I Samuel XV." *Journal of Theological Studies* 12 (1961) 260–1.

Moore, Carey A. "Esther, Book of," *Anchor Bible Dictionary* 2:633–43.

Orlinsky, Harry M. "The Canonization of the Hebrew Bible and the Exclusion of the Apocrypha." *Essays in Biblical and Jewish Culture and Bible Translation*. New York: Ktav, 1974.

Radday, Yehuda T. "Esther with Humour." *On Humour and the Comic in the Hebrew Bible*. Ed. Yehuda T. Radday and Athalya Brenner. Sheffield: Almond Press, 1990.

Sasson, Jack M. "Esther." *The Literary Guide to the Bible*. Ed. Robert Alter and Frank Kermode. Cambridge, Mass.: Harvard University Press, 1987.

Torrey, Charles C. "The Older Book of Esther." *Harvard Theological Review* 37 (1944) 1–40.

White, Sidney Ann. "Esther: A Feminine Model for the Jewish Diaspora." *Gender and Difference in Ancient Israel*. Ed. Peggy L. Day. Minneapolis: Fortress Press, 1989.

Wiesel, Elie. "Esther." *Sages and Dreamers*. New York: Touchstone, 1991.

GENERAL INDEX

INDEX OF SCRIPTURAL REFERENCES